CARYL CHESSMAN

CELL 2455 DEATH ROW

GREENWOOD PRESS, PUBLISHERS
WESTPORT, CONNECTICUT

The Library of Congress cataloged this book as follows:

Chessman, Caryl, 1921–1960.
    Cell 2455; death row. Westport, Conn., Greenwood Press
[1969, °1954]

    361 p. 23 cm.

    Autobiography.

    1. Crime and criminals—California.   2. Prisoners—California—
Personal narratives.   I. Title.

HV6248.C44A3 1969   365'.6'0924 [B]   69–10074
ISBN 0–8371–1631–7   MARC

Library of Congress   [4]

Originally published in 1954 by Prentice-Hall, Inc.,
Englewood Cliffs, N.J.

Reprinted with the permission of Prentice-Hall, Inc.

Reprinted in 1969 by Greenwood Press,
A division of Congressional Information Service, Inc.
88 Post Road West, Westport, Connecticut 06881

Library of Congress catalog card number 69-10074
ISBN 0-8371-1631-7

Printed in the United States ofsAmerica

10

I dedicate this book to the memory
of the gentle Hallie, my mother,
who dreamed a deathless dream.

AUTHOR'S NOTE

Lo, how men blame the gods! From us, they say, comes evil. But through their own perversity, and more than is their due, they meet with sorrow . . .

Thus spoke Zeus, the father of men and gods, through the mouth of Homer.

To understand the evil of one man is to understand the evil of all men. For evil has but one root, but one cause, but one purpose. If they hope to survive, men of good will must learn this lesson soon and well: Evil seeks but the opportunity and the means to destroy itself; only when frustrated and denied its birthright does it turn with savage violence against its tormentors.

Today a dreadful dagger is pointed at the heart of Christendom. And from within a many-faced evil swaggers at noonday, strikes swiftly and terrifyingly during the midnight hours. Our label for this internal evil is Crime.

We know that there are those who walk among us who seemingly are not of us. And because some of them rob and hate and kill and throw away their lives we call them children of the Devil. Quite often they regard themselves as such. But we, as well as they, are wrong, and when we wreak blind vengeance upon them we do a futile and a tragic thing. Unwittingly we seek to propitiate a malignant god whose goal is to rob us of our humanity.

A familiar proverb tells of a blind man who, coming to a wall, declares himself to be at the end of the world. From that proverb is drawn my book's pervasive theme—even a society with excellent vision sometimes has a perverse and tragic tendency to follow the example of the blind man.

I asked myself: *Why?*

Cell 2455, Death Row is an earnest effort at an answer.

I feel impelled to add that the book has been written for one purpose only—because its author is both haunted and angered by the knowledge that his society needlessly persists in confounding itself in dealing with the monstrous twin problems of what to do about crime and what to do with criminals. Pled, consequently, is the cause of the criminally damned and doomed. It's time their voice was heard. And understood.

Caryl Chessman

San Quentin, California

• • • PART ONE • • •

FACILIS EST DESCENSUS AVERNI

CHAPTER

1   DEATH BY LEGAL EXECUTION 3

2   HELL'S ANTEROOM 12

3   THE TWIG 17

4   THE TWIG IS BENT 23

5   AND BENT STILL MORE 33

6   FEAR! 42

7   THE INEVITABLE IMPLOSION 52

8   "IT'S BETTER TO BE ANYTHING THAN AFRAID" . . 59

9   CONQUEST AND THE WALL 69

10   "SONNY BOY, KEEP ON LIKE YOU'RE GOING . . ." . 80

11   A REFORMATION FACTORY 87

12   I CAN KILL! 94

13   AND HE RAN FASTER 100

14   "APPARENTLY YOU DIDN'T LEARN YOUR LESSON" . 113

• • • PART TWO • • •

CUILIBET IN ARTE SUA PERITO
EST CREDENDUM

CHAPTER

15   A Peculiar Art 129

16   "A being darkly wise, and rudely great" . . 135

17   The Fool and the Madman Were One . . 145

18   But This Wasn't Fiction 155

19   The Dark Night's Children 160

20   A Game of Cops and Robbers 173

21   The Game Grows Grimmer 184

22   The Beginning of the End 191

23   *Deus Ex Machina* . . . With a Twist . . . 205

24   Operation Adolf 226

25   The Pull of the Orbit 239

26   Stone Walls Do a Prison Make 252

27   "O villain, villain, smiling, damned villain!" 265

• • • PART THREE • • •

DAMNANT QUOD NON INTELLIGUNT

CHAPTER

28 THREE TIMES AND OUT? 273

29 A FOOL FOR A CLIENT 281

30 "WHAT DO YOU THINK ABOUT IT NOW, SUCKER?" 295

31 SOMETHING NEW IN THE WAY OF VILLAINS . 308

32 "THE CHECK ON CHESSMAN" 314

33 THIS THING CALLED JUDICIAL JUSTICE . . . 320

34 "KILL HIM IF YOU CAN" 326

35 A VICTORY NONE WOULD COMPREHEND . . . 331

36 AN AWAKENING 341

37 THE RETURN FROM OUTER DARKNESS 350

PART ONE

FACILIS EST DESCENSUS AVERNI

Death by Legal Execution

Thursday afternoon, October 30, 1952. Death Row.

The death watch is expected in a few more minutes. Then, one at a time, it will remove two men from their individual cells.

One of the two is Big Red.

Big Red is an uncomplicated, normally jolly Arkansan in his late thirties, who drifted to California to labor at agricultural jobs in the San Joaquin Valley. For years Big Red was plagued with domestic troubles. "Me and the old lady didn't get along." His wife had him locked up several times for nonsupport, which rankled. He failed to see why he should support a wife who refused to live with him and perform her wifely functions. He was convinced "she was carryin' on with another guy," and felt badly because their only daughter had been placed in a state institution. Big Red blamed his wife for the girl's commitment. One night he got himself likkered up and grew broodingly belligerent. The local constabulary jailed him until he sobered up. He was placed in a drunk tank with two other men, neither of whom he had ever seen before in his life. Something in Big Red's alcohol-steeped mind snapped. He beat one of the men to death. A jury found him guilty of first degree murder and fixed his punishment at death. October 31, 1952, was fixed as his execution date.

So Big Red is waiting. He's waiting in Cell 2439, just four cells from the east end of the Row corridor.

Henry is the other man who is waiting. White-faced, he cringes pitifully in Cell 2449. He has withdrawn into a sort of fear-induced stupor.

3

Sex killer! Sex fiend! That's what the newspapers call Henry. With a prior history of sexual misconduct with children, he was convicted of the sex murder of a ten-year-old girl, and doomed. He himself has a defective, child's mind in a man's body. He knows the state intends to gas him to death in the morning. He shivers and trembles with fright.

"Hey, Knuckle-Head!" Big Red's voice booms out, shattering the silence, "Wha' time izzut?"

Knuckle-Head shouts back, "Four minutes o' four, Red."

"Well, it won't be long," Big Red says. "You only gotta put up with me fur a few more minutes."

But Big Red doesn't want to believe this. He knows his attorneys have filed papers for him in a Federal court and he doesn't know he has been denied relief. He's waiting and hoping for an eleventh hour stay. Like most men, he doesn't want to die.

"Hey, Knuckle-Head!"

"Yeah, Red?"

"You know what I'm gonna be eatin', don't you?"

"What, Red?"

"Banana cream pie. An' I ast 'em to put lotsa bananas in it. I'll think about you."

"Okay, Red."

Knuckle-Head is an intelligent Brooklynite who unintelligently shot his sweetheart to death. He and Big Red are tied for first place as the Row's champion eaters and talkers.

Big Red says plaintively, "Only thatsa heckuva way to get pie, ain't it?"

The question is left unanswered.

Knuckle-Head asks, "What else you gonna eat, Red?"

"Black-eyed peas. Southern fried potatoes. Some . . ."

"No chicken?"

"Naw."

"How come?"

"Don't like it. But I'm gonna eat plenty else. I'm gonna eat 'em outa house and home. And I'm gonna have 'em set up the victrola and play me a lotta Eddie Arnold records."

Big Red sings a few snatches of a sad hillbilly song; next he whistles a couple of bars of another and livelier tune.

"Hey, Knuckle-Head!"

"Yeah, Red."

"I still like Ike. Tell Frisco I'd bet 'im a carton o' cigarettes on the election but if I wuz to win he might have a little trouble gettin' the cigarettes to me."

Big Red laughs at his own joke. A babble of voices expresses varied political opinions. Big Red and the slow-speaking "Phantom Sniper" (a newspaper appellation—the Sniper ran around Los Angeles shooting at women with a small bore rifle; one of them died; the Sniper was caught, tried, doomed) are strongly pro-Republican. Knuckle-Head and Frisco are ardent Democrats.

Big Red raises his voice and is given the floor. It is not uncommon for all four of them to be talking at once. Quite often debates are won by the man among them with the healthiest set of vocal cords. This afternoon, however, some of the proprieties are being observed and Big Red enjoys a favored position. He expounds at some length on why he is convinced Dwight David Eisenhower should be the next President of the United States.

Frisco stutteringly demurs. Notwithstanding the fact that he can barely read and write, Frisco is not in the least backward about letting it be known that he is a political pundit of no small stature. When Big Red interrupts, Frisco declares: "Ah, ah, ah, ah; he got the soapbox now; tomorrow, ah, ah, ah, I'll have the soapbox."

Big Red retorts, "I bet if I showed up in fronta Frisco's cell tomorrow night he'd break out."

To this the Sniper mumbles an aside and Big Red roars with laughter. Then—*two bells!* And a sudden, chilling silence.

Big Red knows that give or take two or three minutes, the time is 4:45. (*And this time it's different, Red. This time they're coming for you. Before, it was the other guy. Now you're the other guy, and you're ready; in a way, you're impatient to be on your way.* "Hell, if it's gotta come, I may as well get it over with!" *That's right, Red.*)

"They ain't forgot me. I hear 'em comin'," Big Red says.

"They tied a string around their finger," Knuckle-Head adds.

"Well, I been waitin' eleven months for this." Big Red's mind is now sharply focused on what faces him.

The safety bar squeaks; keys on a ring jangle; bolts slide.

Big Red's voice booms out: "They'll get the biggest pile first." He's referring to himself. Then he adds ruefully, "I think I'll hide under the bed. Tom, you tell 'em I've moved to forty-five." Forty-five—Cell 2445—is Knuckle-Head's cell.

The death watch officers—one of them chews on an unlit cigar—enter the Row corridor and proceed to Big Red's cell.

"I'm gonna take Ike with me," Big Red says. He's referring to a large picture of Eisenhower he has in his cell. When his cell door is opened, he steps out with the picture in his hand. The death watch doesn't protest.

Big Red has a choice: if he wants, he can say goodbye to all or any of the men he's been living with for eleven months, or he can walk straight to the bird cage. He decides to say goodbye. He walks down the corridor and then starts back.

"So long, Chief . . . So long, Tom . . . So long . . ."

"Keep yer chin up, Red. . . . Take it easy, Red. . . . Be seein' ya, Red. . . ."

Big Red is being passed through the bird cage when he quips, "If I got any bigger we all wouldn't fit in here."

There's laughter. A guard asks, "How much you weigh, Red?"

"Two-eighty. I been kiddin' the day sergeant I been tryin' for three hunnerd. Now it don't look like I'm gonna make it."

A gate swings open and then Big Red is gone forever from the sight of the doomed, those he is leaving behind to live out the few days or weeks or months left to them. The ones listening to their headsets know that on the Open House program with Bert Solitaire the Frank Sinatra recording of "Birth of the Blues" is being played.

Condemned Row grows broodingly quiet for a time.

Big Red reminds you of your own plight, and your cell grows smaller in front of your eyes. The walls have a way of closing in. You light a cigarette and you think. The image that forms in your mind is stark and vividly clear. . . .

In the sergeant's office, Big Red changes his blue jeans, denim work shirt, underclothing and slippers for similar but new attire, keeping up a running fire of conversation. A restraining belt is fitted snugly around his huge middle; he's handcuffed, and the handcuffs are attached to the belt by a short length of chain. One of the death watch carries the picture of Ike. Big Red is whisked down the elevator to the ground floor, marched a few feet. The talk—the shielding talk— goes on.

A key is thrust into a lock, a solid steel door is pushed open, and Big Red is ushered through into a short hallway. To his right, a few feet away, are two cells, both brightly lighted. He is placed into the first cell. The handcuffs and restraining belt are removed. He's locked in.

It is here, under constant surveillance, that Big Red will spend a long and final night on earth.

Two of the death watch stay with Big Red; three of the remainder go back upstairs for Henry.

Henry's cell is dark and he is huddled on his cot.

"It's time to go, Henry," the lieutenant says.

"Go? Go where?"

"Downstairs."

"Why?"

"You have to go, Henry."

"But I don't wanta."

They help Henry to his feet. One on each side grips a shoulder and elbow to support him. In this way, his head bobbing on a rubbery neck, his feet dragging, they walk Henry to the bird cage.

The condemned look up to see Henry go by. On their headsets Bert Solitaire is spinning the brassy Kay Starr record of "Comes Along a Love." Then Solitaire says brightly, "For our brainbuster today we asked: How old Joe was when he kicked the bucket? The answer's eighty-four." (Solitaire and his juvenile voice and his juvenile trivia and his jump records—and the Death Row and Big Red and Henry and the mechanics leading up to a "legal execution.")

In the sergeant's office the death watch has to change Henry's clothes for him. Henry has gone limp; he babbles and his face is puffy from shock. He's handcuffed, swiftly taken downstairs.

Big Red catches a glimpse of Henry as the latter is walked by his cell and placed into the adjoining one.

"Don't look like my partner's doin' too good," Big Red observes.

Right at this time the five o'clock news from San Francisco is being broadcast. Most of the condemned have their headsets on, listening. Red must die with Henry, says the newscaster. He has lost his legal action and his request to the warden to be executed at nine A.M. instead of ten, to avoid dying with Henry, has been rejected because, according to the newscaster, the California Attorney General has declared that the wording of Big Red's death warrant won't permit it. "I got kids of my own, Warden," Big Red had told Warden Teets earlier. "If I die with this other guy there'll be a lotta bad publicity, on account of what he did. So can't you let me go an hour earlier?"

With Big Red and Henry brought downstairs, the death watch settles into its long-established routine.

This last night belongs to the condemned man. The death watch caters to his reasonable wants or requests. He can listen to programs on a radio outside the cell or have recordings played for him on an electric record player available to those waiting to die. He's kept supplied with tobacco and steaming hot, freshly brewed coffee. He's offered the traditional "hearty" meal. Reading material is furnished if he requests it, or a deck of cards with which to play solitaire. During the evening the warden and other prison officials may visit him to pass along legal or other news. He may write a last letter to a loved one. He may be visited by a chaplain of his faith who will pray for the salvation of his soul. He may brood or talk or curse or sleep or pace the floor. Such as it is, the choice is his.

Big Red talks and smokes and eats and listens to hillbilly records. The warden comes in and tells him he and Henry will have to die together, the courts have turned him down. Big Red still clings to the hope that a final plea by his attorneys will stay his execution. He kids with those standing the death watch on him. He sleeps for a few hours. He thinks back on almost forty years of life.

Henry lies on his mattress, staring blankly at the wall. He spends the night like that, saying nothing, a picture of what naked fear can do.

Inevitably, morning comes.

"Care for some breakfast?"

Big Red looks at the tray of food and his appetite deserts him. He forces down a few mouthfuls of food, smokes a cigarette, drinks two cups of hot, black coffee. *Death is a tough proposition. Death is a funny feeling, a tightening in the belly; it's a creeping numbness. Death is something too big to understand.*

And for Henry, waiting death is a terrible, lurking, shapeless Thing. The doctors look in upon him, as they have during the night.

Ten o'clock draws near. Big Red is informed all hope for a stay is gone.

Then Henry gets a stay. His attorneys have prevailed on a judge of the local superior court to stop his execution and to require the warden to show cause why he shouldn't certify Henry as being legally insane and hence not liable for execution until his sanity is restored. Guards swiftly remove Henry from his cell, return him to the Row. Supported by two burly guards, Henry babbles hysterically. Over and over he repeats something that sounds like "Eeko, eeko, eeko."

9:50. Big Red puts on the white shirt they give him to wear. He smokes a last cigarette. "Maybe I shoulda played crazy," he says. He grins crookedly. He doesn't blame the men who will put him to death. With them, it's just a job. It's too late to fix blame; it's too late to protest. But still there is something wrong with all this. Big Red feels the wrongness. He wonders: "What'll they gain by killin' me?" He knows he did wrong, but he remembers what a grammar-school teacher once told him: Two wrongs never make a right.

Ten o'clock!

"All right, Red," he's told, "it's time." The cell door is unlocked, opened.

Big Red hesitates an instant. Then he picks up his picture of Ike. (Ike is someone to believe in.) He takes the picture with him. He's marched around a bend in the hallway to the door of the gas chamber. There he stops and hands the picture to a surprised guard.

"Here," he says, "take this. I don't want to take Ike in here with me."

The guard's embarrassment is obvious as he accepts the picture. Big Red enters the chamber. He's quickly seated in one of the two metal chairs, strapped down. One end of an electric stethoscope is taped to his chest. A guard pats him on the back, says, "Good luck." In turn, Big Red quips; others before him—those who didn't curse or pray or remain angrily mute—have done the same.

10:02. The guards hurriedly exit. One of them twirls the spoked wheel that seals the chamber door airtight. Official witnesses stare at Big Red through the thick glass windows of this squat, infallible chamber of death.

His face an expressionless mask, the warden signals the executioner. The executioner swiftly operates his levers.

Big Red hears the *plop, plop, plop* of the deadly cyanide "eggs" as they drop into the acid pan beneath the chair. The chemical reaction is immediate; hydrocyanic acid gas generates, swirls up, envelops him in an invisible fog.

Big Red sniffs tentatively. His nostrils twitch at the pungent, sickening-sweet odor of peach blossoms. He gulps a lungful of the deadly fumes; his senses reel giddily, then swiftly dim. As consciousness recedes into a final darkness, he strains once desperately at his straps. His eyes glaze. They no longer see; they will never see again. His head falls forward, grotesquely, but he's wholly unaware of this. He has fallen into a black and bottomless pit; for ten minutes the process of dying goes on. His body jerks, convulses. Once. Twice. Three times. His heart races, pounds like a sledge hammer; then it slows and slows and slows—and finally stops.

The attending physician stationed outside the chamber takes the stethoscope from his ears and gestures to the warden.

Big Red is irrevocably dead.

At his peril, the warden has failed not.

The witnesses file from the presence of death into a sparkling Indian summer day. The motors behind Big Red whir; blowers drive the lethal gas upward through a pipe and release it into the air high above the chamber. A prankish breeze, coming off the bay, wafts a few molecules of the gas toward the Row, giving its keener-nosed occupants the faintest whiff of things to come. Henry crouches in his cell, the caricature of a man. "Eeko, eeko, eeko," he mumbles. More than an hour after he has been pronounced dead, a special crew removes Big Red's body from the "green room" and takes it to the prison morgue.

But Big Red is oblivious to all of this. His spirit has flown, and for a few editions after its flight he is rather good newspaper copy, what with his keenly felt political views, his taking the picture of Ike to the door of the gas chamber and his getting his wish not to die with Henry a sort of consolation prize. Yet Big Red's news value cools almost as fast as the prison morgue's ice box cools his cadaver. The public promptly forgets him, turning its attention to the fate of living, breathing condemned men, or those on trial for their lives, or those wanted for murder and other capital crimes.

Hell's Anteroom

Cell 2455—a highly guarded, next-to-inaccessible concrete and steel cubicle 4 1/2 feet wide, 10 1/2 feet long and 7 1/2 feet high—is located on the south side of the top tier of the North cell block at the California State Prison at San Quentin. By design, not chance (because here nothing is left to chance), just getting to and into the cell is, in itself, no mean feat.

The initial, ground level leg of the trip carries us, under double escort and the hawk-sharp eyes of rifle-bearing gun rail guards, along a path leading through a garden perennially ablaze with color; past a check station and the old Spanish cell block, quaint, whitewashed remnant of the nineteenth century; past the modern, bustling educational building; past the quonset hut temporarily housing the library; to the western end of the towering North cell block; and then, through an arched and guarded gateway, into the Big Yard, the prison's epicenter, a vast, rectangular expanse of cement surrounded by huge concrete and steel buildings dotted with gun towers and interlaced with gun walks.

On reaching the Big Yard, we veer sharply to the left and walk around what appears to be nothing more than a grouping of thin cement slabs stood upright by some casual, pranking esthete. However, we're familiar with their functional purpose. Concealed within each is an electric eye that zealously probes for metals and clangorously announces its finds. (Since stool pigeons, human or mechanical, are not here generally looked upon as practitioners of a high calling, "The

Eye" is one marvel of modern science whose virtues the inhabitants of this walled city do not enthusiastically acclaim.)

We've entered the Big Yard on a weekday morning a few minutes after the two mess halls have disgorged their small army of break-fasters. The yard seems to bulge with prisoners of all sizes and shapes, each garbed in blue work shirt, jeans, a jacket. Soon they will be on their way to work. The hum and babble of a thousand, two thousand, three thousand voices swells from this concrete canyon, speaking with a collective phonology of its own. Overhead a lone sea gull darts and squawks.

With a hundred briskly-taken steps we've crossed this, the northern end of the yard. We enter the North block rotunda, leaving the sun and the sky and the bright cheeriness of the new day behind. An old man with a wrinkled face and watery eyes looks at us incuriously as we enter. He is the doorkeeper of the rotunda, an ancient inmate who has seen so many come and go. He knows where we are going, but, after all, that is none of his concern.

One of the officers escorting us punches a button on the rotunda's far wall; next to the button are two massive steel doors set one against the other. Both are manually locked and unlocked from the inside.

An eye peeps at us through a slot in the innermost door. The effect is momentarily comical, reminiscent of speakeasy days when the pass-word was "Joe sent me." Then we recall where we are and where we're going, and we're no longer amused.

The two ponderous doors are swung open—one inwardly, one out-wardly—by the owner of the peeping eye, who proves to be a plump-ish gnome with a wide and disarming, somewhat vacant grin. This grinning gnome is a trusty; faithfully, but with malice toward none, he guards these "gates" against interlopers—an incongruous, grinning Cerberus. Yet, strictly speaking, the gnome is really no guard at all, for no one covets access to the dread place above.

In we go, pausing with our escort as the gnome goes briskly about his business of closing and locking the doors behind us. Closed and locked behind us too are all the reassuring sounds, sights and smells which filled our senses a moment before. Too swiftly have these sensory impressions been blotted out.

His doors locked, the gnome tugs twice on a bell rope to signal our coming. From above, we hear a bell clang twice. With only slight assistance from our now stimulated imagination, the elevator cage to which we're guided assumes the appearance of a gaping maw. Flanked by our escort, we ascend, in this gnome-operated cage, the equivalent of five floors, and step out, to the left, into a cramped, caged area.

According to a local wag we are now as close to Heaven as we will ever get; and, for a fact, the only direction one can go is down. That is where the gnome goes. The elevator door clicks shut; gnome and cage disappear.

From behind a bulletproof glass window set in a thick, rivet-warted steel door, the face of the correctional sergeant in charge of the unit is visible, slightly distorted by the poor refractive qualities of the glass. In front of this door is another, a screen-meshed, sliding one. Both, like those opening into the rotunda below, are locked and unlocked from the inside.

Our identity visually established (a phone call has notified the sergeant of our coming), these vault-like doors are quickly opened and we step within and halt. Behind us doors slide and slam; locks snap closed. To our left, in a "gun cage," an armed guard alertly watches us. To the right, commanding a view of the entire length of the building on this side, is the sergeant's office, the control and nerve center of the unit. Adjoining the office is a compact kitchen, and next to it a clothing room.

We're searched. Trained fingers probe our pockets, run along our body down to our ankles, look in our footwear. Then we enter a steel-barred, multi-locked, double-doored enclosure resembling a huge bird cage, are passed through with a jangle of keys and a sliding of bolts, and, still under escort, walk some two hundred feet along a corridor fronting a row of cells and a shower stall. There we find Cell·2455. Its front is steel-barred, steel-slatted, designed for maximum security. Across the top of its door is a "safety bar"; when locked in position, this bar prevents the door from being opened, even when unlocked. On each side of the cell the walls jut out two feet into the corridor. The cell's interior is functional, almost sterile, containing only a wooden table and stool, a sink and a toilet attached to the back wall, a cot and a board shelf above the cot which holds, neatly arranged, permitted articles and books. A set of earphones, with a ten-foot cord, hangs by a headband from a jack securely bolted to the back wall.

The safety bar across the top of the cell doors for the lower or far half of the cells away from the sergeant's office is under the control of the armed guard who patrols behind a barred and screened walkway that runs the length of the corridor fronting the cells. When signaled to do so by our escort, the armed guard pulls the lever at the west end of the corridor and just outside the fenced-in area. Up goes the bar. One of the officers unlocks and opens the door. He motions us to enter. We step within. The door is shut, locked. With a squeak, the safety bar drops back into place.

There we are.

That, physically, is how we get to and into Cell 2455. Getting permanently out of the cell and living to tell about it, once having been lodged therein as a guest of the State of California, presents an infinitely more difficult problem. Considerably more than a few dozen odd doors, locks, bolts, bars, gnomes and armed guards stand in the way.

Cell 2455, you see, is a death cell.

And . . . Whit is in Cell 2455, twice doomed.

Whit is a broad-shouldered, 190-pound six footer in perfect health and physical condition, a trained and functional fighting machine who has survived the rigors of almost six years on Death Row. His appearance bears eloquent testimony to the life he has lived. His brown, wavy hair is cut short and is beginning to thin in front. His lips have been smashed almost shapeless, and his nose is battered and broken. He wears a four-tooth bridge; the teeth missing were knocked out. Scar tissue has formed above the alert hazel eyes which glitter when he's angry, and there are innumerable turkey tracks beneath and beside them. His forehead is corrugated; his chin, scarred. An old injury to his left leg causes him to walk with a combined limp and bounce which is noticeable but which does not prevent full use of the leg.

By the most charitable standards, his face is not handsome or esthetically pleasing. It is a face that has seen too much, a young-old face, scarred by violence. With its broken, humped nose, its washboard brow, its glittering, gold-flecked eyes, and when alerted to danger its aspect of bold, the-consequences-be-damned insolence, it is a predatory face that seemingly has found its rightful place in the gallery of the doomed.

Yet further observation reveals a disturbing quality about it which suggests the paradoxical duality of its possessor, for it is a face capable of grinning disarmingly, of laughing in great good humor, and when comically split by a grin or crinkled by laughter it becomes a homely, friendly face, devoid of ugly or fearful physical connotations. At those times, one realizes that much has been superimposed upon Nature's original design, that violence, hatred and rebellion have remodeled it to suit their harsh, brutal fancies. Apparent, too, is the fact that its owner is wryly amused by its present, unlovely appearance. He remembers it was once a young, sensitive, wholesome face.

What changed it—and him?

That was long, long ago.

What brings a man to Death Row?

• *3* •

The Twig

It was 1921, a fine late spring day. May 27.

The war in Europe had been over for almost three years. And had not that war been fought to end all wars?

The third decade of the twentieth century had not yet begun to roar; the bleak, depression-ridden thirties were undreamed of. Fortunately, dreamers do not dream black dreams.

And Hallie was a dreamer, at heart a poetess with both feet firmly planted on the ground and her soft, searching blue eyes in the heavens. This day her most cherished dream was to be realized.

It is on this day the life and story of Whit begins—at Saint Joseph, Michigan. It begins unheralded in an unpretentious but sturdy house on a quiet residential street. In the front bedroom a young, reddish-haired woman is in labor. This is Hallie, the gentle Hallie, destined to suffer so much and to die so terribly. The soft cries occasionally escaping her lips are involuntary, for her heart sings a joyous song. Soon she will have brought her first child into the world, and the pain is therefore nothing. She resolutely closes her eyes and clenches her teeth against it. . . .

The pain receded. When Hallie opened her eyes she saw the good Dutch countenance of the lady doctor, who would deliver her baby, looking smilingly down upon her.

"Well, Hallie, we're all in readiness for the new heir."

Hallie nodded happily. "Serl? Is he . . . ?"

17

"Like all fathers. Fidgety. Keeps getting in the way."

The tiny, silver-haired old lady standing at the head of Hallie's bed was Hallie's foster mother, a God-fearing Baptist who saw the whole of life in terms of duty to her Maker.

The pain stabbed at Hallie again. She clutched the edges of the bed and gritted her teeth. She cried out, then moaned softly.

Delivery proved complicated. The woman was so small, the child so relatively huge! And so obstinate!

Hallie fainted. Mother Cottle wrung her hands and began to pray aloud.

The doctor spoke sharply to Mother Cottle. "There's no time for that and I'm sure *He* understands our problem. Now, quickly, do what I tell you!"

This courageous lady doctor who was Hallie's friend redoubled her efforts to deliver the infant. She threw herself into the task like one possessed or inspired. She kept Mother Cottle hopping.

For long minutes the life of both Hallie and her unborn son hung in the balance. Providence was playing a familiar game. This time it ended on a note of triumph.

"Now I have you, you fat little rascal!"

The lady doctor held the newborn babe aloft by his pudgy legs.

Later Hallie opened her eyes. "I'm fine," she insisted weakly. "And so is he." She indicated the sleeping bundle snuggled in her arm. "Yet I must admit I didn't expect him to be so big."

"Judging from the size of him now, I predict he'll be a six footer when he's full grown," the doctor said.

"Really?" Hallie said. This was wonderful news, for there hadn't been a six footer on Serl's side for generations. Of her own parents and ancestors, Hallie knew nothing. She was a foundling who had been legally adopted and raised by Mother and Dad Cottle. Hallie added, "And my little man is going to have several brothers and sisters." Already the agony of giving birth had been entirely forgotten.

The doctor frowned but said nothing. She was unable to bring herself then to tell Hallie that she could never bear another child. *I must wait to see if possible complications develop and pray they do not.*

No complications developed. Hallie quickly regained her strength; she was soon back on her feet. When told she could have no more children, she did not become sad. Surely, she thought, this fat, jolly, golden-haired little man was enough. She was inexpressibly thankful for him. She took him in her arms and assured him of this time and again.

Late November was dark and cold; an icy wind whipped in from the lake. California, with its promise of sunny blue skies and golden opportunities, beckoned Hallie and Serl. Hallie especially was certain that her Whit was not a winter's child. So they came west to the Golden State and established residence in the booming Los Angeles area. They found a cottage on Greensward Road which suited them ideally.

The seasons rolled around and all went well for this little family. The gentle Hallie lavished on her toddler the love and affection she herself had never known. They were great and inseparable pals, these two. Whit's dad, too, was his pal, and romped with him each evening on returning home from the studio where he was learning to make moving pictures.

Almost from the hour of his birth, Whit gave evidence of precocity. When he should still have been crawling in his play pen, he stood upon his fat, sturdy legs and began to walk. When his vocabulary should have been limited to gurgles and coos, words spilled intelligibly from his delighted lips. Hallie found him trying to make out words in a book and taught him how to play a fascinating game called reading, and another called writing. When given a set of crayons and some paper, he needed no encouragement to begin drawing pictures, and they were very promising pictures for such a tot.

Serl laughingly referred to his son as "The Little Professor." The nickname was an apt one, for Whit was a keenly inquisitive boy, anxious to learn.

From Hallie, Whit came to know God. God was the wise and good Father; they were all God's children. God looked down upon them and protected those who sought and needed His protection. God expected them to help one another, to be kind and good to one another, and to find and pass on, in the way in which each was best qualified, the beauty and the meaning of life.

Whit and his dad tinkered and made things together. Whit was particularly fascinated with the family car, a Star coupe, and what made it run. Gravely he listened to his dad's simplified explanation of the principle of the internal combustion engine. On the boulevard nearby was a garage; Whit made friends with the two mechanics and they let him go down in the grease pit with them. They let him "help."

Hallie had an inexhaustible supply of exciting children's stories at the tip of her tongue. In the evenings, after supper, Whit would curl himself up in his mother's lap, and listen with rapt delight to the adventures of Peter Pan or Alice or Jack who had climbed the beanstalk. There were stories from the Bible too.

Weekends and vacation time the three had great fun together. There were trips to the ocean where, with tiny pail and shovel, Whit discovered wonders in the sand. Then the happy boy would stand and listen to the booming roar of the surf.

"It's talking, Mommy!" he would exclaim delightedly. "The ocean's talking to me!"

And Hallie would smile; she would give thanks to God that her sturdy son was aware that Nature could speak to those who would listen.

Whit was three and a half, going on four, and it was the Christmas season of the year 1924. The family purchased a huge tree for the front room and he helped his mother decorate it. The tree was a wonderful, dazzling sight. That evening, after they had lit the candles on the tree and turned out the living room lights, Whit listened, wide-eyed, to his mother's recitation of the visit of St. Nick. Later, Hallie and Serl heard him in his room, apparently talking to someone. They looked in upon him.

Whit had his teddy bear propped up in front of him and was reciting to Teddy, word for word, " 'Twas the night before Christmas . . ."

They exchanged startled glances. So far as they knew, Whit had heard the poem but once!

Returning to the living room, Serl chuckled. This was not the first time his son had shown an ability to remember practically everything he heard or read or saw. "The little professor is some guy," he said approvingly.

Hallie's gentle face wore a worried frown. She said, "Sometimes I'm afraid for him, Serl."

"Afraid? In the name of creation, why?"

"I'm not sure I can put it into words. Perhaps it's nothing more than a feeling or a premonition."

Serl wasn't a complex man and he strongly resented even the suggestion of the presence of fear in his household. Further, it wasn't like his wife to voice such thoughts. That the boy was smart as a whip was certainly no cause for alarm as far as Serl was concerned, and he told his wife so.

Hallie smiled and said agreeably, "You're probably right, Serl."

She loved her husband and her son quite as much as she loved life. Actually they were her life, and her loyalty to both was fierce, unqualified. Yet there was a loyalty she owed to her dream and it need not conflict, she thought, with her loyalty and devotion to her husband and son. When she was younger, there had been creative fire in this small, plain-faced young woman. It had been a need and a demand. She had wanted to write, to be a poetess; yet, the two who had adopted and raised her—and another, near-blind child—had stifled her desire.

So, under this pressure, Hallie had channeled this creative fire into secretarial work and had become a competent and skilled private secretary to a man who had forged a multimillion-dollar business empire.

She had done this and waited. Then she had met Serl. And Serl had given her a new life. Her dream hadn't died, yet it no longer was hers alone.

There was a meaning and a beauty to be found, to be set to words or to music or on a canvas, and from the day of his birth, Hallie had never wavered in her conviction that her son would one day find and express in his chosen way this meaning and beauty. Hadn't her toddler heard and understood the voice of the surf? The knowledge was as frightening as it was wonderful, for it told Hallie that her little man would suffer and be sad and often walk alone. But this was not too great a price to pay for what would then be his.

• *4* •

The Twig Is Bent

Winter came, and with it days of fog and rain. Whit caught a cold; when he began to sniffle Hallie wanted to keep him home from school, but he begged his mother to let him continue. Against her better judgment, Hallie gave in to his plea. Then school was out for the Christmas vacation. The cold had stayed with Whit. He ran a light fever. But his spirits were so buoyant his mother found it almost impossible to keep him in bed. She gave him the run of the house. Then, when the rains let up briefly, she permitted him to go outside and play with his small friends. After a few minutes he found his breath coming in short gasps.

"Let's rest," he said, and usually he was the last one ever to want to rest.

"Sissy!" they cried.

So Whit played all the harder. He returned indoors chilled through and through and wheezing. His fever rose. He became dizzy, then nauseated. He had to fight to breathe.

By the time Serl got home, Hallie was frantic. They dressed Whit in his warmest clothes, bundled him in a blanket and drove him to the family doctor. Serl had telephoned ahead and had been instructed to bring Whit to a nearby hospital where the doctor would be waiting.

On the way to the hospital, Whit began to turn blue.

"I can't breathe, Mommy!" he cried. "I can't breathe!"

Then Whit lost consciousness. He appeared to stop breathing.

23

Hallie looked in horror at her son. "Oh, God, Serl," she cried, "hurry! Hurry!"

The doctor was waiting. Whit was placed on a table in minor surgery and the clothes from his upper body were stripped off. The doctor plunged the hypodermic needle directly into Whit's heart. The adrenalin did its lifesaving work swiftly. Whit's eyelids fluttered. He recognized his parents and smiled wanly. He began once more his fight to breathe. They took Whit to a private room. They put him in an oxygen tent. He got worse, lost consciousness and began repeating over and over the simple child's prayer his mother had taught him:

"If I should die before I wake . . ."

"Frankly," said the doctor, "he hasn't much chance."

For forty-eight hours, Hallie and Serl kept a vigil at their child's hospital bedside. The torment of watching this small son hang precariously between life and death was almost more than they could stand. Pneumococci were rampaging in both of Whit's lungs; as well, his bronchial tubes were inflamed and clogged. When the doctors attending Whit despaired of his life, Hallie prayed with a quiet, intense desperation.

"Dear Lord, please don't take our son. Let us keep him."

Whit lived, and Hallie gave the credit to God.

By the time the crisis had passed, Whit's body was thin and his face sunken. Brought home, he spent many days abed, as many more indoors. Physically he was a pathetic caricature of his former chubby self.

One day, his eyes sadder than usual, he stood watching his mother. "I'm sorry, Mommy," he said. "I'm awful sorry for all the trouble I caused you and Dad."

Hallie cried. She couldn't help it. Impulsively, with the tears running down her cheeks, she took this little man of hers in her arms and held him tight.

"Don't cry, Mommy," Whit begged. "Some day I'll be big and strong and then you won't have to worry about me any more."

Whit returned to school just as winter was reluctantly giving way to spring. There, with paints, paper, cardboard, glue and imagination, he made a "present" for his mother. He wanted to make her happy again.

The wind blew up a rain. Whit didn't want the rain to spoil his present so he took his heavy coat he had worn to school and covered the present. He was hurrying home when an older boy came along on his bicycle.

"Hi, Louie," Whit called out. Louie lived down the street from Whit and before Whit had gone to the hospital Louie had often ridden him around while he delivered his paper route.

"What've you got there?" Louie asked, braking his bike to a stop beside Whit.

"This," Whit said. He lifted his coat so Louie could see. "I made it for my mother. Do you think she'll like it?"

"She sure won't like you getting yourself all wet just when you're starting to get well," Louie said. "Hop up on the handlebars and I'll give you a ride home."

Whit perched himself on the handlebars of Louie's bike, still clutching his present with one hand. A car suddenly came skidding around the corner, going too fast. Six or seven high-school students were piled inside. Louie had to swerve sharply to avoid being run over. He and Whit took a bad spill. The teen-agers laughed loudly and kept going.

Louie snatched little Whit from the rain-swollen gutter. The latter looked like a drowned thing, but he still clung desperately to his present, which was in a pitifully bedraggled state.

Louie got Whit home as fast as he could and explained to Hallie about their accident. Whit was shivering. While his mother stripped off his wet clothes, he tried not to cry over the loss of his present. He had wanted so much to make his mother happy with the present, and now it was ruined. He began to wheeze and Hallie had dreadful visions of losing this only and beloved son. As soon as she had Whit out of his wet clothes, dried off and in bed, she called the family doctor, imploring him to come as quickly as it was humanly possible.

With the passing minutes, it became increasingly more difficult for Whit to breathe. His thin chest heaved violently as he gasped for breath. He had to sit up to get air into his lungs.

Then the doctor came. Whit was promptly given another shot of adrenalin, this one being injected into his arm. The shot relieved him sufficiently to allow fitful, labored sleep. He slept sitting up in bed.

Whit had bronchial asthma. For years to come periodic attacks would subject him to a hellish torment. Apparently they were brought on by a combination of overexertion, damp, cold weather, dust or certain pollens and hairs (especially from some animals), his state of mind contributing to the severity and duration of an attack.

Hallie and Serl tried every remedy. The doctors agreed Whit would probably "outgrow" the condition. Meanwhile Whit was given medicines, put on special diets. During attacks, a tent was built around him and various preparations were burned.

Whit's initial reaction to these attacks had been one of fright. Fortunately, his parents hadn't babied him or revealed their own fears. When Whit had asked, "Mommy, what's happened to me?" his mother had told him, in a matter-of-fact way, that his asthma was a result of weakened lungs; in time it would go away; meanwhile she and his father would do everything possible to help him get well; he should have trust in them, be brave and pray to God to be cured; and he must never think for an instant they loved him any less because of his asthmatic condition.

This condition acted as a governor on Whit's physical activities. Being an extremely active little boy physically, he soon discovered the price he must pay for overexertion. In a way he couldn't explain, he regarded his asthma as a thing of personal weakness and even of shame. The need to be strong became more demanding with each passing attack; it lurked in his mind and overpowered reason. Yet, on the surface, he remained a friendly, shyly happy child.

Hallie and Serl moved several times in the next few years, seeking a climate less irritating to their child's hypersensitive lungs and bronchial tubes, as well as a community where Whit could find new friends and interests, where he could grow and, so far as possible, be a normal little boy. At length they settled in Pasadena. Whit was then seven, thin, wasted and short for his age. The asthmatic attacks seemed to be stunting his growth.

Whit lost no time in falling in love with the district. Almost at the front door of his home, the Flintridge Hills rose steeply, abruptly; to the north, not far away, were the majestic Sierra Madres. Even as a sickly slip of a boy, the nearness of the hills and mountains awoke something within him, and when he was troubled and physically able he would go alone high into them and stand and look down.

Although he remained small and not strong physically, Whit improved tremendously in his new environment. The law of compensation had begun to assert itself. The foundations of Whit's world had been shaken because he had been; the realization, without being thought out, came to him that only he had changed: there was still an order and an unshaken centrality outside himself.

Whit did exceptionally well in school. He made friends with all his schoolmates. Hallie arranged for him to receive private tutoring in French. Each day was an adventure.

As it should, the classroom led Whit away from the classroom. Annabelle was an exquisite, imperious creature Whit's own age. She stirred Whit profoundly. She first deigned to notice his existence one day at recess. The other youngsters were busily and noisily at play. Whit stood apart and watched, and doing so he was watching and apart from himself as well—a short, brown-eyed, tousle-haired lad in search of a dream with a special meaning.

Annabelle marched over to him. "Why are you looking at *me* like that?" she demanded. "You're always doing it."

Whit was startled. At the time he hadn't even been aware of Annabelle's presence. It was on the tip of his tongue to say so, yet spontaneously he said something not less truthful but more satisfying to his beautiful questioner. "I was daydreaming, I guess," Whit said, "and my eyes just seemed to pick you out to look at all by themselves. But I don't think they made a mistake, do you?"

This was the beginning of a friendship. That it was a friendship Annabelle treated rather casually did not trouble Whit. It didn't matter that she considered him more a plaything than a playmate. Whit loved Annabelle—her beauty enchanted him—and he became her magic mirror on the wall. A child of wealthy and socially prominent parents, this goddess and her three brothers and three sisters dwelt with those parents and a grandmother, attended by a staff of nurses and servants, in a splendid mansion surrounded by spacious grounds not half a mile from Whit's home. He often was invited there to play. One day he discovered a large collection of classical and semi-classical records in the cabinet of an expensive phonograph. He was given permission to play the records and sometimes would sit for hours listening raptly, until the patience of Annabelle was taxed beyond endurance.

Annabelle's mother, however, was more indulgent and greatly amused by his absorbed listening. One afternoon she asked Whit why it was the music fascinated him so much.

"It's because I like the colors," Whit shyly replied.

This answer visibly astonished Annabelle's parent, who looked at Whit sharply. "You *what?*"

Whit was mildly frightened, suddenly ill at ease. To him it was a natural enough phenomenon—he heard music and he "saw" colors. Only there was a greater intimacy, a more perfect oneness. In a way he couldn't possibly explain, music was color.

Whit explained all this as best he could. When his young friend's parent still did not seem to understand, and voiced the hint of a suspicion Whit was trying to make her the butt of some childish joke, he went to the piano and demonstrated, picking out with two fingers melodic fragments of a work he especially enjoyed.

"Don't you see the colors?" he asked hopefully. "Don't you see them now?"

Still Annabelle's mother did not *see,* but this suddenly was not important. For it had dawned on Whit what he had done—he had played the piano and he didn't know how!

That evening at the supper table he excitedly recounted the events of the afternoon.

Hallie listened attentively, letting Whit talk himself out. Then she put several preliminary questions to her son before asking, "Would you like to take piano lessons, Whit?"

Whit's answer was an enthusiastic yes.

For Whit, learning to read music was no chore. He raced through his lessons, striding with seven-league boots toward an ultimate, toward the day when he might have his own say. He didn't try to explain his paradoxically disciplined impatience, not even to himself. What mattered and what motivated him was the fact that there was something inside him and it did not belong to him; it was good and warm and bright and he knew that he must somehow find a way to articulate it, let it flow out of him.

Whit's teacher soon became enthusiastic over her peculiar pupil. She marked him as one whose future held bright promise of a musical career. He was such an odd little boy, so sure of himself, so friendly, so polite, so anxious to become a perfectionist according to his own estimate of perfection.

Whit remained, as well, a human little boy, not above cutting short a practice period to go out and play.

The spring of the year turned to summer and school was out for the annual vacation period. Whit tramped his beloved hills alone. He joined in the games of his many friends. He went to the city with his mother or to a ball game with his dad. He rode the racing bike his father had bought for him.

One summer day he returned home tired and feverish. That day and for several preceding days he had been building a cave with two pals near a creek. He had been stung several times by mosquitoes but had paid the bites no heed. That night his condition worsened; his fever rose. A lethargy settled upon him. A doctor was hastily summoned and at first thought Whit was suffering from the flu. That diagnosis was later changed—and changed, too, was the whole course and pattern of Whit's life.

Whit had been attacked by encephalitis. The disease apparently destroyed, literally ate away, that portion of his brain which gave him his tonal sense. He was left tone deaf. Except mechanically, he was never able to play again. He never tried. Gone were the beautiful colors, the lively, wonderful colors, the friendly colors; left behind was a murky residue, gray, inanimate, dead.

This disease ravaged Whit's personality as well as his physical self. As a consequence, he became a quiet, brooding child. His sense of loss was so great and so personal, and the wound it inflicted so raw and so ugly, that the only protection he had was to embrace the fiction that what had happened didn't matter, was of no consequence. His external world surrounded Whit with cruel contradictions and those contradictions, in turn, caused internal conflicts which he was able neither to resolve nor accept.

If reprimanded in school for some minor infraction, Whit would burst into tears, or explode into a tantrum of temper. Once, irrationally angered, he climbed through an open window of the school on a Saturday morning and wrote an unexpurgated opinion of one of his teachers on the blackboard. He did this because the teacher had wrongly accused him of something he hadn't done, and had lectured him in front of the class.

As well, Whit manifested a cruel streak, directing it particularly against those he loved best. On one occasion his parents saw him kick the family's fat little dog Tippy when she came running to meet him, joyously wagging her stumpy tail. Scolded by his dad, Whit sobbed and ran, with Tippy loyally running after him. He ran until he dropped from exhaustion, falling in a heap, convulsed with sobs.

Tippy watched Whit piteously. She whined to draw his attention. He called to her; without hesitation, the little dog ran to him, licking his tear-stained face and wagging her stump of a tail.

"Tippy," Whit cried, "something's wrong with me! I do things I don't want to do but I can't keep from doing them!"

Whit didn't understand. He didn't understand that he desperately needed love and yet felt he didn't deserve it. The cruelty was sign language; it was the only way he had of asking for help and still not knowing he was asking. Too, the cruelty expressed the conflict inside him, and the unhealthy need for "enemies" that conflict created.

A few days after he had kicked Tippy, Whit was swinging aimlessly, in wide, vicious arcs, a huge bullwhip another youngster had loaned him and which his father had ordered him to give back. He was playing close to their garage when his mother unwittingly stepped from the garage directly into the path of the whip. Hallie was struck and knocked to the ground. Her cry brought Serl on the run. Whit's dad took one horrified glance at his wife writhing on the ground, saw Whit still holding the whip and concluded his son had deliberately struck his mother. In a rage, Serl snatched the whip and began striking his son with it. His wife's protesting cries finally brought the father to his senses.

As the whip bit into him, Whit stood perfectly still; he uttered no word, made no effort to ward off the attack. Actually, he had not known his parents had been in the garage or even at home when he had returned from a neighbor's and had begun to play with the whip. When his father abruptly stopped striking him, he looked once at his mother, and his shame and confusion became so overwhelming that he ran and hid himself and implored God to strike him dead.

Much later, near midnight, with the faithful Tippy's help, his mother found him. She took him in her arms, shut off his bitter words of self-reproach and assured him over and over that she and his father knew he had not struck her purposely.

In days after this incident, Whit withdrew completely into himself. He would shut himself in his room and for hours at a time sketch frightening scenes depicting the terrible fear festering within him. Whit was afraid of himself, certain that God had become displeased and angered with him. The world for him had become a strange and sinister place and he felt, for reasons he could not fathom, that Providence had given him a once strong body only so it could be ravaged by sickness and disease, two hands only so they could be used to inflict pain, and special talents only so they could, one by one, be snatched away from him. He believed sincerely, then, that he should never hope to be anything but a sickly, obscure little boy; if he remained such a little boy, he would bring no further misery and heartache into his parents' and his own life.

This was why he softly gave for reply a simple "no" when his dad later asked him if he would like to take art lessons. Earlier, without his knowledge, his parents had taken some of his drawings to a doctor and then to a psychologist and had been advised, after the doctor had had a talk with Whit, that these lessons might give him an opportunity to work out of his mind the irrational horror gripping it and, since his sketches revealed a natural aptitude, might also compensate for the loss of his music.

Whit did not and could not explain to his mother and father his fear that if he should become an artist God might contrive to cut off his hands. He did not and could not explain that he was afraid of his hands because they once had held a whip and inflicted pain. And where his sketches at first showed considerable skill, they became clumsy, crude scratchings after the offer of art lessons.

It is not in the nature of the young, however, to remain in the company of terror when flight is open to them. Time and his parents' loving care eventually blunted Whit's fears and, with the passing months, his life again assumed a reasonably normal, reasonably happy pattern. The family unit had remained tightly knit. Whit's dad continued to do well with his work, so there were no financial cares. And he himself continued to do excellently in school. Yet Whit, better than anyone, sensed he was simply marking time. He knew that colorless anonymity, when the time came, would offer no protection against what he was certain awaited him. He was a lad whom fate had not treated kindly, and he found it impossible to ignore, to stifle the creative urge inside himself.

Whit became a mother's boy, shy, obedient and, on the surface, altogether lacking the normal, healthy aggressions of lads his age. For the most part he preferred his mother's company to that of his playmates, and each day after school he and his mother took a long walk together, chatting happily. On one of these walks the sight of an injured sparrow filled Whit with such compassion and sadness he wept openly. With his mother's permission, he took the bird home and nursed it back to health. When the sparrow had fully recovered, he and his mother released it.

As soon as the bird was lost to their sight, Whit turned and looked up at his mother. "The sparrow's gone, Mom," he said sadly, "and it never once looked back."

· 5 ·

And Bent Still More

Disaster senselessly singled out the little family and struck with the force of lightning that beautiful day a friend of Whit's family drove his mother, himself and his Aunty Victoria to the city in the friend's new Ford roadster.

At a busy intersection their car was struck almost broadside at high speed by a much heavier car whose driver had ignored a stop sign. There was a screech of rending metal, a sickening instant when the world seemed to have exploded. Whit was catapulted from the rumble seat and thrown to the curb. The adults, seated three abreast in the front seat, did not fare so well. The Ford spun around, then rolled over. The family friend who was driving struck the steering wheel and was painfully but not critically injured. His aunt was thrown under the car; her skull smashed open like an egg. She died three days later without recovering consciousness. The force of the impact snapped vertebrae in his mother's back. Her skull was fractured when her head struck the dashboard. When the Ford spun around she was spilled, broken and bleeding, to the street.

Whit ran to comfort her. He remained with her during the siren-screaming ride in the ambulance to the hospital and while the nurses were waiting to wheel her into surgery. He furnished hospital personnel with their names and his father's business address, not mentioning then how painful it was for him to speak. The next day, when his jaw and his nose had swollen badly, they learned both were fractured.

Just before his mother was wheeled into surgery, the driver of the

33

auto which had struck theirs, a tall, wild-looking woman with di-sheveled hair, somehow had managed to locate their whereabouts. Dashing by startled hospital attendants, she rushed belligerently to where his mother lay, half conscious, on a gurney. It was later learned that this woman belonged to a religious cult which denied, if the mind willed it, the existence of physical injury or disease. Herself then in a profound state of shock, she shouted hysterically at Whit's mother:

"Get up! Get up! You're not fooling anybody. You're not hurt. You're just trying to pretend so you'll get my husband's money!"

Whit ran at the woman and struck at her with his fists.

Hallie, miraculously, did not die; yet she spent many, many weeks hospitalized. During several of those weeks, Whit's busy, worried father boarded him with an old Scots couple whose good gentleness Whit never forgot.

Once or more each week, Whit visited his mother at the hospital. Each time he had to fight back his tears at seeing her swathed in bandages and straitjacketed in a body cast. He talked to her eagerly of the good times they would have when she returned home to them, of the long walks they would take together. He told her he was doing fine and how well "Uncle Bob and Aunty Helen" were looking out for him.

Whit learned from his dad that his mother would soon be coming home. His dad explained that was why they were moving to a one-story house two blocks away. Whit was so overjoyed at the news he didn't think anything about why they were moving. Yet he thought it strange when they brought his mother home in an ambulance. He was permitted to see her as soon as they had established her in her room. She was still in bed, a special bed with cranks, pulleys and other odd devices, propped up with pillows. He was troubled.

"Gee, Mom," he said, after she had embraced him warmly, "I'm sure glad to see you home, but how come you're still in bed?"

Hallie then signaled the others—his father, Pat, the special nurse, the friends present—to leave the room. Alone with her son, Hallie explained to him, as matter-of-factly as possible. Her back had been broken in the accident, leaving her completely paralyzed from the waist down. She could not walk as she had no control over her legs.

"You mean—?" Whit asked, his eyes saucer large.

His mother nodded affirmatively, sensing all her boy wanted to know.

Whit cried, "But why, Mom? Why?"

Hallie told him simply, giving the only answer she knew. "It's God's will, Whit."

If that were the case, Whit reasoned to himself, then perhaps God could be induced to change His mind. In his room that night, and on successive nights, the boy prayed fervently. "Please, God, let me take my mother's place. Hurt me, not her. *Please!*"

Weeks passed. His mother's condition remained the same. In desperation, Whit sought out his dad. He told his father of the bargain he had tried to make with God and asked, in perfect earnestness, if there wasn't some way God could be persuaded. Serl sadly pointed out to his son that God must have a reason for what He had done—a reason beyond their understanding—and that it was therefore probable the Creator would not allow Whit to take his mother's place. Whit realized this, but still he was unable to bear the thought of his mother bedridden for life.

"Then isn't there something *you* can do, Dad?" he implored.

Serl solemnly promised his son, "I'll do everything I can." And he did. He had specialist after specialist examine his wife. Always the verdict was the same: Hallie was a hopeless paralytic. But until the last dollar was spent and credit exhausted, Serl stubbornly refused to accept that verdict. Heroically he resisted it, seeking and praying for a miracle that would never come to pass.

There was renewed confusion within Whit. What had happened to his mother was simply not right. It was a cruel, bad thing. It was a terrible thing. But his mother did not complain, and that made it more complicated. She was always cheerful and it was not a counterfeit cheerfulness. When Whit appeared sad, his mother told him they should be thankful God had spared her life. And he agreed, for he was most thankful for this. Yet, if God were truly responsible, why had He caused or allowed this to happen to his mother? And if God were not responsible, who or what was? These were questions the boy was not prepared to answer; he didn't want, then, to try to answer, for a suspicion lurked behind the questions, a frightening suspicion of what the answers might mean, and he desperately wanted to believe in God and good, and an ordered, controlled Reality. Such a Reality gave strength to those who lived within it; they had the assurance they dwelled in the dominion of One who was all-wise and strong. And so far as Whit then knew, the only alternative to this Reality, as a way of life, was a denial of it. But why deny what you needed? What object in denying meaning? Where did that lead?

Whit wasn't ready to defy and to deny. He still desperately wanted to serve a more significant master than his own mind. He wasn't strong and he needed strength; he had been taught to believe it could be found in Faith—blind faith. Now there was doubt and doubt had spawned a conflict he had to resolve and could not.

He had to wait. He continued to do well in school. He continued to play with his young friends. He remained close to his mother and father. He was, on the surface, a shy, bright, friendly boy.

Within him, there had taken place a transmutation: a spiritual creative urge had become a psychologic compulsion. He must, somehow, win a way back to grace. Somehow he had been responsible, by his thoughts or acts or otherwise, for the position in which he presently found himself. He felt certain that once he had enjoyed favor and now he didn't. That was *wrong*. What was *right*?

Whit would come out of his shell and go back into it. For the next six years of his life he would continue to do that, and simultaneously he would be living in two worlds—the one around him and a private, inner one of his own. More and more he roamed his beloved hills alone, and less and less did he feel a close emotional kinship to other people. He spent much of his time in this secret world, refusing to share it with anyone. Yet he never for an instant lost contact with the external world or denied the manifest reality of it. Indeed, the contrasting quality of his two worlds demonstrated beyond dispute the existence of the one without and the corresponding need for the one within.

One sunny summer day he came down from the cabin high in his hills, B.B. gun in hand, and stood at the edge of a bank looking down at a car—and the three people in it—parked where the street ended at the foot of the hills. In the back seat of the car a nearly naked couple were engaging in a sex act. A tiny, crying girl stood on the front seat and called pitifully for mama. The woman kept shushing her child and all the while responding to the huge, hairy man. Then the tiny girl set up a more insistent wail for her mama and climbed up on the back of the front seat. With a curse, the man reached out and struck the girl down. While the child cowered and whimpered in the front seat, the mother and her lover proceeded to concentrate on the gratification of their lust. They didn't proceed very far.

In a flash, Whit raised, aimed and then squeezed the trigger of his B.B. gun. A moment later a bellow of pain issued from the throat of the hairy individual and a surprising amount of activity, none of it coordinated, took place in the back seat of the car. Whit ran off down a trail; he didn't want to see any more.

Did the Devil make the hairy man and the mother do what they had been doing? Whit didn't know; nor did he know whether Providence or chance had led him to the car. And which was more important, the fact that *he* had witnessed the event, or the event itself, witnessed or unwitnessed? Another paradox had put in an appearance in his thought world: the mere asking of questions, the bare fact of their formulation, was shaping him and influencing the direction he was to take. And the capacity to ask himself puzzling questions implied something more. Creative imagination, given the objective methodology, could lead one to the answers, as well as to the reasons that motivated one to ask the questions.

Whit made his decision alone, and he kept it a secret. Not only would he believe in God, but he would find God. (His mind was made up; it was then simply a question of how.) Why should God stay in hiding? Why should God be unwilling to tell Whit why he had been made? . . . .

Swamped with debts, confronted with the necessity of paying for nurses, regular doctors' visits and medication for the bedridden Hallie, and determined to meet the other expenses of daily living and his son's upbringing, Serl, during those dark, bleak depression years of the early and middle 1930's, worked himself to exhaustion, and in doing so permanently undermined his health. Several of his business ventures flopped. The family savings and the substantial settlement received from the accident that had left Hallie paralyzed had soon been spent trying to give her back the use of her legs.

The family was forced to move to another district where the rent was much cheaper. They were obliged to economize sharply on clothing and food. They faced a bitter fight for survival. Serl swallowed his pride and accepted relief from the county.

The final blow fell when Whit, then fifteen, caught and almost died of diphtheria and the consequent heart strain, aggravated by his recurring asthmatic condition. He was released from the county hospital to his father's care with a warning from one of the doctors that his heart had been seriously overtaxed. The doctor made it clear that if Whit did not have complete bed rest for many weeks, he might not live another six months. This was more than Serl could stand. He made up his mind fate would not be given another opportunity to torment his little family.

Late one night, when Hallie and Whit were fast asleep, Serl went to the kitchen and turned on the gas in the oven. With a prayer for forgiveness, he thrust his head near the burner and inhaled deeply. When he lost consciousness he fell to the floor. The sound of his falling awakened Hallie and the sound of the escaping gas told her immediately what had happened.

"Oh my God!" she gasped, and jerked open a window within reach of her bed. She forced her voice to be calm when she called to her son.

"Yes, Mother?" Whit answered.

"I think your father has had an accident in the kitchen," she said. "Can you make it back there and turn off the gas and then get help?"

"I think so, Mom. I'll try."

Whit crawled to the kitchen and turned off the gas. Then he crawled to the back porch and shouted to a neighbor. His dad quickly revived and immediately regretted his act (although he made a second attempt hardly more than a year later). If anything, the incident brought Hallie, Serl and Whit closer together. They sat up the rest of the night and made brave plans for the future. Whit then told his parents of his decision to learn to walk again as soon as possible. He said he was certain the doctors were wrong about his heart and gently brushed aside their entreaties that he return to bed.

He had been in bed so long that learning to walk was a slow and painful process. An attack of asthma interrupted his progress—but only for a day. Within a week he had regained a shaky use of his legs; within two weeks, he was helping around the house.

Not long after the kitchen incident, two friends happened to be at Whit's home when his dad returned with foodstuffs doled out to those on relief. The packages were plainly marked NOT FOR SALE and one of his friends, Joey, recognized their source from the markings.

"Gosh," Joey remarked, "you sure must be awful poor to have to eat that stuff. I feel sorry for you."

Joey's words stung. A trigger, they set off something dangerous inside Whit. That night he told his parents he had arranged to take over his old paper route again, beginning at once. He assured them he felt strong enough. At four o'clock the following morning he rode off on his bicycle. The paper route, however, was a fiction.

Whit pedaled to a grocery store a couple of miles from where he lived. In the past he had watched truck drivers leave at the back of the store, before it opened, milk, vegetables and bakery goods. He knew of other stores, too, where this practice was followed. Once at the store, he made certain he was not being watched; then he filled his newspaper bag with two loaves of bread, two coffee cakes, two quarts of milk, a pint of cream and three cantaloupes. After that he rode off to a nearby park and waited out the time it would have taken him to deliver his old route. Returning home, he explained the food by saying his boss on the paper route had given him an advance. The family had a hearty breakfast that morning. Whit refused to regret what he had done.

He continued to steal and he kept a detailed list of each theft. To hide what he was doing, he actually got another early morning paper route. He committed minor burglaries, he purchased food with forged personal checks and got, in addition to the food, a dollar or two back in cash. In subsequent weeks, he grew increasingly more ingenious at inventing plausible stories to account for the source of the money he used to "buy" food, medicine, a little present for his mother or some other item his family needed. His thievery, added up, amounted to very little, perhaps at most four or five hundred dollars, yet without it to augment the family income, his family would have gone hungry. And with it life was still grim and hard for them.

Whit had taken no pleasure in the success of his deception or in having become a sneak thief. But had he truthfully told his mother and father the food and other items he had been bringing home were stolen, he knew his parents would have made him return them; he knew they would have preferred to go hungry and do without other necessities. He had made up his mind the choice should not be theirs. He had determined they should never know the truth.

For the first time in his life Whit was helping his parents when they needed help most. He desperately wanted and needed to do that, even when the price he paid was to become a thief and a liar. He believed, when he bargained to pay that price, that he did not have long to live. He was willing—yes, and anxious—God should punish him in any way He saw fit after death. He believed he deserved to be punished—even sent to Hell—for what he was doing. But he prayed this deserved punishment be withheld until death closed his eyes for-ever; he prayed that his parents should never know the truth, that they would remember him as a good and loving son who, during his last days, had been helpful to them. He failed to realize that he was asking too much.

Whit concealed his fright as best he could the day he became violently ill with stomach cramps and, believing his hour of reckoning to be at hand, insisted upon kissing his mother goodbye before he allowed his father to drive him to the doctor. Although nauseated and terrified beyond belief at what he thought lay before him, and with his conscience demanding he blurt out the whole story to his dad, Whit still held his tongue, determined not to betray himself. It was too late, he told himself, to cry out for help or to beg his dad or his Maker for another chance.

6

Fear!

In the doctor's office Whit began to retch. Presently a quantity of partially digested green peaches was deposited on the office floor.

Whit was given something to soothe his outraged stomach. In a matter of minutes, he was much improved and asked his father to take him home. After becoming ill, he had forgotten completely the peaches he had eaten, and had thought himself about to die. Confusion and embarrassment restored the color to his face and made him stutter.

Serl, knowing nothing of his son's thoughts and not fully recovered from the scare he had had, asked the doctor to give the boy a complete physical examination, "to be on the safe side."

This examination over, the old doctor spoke with kindly assurance. "The boy, as you can see, is underweight and rather small for his age. He has an audible congestion in his bronchial tubes caused by his asthma. But his heart is sound as a dollar. Youngsters his age have amazing recuperative powers and the boy seems to be no exception. In fact, I find no indication whatever that he hasn't completely recovered from his bout with diphtheria."

These words had an almost paralyzing effect on Whit. They meant he would not die! They meant that mere sickly slips of humanity did not dictate terms to God. He knew then what he should have known all along. It appeared certain, therefore, that God had made a fool of him, and had left him trapped.

He didn't speak on the way home. His dad tried to talk to him and became irritated with his whipped-cur attitude. His mother was overjoyed to hear the good news about his heart. She couldn't understand why when he went to his room and stayed there.

Sleep wouldn't come to Whit that night, so chaotic were his thoughts. A vague but intense fear gripped him; it was as though clammy hands had taken hold of him and would not let go. A familiar sound, which ordinarily would have passed unnoticed, brought him upright with a jerk, wide-eyed and panicky. He would not have been surprised then to have seen the Devil himself, with flowing crimson cape, horns and sinuous, pointed tail, standing there leering at him, mocking him. Instead, in the pale gloom of the bedroom shared by him and his father, he saw the authoress of the sound, faithful old Tippy, industriously scratching herself.

"Tippy," Whit called quietly, and she waddled over to his cot, jumped up onto it and nuzzled him. In another moment, lying there beside him, she was fast asleep, again leaving him alone and terribly afraid. An overpowering sense of guilt, theretofore locked in a dark corner of his mind, had found release when he had learned he would not die. Fear was there, too——shapeless, threatening. It filled the room. It filled his mind.

From across the room he heard the sound of his dad's deep, regular breathing. He visualized in his mind the composed face of his mother as he had seen it in sleep, with the lines of worry and physical suffering briefly erased.

Over and over he told himself: They must never know! They must never know! But he recognized this for the delusion it was; they would know. They would know their only son was a thief, a liar, a deceiver. They would know he was not a good son. The realization made him burn with shame. They would be ashamed and hurt; yet so selfless was their love for their child, they would conceal their shame and hurt and do their best to protect him. They would, furthermore, make impossible sacrifices, denying themselves even food in order to repay every cent he had stolen. And they would forgive him for what he had done, fixing the blame on themselves for somehow having failed him. All this he knew, and the knowledge was bitter wormwood. It was all wrong.

God had no right to punish his parents for what he had done! Already they had been made to suffer too much. Already they had made too many sacrifices for him. He, alone, deserved punishment. His pride, his cowardly refusal to live in poverty, his selfish belief he could do good by being bad, had led him into a maze from which there was no apparent escape. The very nature of his conduct had alienated him from his beloved parents when he needed them most. He dared not turn to them without transferring his guilt and his shame to them, and that he could not do.

Whit had to find his own way. He realized then, with bitterness, what an uncourageous thing he was, standing alone and unshielded. All places of concealment had been sealed off; the past could not be blotted out. And it seemed to him that past was a steamroller bearing down upon him. He stood directly in its path, transfixed by fear, knowing that unless he could first conquer that fear, there would be no escape.

He saw himself for what he was: a scrawny, fifteen-year-old boy, barely five feet tall and weighing not more than one hundred ten pounds. An asthmatic, puny, wheezing machine. A poor anonymous nothing who wanted to be a something. A neurotically anxious nothing. And he saw himself for what he wanted to be: A man. Tall and strong. A man who couldn't be hurt. A man who knew and made his way without doubt. A man who couldn't be scared.

Whit was thankful for the morning and the opportunity for physical activity it afforded. After dressing without awakening his parents, he pedaled off on his bicycle just as the sun's warm rays knifed through the haze over the sleeping city. There was, however, no warmth inside him; only a cold and wintry desolation. He rode along aimlessly, waiting for the hours to pass and for the time to come when he might make the visit he proposed.

At a few minutes before eight, he parked his bicycle at the curb fronting a small cottage dwarfed by a church that loomed beside it. At that moment the towering house of God was sternly symbolic to him of the Creator's might; while the tiny parsonage nestled in its shadow represented the strength of man.

It was in this church that Whit had been baptized. Here, each week, he had attended Sunday School. This was the fount of the world of God he had found. He recalled how his teacher one Sunday had flourished a piece of snowy white paper and told the class: That, when man was born, was the color of his soul; each time man sinned he smudged his soul. God was, she warned the class, a God of love and a God of wrath.

Whit had sinned. He had felt God's wrath. His sense of spiritual guilt, aggravated by a creative imagination denied legitimate expression, had become an exquisite horror, and perhaps helped satisfy the need he felt to suffer.

He had come to beg for intercession. He ran to the door of the parsonage and banged on it until it was opened by the minister, whose sleep-filled eyes opened wide at the sight of this wild-looking young member of his flock.

"I've got to tell you something, Reverend," Whit blurted out. The story of his thefts and deception spilled from his lips in a torrent of words.

The man of God heard and was profoundly shocked. He declared the boy had no choice but to go promptly to his parents and to the police and confess.

"But I just can't," Whit sobbed, stubbornly.

"In that case," said the then stern-visaged cleric, "I shall be forced to tell them myself."

"But isn't there some other way, Reverend?" Whit pled. "Isn't there some way you can fix it up with God? I know everything I took. I kept a list. And I thought if I came to you, you could make God understand. I promise I'll pay it all back."

"See here, young man," the minister said, "I want you to understand right here and now that the good Lord is never a party to thievery."

Whit fearfully persisted. "But, Reverend," he said, "can't you see? It's partly God's fault in the first place."

The minister regarded the words as blasphemous. His jaw muscles knotted; his countenance registered righteous horror. He demanded, carefully spacing each word: "Just exactly what do you mean by that?"

"Well," Whit replied, anxious to try to explain, "Mom told me it was God's will that she was paralyzed and I used to pray to Him every night to let me take her place, to paralyze me and let her walk again. Then when I went to my dad he told me God probably wouldn't do that because He must have had some reason for letting Mom get her back broken."

"And what your father told you was unquestionably right," the minister interrupted.

"Well," Whit continued, "Dad spent all his money on doctors trying to help Mom. Finally he went broke and pretty soon we didn't even have enough to eat. Then, like I told you, I caught diphtheria and we went on relief and I just couldn't stand living like we were after my dad turned on the gas and after the day Joey saw we were on relief and said what he did. I figured then God wouldn't be too mad at me if I took something for us to eat. I just had to help my folks. I couldn't stop myself. Besides, I thought I only had six months left to live and I figured if God wanted to punish me He could do it after I was dead and Mom and Dad would never know anything about it."

"I see," the minister said, clasping his hands together and looking ceilingward through half-closed eyes. He remained silent for many long seconds, which were ticked off by a grandfather clock in a corner of the room. At length he said, "Perhaps, son, you had better give me a few days to think the matter over and pray for guidance. In the meantime, you have my permission not to say anything to anyone about what you have told me, and I shan't either."

"Yes, sir," Whit said. "Thank you, sir."

He rubbed his eyes and started for the door, still gripped by despair. It was still he, alone and unaided, who would have to liberate himself, and he realized his problem, at heart, was not simply the winning of spiritual amnesty or the repayment of something taken which had not belonged to him—it was finding himself and the meaning of himself. Too, in a way, it was finding reality, no matter how ugly reality might be.

This meant he first had to conquer the fear inside him; for so long as fear remained his master, his life would be an unbearable parody filled with the tempests of petty crises. Until he rid himself of fear, he would simply be a wretched puppet, jumping this way and that as fear jerked the strings.

At the door, Whit turned. "You know, Reverend," he said, "I think God made a mistake when He didn't let me die like the doctors said I would."

Then he walked out into the sunlight, his eyes blinking against the brightness of the spring morning.

Whit went home and helped around the house, doing the dishes and other odd chores. It was a ramshackle wooden house and poorly furnished with old and odd pieces of furniture. It was a visible symbol, and he couldn't deny he hated it and all it stood for: the shame and the degradation of their poverty—that particularly. He made his mother some lunch and sat by her bedside while she ate.

When his dad came home Whit said he was going to a show. He washed and put on a clean shirt. He walked slowly through the early afternoon sunlight. Somewhere, just out of reach, he felt there was a solution, an answer.

Barbara was waiting for him in the foyer of the theatre. She was a plump, pretty girl whose parents were strict with her. About the only time they were able to spend together was at these Saturday matinees which were watched over by mothers from the P.T.A.

They took seats together, halfway down, on the left hand side of the theatre. When the main feature was half over, two boys seated themselves directly behind them. One of the two was an overgrown, loud-mouthed bully whom we'll call Sonny who had taken a fancy to Barbara several weeks before and who had been bothering her since. Sonny had been enraged when Barbara had made it plain to him she preferred Whit's company to his.

Sonny immediately began making insulting cracks about Whit, coupled with foul insinuations concerning Barbara, which were echoed by Sonny's leering companion, whom we'll call Charley.

Whit turned in his seat but before he could voice protest Sonny thrust his coarse-featured face close to his and said in a stage whisper, "You know something, you scrawny little runt? I don't think you got a gut in your body."

"Why don't you leave us alone?" Whit asked. "We're not bothering you."

Sonny said, "You're bothering me by just being alive. Barbara's my girl from here on. Now beat it home to mama before I punch you in the nose."

Barbara turned angrily. "I'm not your girl and I never will be. I'm his and you leave him alone."

In one swift motion, Sonny reached out and gripped Whit by the shirt front, ripping it. He made a fist of his free hand. "You're either my girl or I beat the hell out of this yellowbelly right now."

The incident drew the attention of the ushers and the P.T.A. mothers. They descended in a body and made Sonny and Charley leave the theatre. Barbara took Whit's trembling hand and held it until the show was over.

Whit was walking Barbara home when Sonny and Charley, who had been lying in wait behind a sign board, again accosted them. Whit involuntarily sobbed.

Sonny's long face wore a mean, triumphant expression. He gloated over Whit's obvious fright. "What's the matter, punk, scared? You didn't think I was gonna let you off that easy, did you?"

Sonny shoved Whit, sending him sprawling to the sidewalk. Before Whit could get up, Sonny laughed and kicked him. Whit looked up. Sonny stood over him, the coarse features of his long face registering his pleasure. Whit was unable to comprehend why this tall, strong boy who towered above him like a giant should find pleasure in picking on such a small and weak creature.

"Please, Sonny," he said, "please don't beat me up."

"Why shouldn't I?" Sonny demanded, kicking him again, viciously, and making him cry out in pain.

"Listen to this punk whine, Charley," Sonny gloated. "I told you he was a gutless wonder."

"Some jellyfish, all right," Charley agreed. "Let's see you make him squirm some more. Might do him some good."

"Sounds like from the way he's crying, Charley, the punk is gonna die of fright before I get a chance to give him a little workout," Sonny said, watching Barbara for the effect his words would have on her.

Barbara was white-faced. She, too, was afraid, but her fear was for Whit, not herself. At first she hadn't known what to do and her mind had raced. Then, when Sonny looked at her, she knew what she had to do.

"Leave him alone, Sonny," Barbara said.

"Sure," Sonny replied, his voice mocking her. "Sure, I'll leave him alone—provided I can have you."

Barbara stepped closer to Sonny and the expression on her face should have warned him.

"All right, Sonny," she said, facing him. "You can have me—like this!"

Barbara raked her fingernails down Sonny's cheek; in a frenzy of anger, she kicked and scratched him until a blow sent her reeling back.

Whit leaped to his feet and rushed at Sonny, only to be struck solid, sickening blows that dazed him. Sonny hit him twice more and Barbara shouted, "Run!"

Whit ran, with Sonny and Charley chasing after him, cursing him. He thought his lungs would burst before he managed to elude them. Then he stumbled into a restroom at a service station and vomited until he was too weak to stand. He sobbed with shame and humiliation.

Late that night he stole quietly from his cot, dressed and wrote this brief note to his parents:

> Dearest Mom and Dad:
> I am running away because it is best. I can't tell you why. Please don't try to find me. I will come back as soon as I can. God bless you both.
>
> Your loving son,
> Whit

He placed the note on his pillow, tiptoed silently from the house, and had just reached the sidewalk when a figure stepped out from be·hind a hedge.

"Barbara!" he exclaimed.

"Shhh," Barbara told him.

"Gee," he whispered, "what're you doing here?"

"I came to warn you."

"About what?"

"Something awful has happened," Barbara said. "Sonny called up and said he knew we had been doing something bad. You know what I mean. He said you had been bragging about it."

"But it isn't true! It's a dirty lie!"

"Of course it isn't true, but they won't believe it. At first they were so mad they said they were going to kill you and me both. But after they quieted down they said they were going to the police station in the morning and get you put in jail. And send me away. I waited until they went to bed and then I sneaked out my bedroom window and came to warn you. I was just going around to the back of your house and try to wake you up so I could tell you when you came out. How did you know I was out here?"

"I didn't," Whit said.

"Then what—?"

"I was running away," he told her.

"Why?"

"Partly because of what happened this afternoon; partly because of some other reasons. Can't you see, Barbara? I'm no good and a coward on top of it. Everybody concerned will be better off if I'm not around."

Barbara said feelingly, "You mustn't talk like that. You *mustn't!* You're *not* a coward. I know you're not."

"But I ran away," Whit said bitterly. "And now I'm running even farther away. I'm like a rabbit; I run every time I get scared."

Barbara's answer died on her lips when a sedan rounded a corner up the street. The beam from the headlights caught and outlined them for an instant. The auto accelerated, racing toward them and then braked, tires squealing, to a stop.

"Quick, run!" Barbara cried. "Here they come."

They ran, together, down the driveway. They climbed the back fence, dashed through a back yard, up a second driveway, scooted across a street and concealed themselves in the thick shrubbery in front of a school. There, panting, they crouched and listened anxiously for sounds of pursuit. There were none.

"They sure will be sore now," Barbara said.

"What'll we do?" Whit asked.

With a boldness to hearten Whit's timidity, Barbara said, "We'll both run away. We'll run away together where nobody can find us."

7

The Inevitable Implosion

Whit said, "It wouldn't be right for a girl to run away, at least not with a boy."

"All right," Barbara replied, hurt and a little angry. "Then I'll go home. And you know what will happen?"

"What?"

"I'll get beaten again real bad, that's what. I might even get killed. And if not, I'll probably get sent away—maybe to a reform school— and you'll never see me again. *Never!* Is that what you want to happen?"

"Gosh, no," he said, frightened. The mental picture conjured up by the girl's words and magnified by his own imagination made him shake so much his knees knocked together. "But just the same I don't want you to get in trouble."

Barbara laughed and looked at Whit sharply in the near-darkness of their hiding place. "I'm already in trouble. Besides, there's nothing wrong with a girl and a boy running away together if they're in love and want to get married."

"But we're too young to get married," Whit protested.

"There's a way we could do it," Barbara said.

"How?"

"If I was going to have a baby. I knew a girl it happened to once. They made them get married."

This suggestion frightened Whit so badly he had to lean against the shrubbery for support. He remembered a long-ago day in the hills, and a hairy man, a tiny girl and a woman.

"Please, Barbara," he said. "Please don't talk like that. It scares me so bad it makes me die inside."

"Why?" Barbara demanded.

Whit said the words but they didn't sound convincing even to him. They were just words. "Because . . . because I love you. I love you so much it makes me sick just to think about hurting you. If we got married for that reason people would talk about you. They would say you were a bad girl and it would be my fault."

Pouting, Barbara said, "I wouldn't care what anybody said so long as we were able to get married and be together."

"But I would," Whit said. He tried to make Barbara understand, and in doing so he was really trying to convince himself that he was doing the "right" thing voluntarily rather than the thing fear insisted he do. The words he used were a kind of emotional dialectic. "Can't you see? You're a good girl, Barbara. You've got to stay that way for me. You've got to make me good, instead of letting me make you bad. Right now I'm all mixed up and scared. I've done something bad and I'm running away. I've just got to run away. But I've got to have something to believe in while I'm scared and running."

He paused and then he said, "One of these days I think God will make everything all right for me again. Then I won't be scared and I won't have to run any more. Then, when I'm good again, I can come back to you. Then I'll have a right to you I don't have now. If I took you with me now I'd be taking something that doesn't really belong to me and I'd always hate myself for doing it."

Barbara began to cry. He was letting words get between them. He was right but he was wrong, and she knew he would be sorry. "I understand," she said, because she *did* understand. Understanding did not make it easier. "But I'm still awful afraid if I go home now I'll never see you again, that they will send me away where you can't find me."

"I'll find you," Whit promised fervently. "Besides, I have an idea I think will make everything easier for us."

He told her his idea. Then they walked to an all-night drugstore and used the pay telephone, both crowding into the booth. Whit dialed the number of Barbara's home. He let the phone ring five times before he hung up and waited. Twenty minutes later he dialed the number again. This time a woman's voice answered. Whit identified himself.

"Oh," the woman said, surprised, "we've been looking all over for you. Where are you now? What've you done with Barbara?"

"She's safe," Whit replied. He heard another, a gruff voice demand, "Who is it, that kid? If it is, let me talk to him." The woman told this other party, "Wait just a minute. Let me ask him a question first."

Speaking into the phone, she asked, "Where is Barbara now?"

"Right here with me," Whit said, purposely not being more specific. Then he let Barbara talk.

"Please, listen to me. I'm all right. I'm coming home. But first we want to talk to him."

"I don't know if you should. He's . . ."

"Give me that damn phone," they heard the gruff voice angrily demand. "What kind of a stunt do you think you're up to now?"

"Sir, Sonny told you a lot of dirty lies about Barbara and me. None of that stuff he told you is true. I swear it isn't."

The gruff voice snorted derisively. "And I suppose you'll swear she didn't sneak out her bedroom window and that I didn't see you and her run when I drove up to your house?"

"No, she sneaked out all right," Whit admitted. "But she only did it to warn me about the lies Sonny had told you about us and because she didn't want me to get into any trouble over them."

"Yeah, then why'd you both run? Answer me that one."

"Because we were scared you would whip her again if you caught her."

"She had a whipping coming."

"No, she didn't. She hasn't done anything bad."

"How do I know that?"

"Well, if you won't take our word for it you can take her to a doctor and he'll tell you."

Then he did shout: "How the hell can I take her anywhere?"

And Whit answered quietly, "Because she's coming home. Barbara's a good girl and she wants to come home."

"Well, nothing's stopping her, is there?" the gruff voice snapped back.

"Not if you'll promise not to beat her and not to send her away. I don't care what you tell the cops about me, but I want you to promise you won't tell them anything bad about her. And if you let her stay home, sir, I promise you I won't ever try to see her again until we're old enough to get married."

The voice fumed unintelligibly, called Whit a nervy, presumptuous little bastard, swore Whit would be put behind bars until hell froze over. He might have been talked out of calling the cops once last night and again this morning, but it couldn't be done again—not unless it was over his dead body.

"And if that girl isn't home here in thirty minutes," the voice concluded ominously, "I'll have every cop in the country out looking for you. Get that?"

Whit heard a woman's voice pleading for calmness and understanding.

"I don't think we're asking too much," Whit said. "So why don't you promise?"

Finally, with bad grace, the gruff voice gave in. "All right, I promise. But I'm going to tell you one thing right now: if I ever catch you around Barbara again I'm going to beat you to within an inch of your life."

Whit hung up.

He and Barbara stopped walking when they reached the railroad tracks where she lived. The first streaks of dawn had appeared in the east. The morning was cold.

"I guess we better say goodbye here, Barbara," Whit said.

Impulsively, Barbara threw herself into Whit's arms, pressing her trembling young body against his.

"Don't forget to leave a note in that hole in the palm tree so I'll know if they keep their promise."

"I won't," she replied, small-voiced.

"Goodbye, Barbara. Goodbye for a little while."

"For two and a half years," Barbara said.

"The time will go fast," Whit said. "And it's best this way."

"If you say so," she whispered, and then, with a longing she could not put into words, she kissed him.

Whit had his first taste of manhood. He wanted to take the girl with him. It was a sudden, consuming desire and it almost overpowered him. But he knew he couldn't take Barbara with him; he was still a puppet on a string.

Gently, reluctantly, Barbara loosed herself from Whit's arms, looked once deeply into his troubled, haunted eyes, forced herself to smile and said softly, "Goodbye."

She walked away quickly, almost running. "Remember," she called back, "always remember I wanted to go with you." She ran then, swiftly.

Whit would remember. He turned slowly, his heart sick and ineffably sad. "I love you, Barbara," he said in a barely audible voice. "I love you so much I know I will probably never see you again."

He hid himself in the nearby hills of his childhood, away from all of his kind. A few years earlier, he and a pal named Tim had built a crude log cabin in these hills, and it was to this cabin he crept. Here he lay, staring at the ceiling, not eating, refusing to think, waiting. He ventured out only to get an occasional drink of water 'from a reservoir close by. Although the days were warm and sunny, for it was late spring, the nights were biting cold and through them he wheezed and shivered, but unmindfully, so complete was his sense of loss and loneliness.

Still with him, mocking him, terrifying him, was a dark, unnatural fear that his imagination, events outside himself and a sense of guilt had turned into a monster which threatened to destroy him.

He lay hidden in the cabin for three days. Then, late the third evening, he came down from the hills on hunger-weakened legs. He found Barbara's promised note in the hole in the palm tree near her house.

Beneath a street light he unfolded the note with trembling hands. He read:

> My darling:
>
> I have to write this in a hurry. My family aren't keeping any of their promises except they haven't called the police on you. We're leaving in the morning. I don't know where we're going but as soon as I learn I'll send our new address to your mother. When you get it don't try to write because if they found out they probably would move again. Remember I love you now and I always will. Please, please come after me. I'll be waiting and counting the days.
>
> All my love forever,
> Barbara

Barbara had been stolen from him!

Whit felt numb even though he had known this very thing would happen. He had known but he had refused to believe. His mind and his heart told him he had been cheated, cruelly, unnecessarily.

And why? He didn't, he couldn't fool himself any longer. He didn't try. He knew why. But not rationally. Emotionally. Arbitrarily. That was how he knew. And knowing required no proof.

It was then that Hate and Rebellion took off their masks and introduced themselves. They had been hiding within Whit for a long time, playing a waiting game—for sickness, frustration, resentment, hostility, fear, confusion to build into an intolerable tension—for anxiety to generate a pressure that could not be withstood. Waiting for the inevitable psychical implosion. And then it came, and was soundless, and did its devastating work.

Hate had showered sparks and the sparks had kindled a fire in the midst of the devastation; Whit vowed he would fan and feed that fire until it became a roaring inferno.

I'll get even! (It didn't matter against whom or what.)
I'll make "them" sorry!
"They" think I'm afraid—I'll show them!
I'll show them I don't care!
And I don't.

8

"It's Better to Be Anything than Afraid."

Night passed and day came unnoticed by Whit. The sun rose. The city awoke. City sounds and smells filled the air. Pedestrians were all about when hunger and fatigue finally brought Whit out of his funk and he became aware that he had been trudging blindly along a sidewalk on the main street of the city, oblivious to his surroundings. He saw where he was. Simultaneously, the sounds of the city became audible, and delicious food smells from a restaurant increased the hunger pangs in his belly.

He was dog tired. He leaned against a building to rest. Then he noticed Barbara's crumpled note, still clutched in his hand. He smoothed it out, folded it and placed it in his wallet. He didn't think about it. He thought about where he intended going. He walked unsteadily south to an intersection. When a business coupe was halted by the traffic signal, he stepped off the curb and asked its operator, "Ride, mister?" The driver motioned him to get in.

He got a ride to within a block of Tim's home and walked the rest of the way. His pal Tim was a short, husky, healthy youngster his own age. Tim's father had died when Tim was a toddler. When smaller, his pal had been shunted around among his relatives to live. When they had refused to keep him longer, the mother had re-established a home of sorts. She had made no great pretense, however, of loving her child and, in turn, Tim had felt no particular devotion or attachment to his mother. A rather wild youngster with an urge, perhaps defensive, to be a tough, cynical guy, Tim had already had several minor brushes with the law. He was a member in good standing of a gang composed of would-be young toughs and their girl friends and had made several unsuccessful efforts in the past to get Whit to join his "club."

Whit found Tim at home. With him were two teen-agers Whit knew casually. One was Tim's girl, Bobby, sharp-tongued young sophisticate with a cute, overpainted face. The other was a girl we'll call Virginia, who, with ample justification, considered herself sexy and a seductress. Virginia was certain she knew all the answers. Both girls regarded Whit with open contempt because they thought him a goody goody mama's boy, more interested in books than girls. They didn't think he knew the score.

"Hey," Tim said, "where the heck've you been? You look awful, like you been run through a wringer. And your dad's been here looking for you. What happened?"

"I ran away from home," Whit said.

"*You* ran away from home! I'll be . . . Where you been?"

"Hiding in the hills."

"What's the matter, the bulls after you?"

"I don't think so. Not unless my dad turned me in."

"Well, if the bulls ain't after you what've you been hiding from then?" Tim asked, perplexed.

Whit flushed with embarrassment and then became angered with himself for having done so. He said, "I guess you could say I've been hiding from myself."

Bobby squealed with mirth.

All expression left Whit's face; the color drained from it. "Go ahead and laugh," he told her in a voice that sounded harsh and strange even to himself. "I think it's funny, too. I think it's the funniest thing I ever knew of happening to anybody. And you know why? Well, let me tell you the whole story and then you'll know why. Then you'll really get a laugh."

Whit told them, in hard, plain words, about himself. He made what had happened to him come vividly to life before their eyes. He showed them Barbara's note. He made them read it.

He said, "That's the story. Now go ahead and have a good laugh."

Bobby squirmed in her chair, avoiding Whit's eyes. She had seen Whit's soul; it had frightened her. She stammered, "I don't think it's so funny now."

"Then you've missed the point or you've got no sense of humor," Whit said. "Because it is funny. It all started because I wasn't satisfied with being ordinary and plain and poor, but there wasn't much I could do about changing it on the outside. So I changed the inside. I let my imagination make me a special world. I created a lot of symbolism with religion and people and things, like I used to do with my music and drawings. After that everything that happened was symbolic; it had a special meaning that only I understood, and it made me feel important. But after I'd started to steal and then found out I wasn't going to die, it got out of control. I found out I'd created something a lot worse than just being plain and poor. It was like being in a nightmare when something awful is chasing you and you can't run, no matter how hard you try. You're sick with fear and yet you aren't even too sure why. And somehow you know it's only a nightmare but you can't wake up. Then, finally, the awful thing does catch up with you and that's when you do wake up. You wake up and find you haven't been sleeping. You find out that you've been unconscious, and you've been that way because you've been taking something like dope. You know you don't ever dare take the dope again, not ever, because the thing will be waiting for you. And yet without the dope you're so confused you don't know for sure what's right and what's wrong or what's real and what isn't. But you have to find out—above everything else you have to do that—and you're sure of only one thing: It's better to be anything than afraid."

Tim didn't understand the import of what Whit had said, but he possessed a form of cunning which told him his timid friend stood where the road branched. Tim long since had concluded that only suckers took the "right" road; so he asked, "Does that include the cops?"

Whit's eyes glittered strangely. "That includes the Devil himself," he said quietly, meaning it.

Virginia looked at him with bold, interested eyes. "You talk big," she said. "But I bet you're even afraid of me."

Bobby giggled. The talk had returned to a level she understood. Tim snickered.

The color rushed back into Whit's face; for an instant there was renewed confusion inside him. He fought it down and said, "Not if I had something to eat first."

Tim knew then his pal had really changed. "How long since you had something to eat?" he asked.

"Three or four days," Whit said. "And I feel kind of weak and dizzy."

"Jeez," Tim said, "no wonder." He told Bobby and Virginia to fix his pal a breakfast. "My old lady'll raise Cain. She does every time there's anything missing. But I don't care. I like to hear her squawk."

Whit wolfed down the meal the girls prepared for him, listening to their chatter and Tim's expansive talk. He learned the other three were ditching school. Virginia cleared away his dishes and poured them all coffee. Then she opened a package of cigarettes, passing them around. Whit didn't smoke, but he took a cigarette and puffed on it experimentally.

Tim said, "What we need now is something to drink. There's a bottle stashed around here some place. Let's find it."

They all began searching for the bottle. Bobby found it on the top shelf of a cupboard behind some canned goods, an unopened fifth of Scotch. Tim opened it while Bobby rinsed out four water tumblers and Virginia got a quart bottle of a cola drink from the refrigerator to mix with it. Tim filled the tumblers half full of the Scotch and then poured in the cola until they were full.

The first few swallows burned Whit's mouth and throat. When the drink reached his stomach he wanted to gag but managed not to. After that the mixture went down easier and he began to feel pleasantly lightheaded.

Tim's mother returned home unexpectedly and found them noisy drunk. She snatched up a dust mop and routed them from the house.

The alcohol had accentuated Tim's tough-guy complex; he snarled ludicrously at his mother.

They made their way, none too steadily, along the tree-shaded street on which Tim lived, with Tim muttering imprecations and Bobby and Virginia singing until Bobby got the hiccups. They cut across a dusty vacant lot to a boulevard and continued on toward the business section of the city. The day was scorching hot. The sun was beginning to spoil their drunken fun when ahead of them they saw a portly gentleman park his late-model sedan at the curb and enter a drugstore, leaving a door of the car open and its motor running.

Of one mind, they walked quickly to the car. "Well, lookee here," Bobby said. "Do you see what I see and are you thinking what I'm thinking?"

"I'm thinking," Virginia replied, "that my feet are getting tired. I think I feel like riding for a while."

"In that case," Tim said, still playing the tough guy, "quit gabbing so much and get in. Let's go for a ride."

"Yeah," Whit said, almost soberly, repeating Tim's words, "let's go for a ride. Let's go for a ride to Hell. I'll do the driving."

Whit shoved Virginia over and got behind the wheel while Tim and Bobby scrambled into the back seat. Whit, whose dad had taught him to drive their pickup truck, eased the sedan from the curb. Then he honked the horn in one long, continuous blast until the portly owner of the car came running from the drugstore, shouting at them. Then Whit sent the sedan speeding off.

Virginia moved over in the seat. She pressed her leg against his suggestively. She tuned the car radio to some dance music.

Then she asked, "Which way is Hell?"

Whit knew she was trying to make fun of him. He didn't intend to let her get away with it. Having the powerful car under his control wrought a change in him. It opened up, with alcohol's help, a new world, a world a man could conquer and do with what he pleased.

"I'm not so sure which way Hell is," he said, "but I'm looking for street signs now."

Virginia laughed in a sly way. "I know a shortcut in case you're interested," she said, and pointed to an intersection up ahead of them. There sat a cop on a motorcycle, watching traffic. Whit tensed; fear pulsed through him. He wanted to disappear, to hide; but he couldn't. He had to keep going, to act natural. With an effort, that is what he did. He was "walking" forward into danger.

The cop didn't impress Virginia. When Whit made the boulevard stop, his heart in his mouth, Virginia waved at the cop and the cop waved back, then not paying any more attention to the car or its occupants. Virginia said, "The stupid bastard."

Then she spoke to Whit, "Did the big bad policeman scare you, little man?"

"No," Whit said, anger taking the place of fear. He had to show her he wasn't afraid; he had to show himself that, too.

He pushed down on the accelerator. The car leaped ahead, around a corner, onto the open highway. The speedometer needle climbed. The windows were open and the wind roared in their ears. Whit shot through a stop sign and Virginia wasn't relaxed any more.

Behind them a siren screamed faintly.

Tim shouted, "What the hell's the score?"

"Virginia's in a hurry to get to Hell," Whit shouted back. He fought the big, sleek sedan around an S-turn. Then he pushed the gas pedal down to the floorboard. For a half mile the car continued to pick up speed. Two motorcycle cops were after them, gaining on them. The speedometer read eighty, eighty-five. They were approaching a jammed intersection. Whit kept his foot on the accelerator. Virginia screamed and made a grab for the steering wheel. Whit cursed and shoved her away. He knew, then, he would get through; he had a reason. Virginia could be scared, too. He had the power to scare her.

Somehow a space opened up for him at the intersection and he got through, not expertly, perhaps even miraculously, but he got through. He turned onto a side street, then another. He had ditched the bulls, as Tim called them.

This premise came from the experience: If you used your head and your guts, you could do what you wanted and get away with it. The premise lit up in his mind like a neon sign, and suddenly Hell took on a special allure of its own.

Whit laughed, even though his body was trembling and his hands on the steering wheel were wet with perspiration. He had to hide his own physical reaction.

"Don't ever grab at the wheel again," he told Virginia. "I know what I'm doing." He tried to sound tough.

"You were just lucky," Virginia said. She wouldn't give him any credit. That made him angry.

"Yeah? Well, let's see if I can be lucky again." He swung the sedan around in a U-turn, headed it toward the main highway again.

"Never mind, little man," Virginia said. "I've got a date. And my date's got his own car and plenty of money. He's not just a half-pint show-off who's been living in some screwy dream world."

Her words hurt him. They cut like a knife. He had to get over that. He had to reach the point where nothing anybody said could hurt him. He didn't get a chance to reply.

Tim said, "What the hell!"

Bobby was giggling. "I wet my pants," she said, making a joke out of it.

"I'll be damned!" Tim said, and then he laughed. They all laughed. They weren't drunk any longer; they were cold sober, and they were having a reaction and trying not to show it.

"Where do you want to be left off?" Whit asked Virginia.

"At Bobby's. I'll show you how to get there."

When he stopped in front of Bobby's house, he had already thought out what he wanted to say to Virginia. "I thought you were going to show me a short cut to Hell. What's the matter, change your mind?"

"You're too little, little man. I don't think they'd let you in," Virginia said, composed again.

"I don't think they could keep me out," he said. "The whole damn bunch of them couldn't keep me out."

Her eyes were cat's eyes. They measured him contemptuously. "Meet me at the malt shop tomorrow after school and I'll make you run back home to mama, yelling for help."

Whit nodded; then he drove off, fast. Tim climbed over the back of the front seat, slid down and lit a cigarette.

"What do we do now?" he asked.

"You going home?"

"Hell, no," Tim said. "Not until my old lady cools off."

"I'm going home in the morning, not tonight. I've got some business to attend to tonight. And the first thing we better do is get rid of this crate. Every cop in the country will be looking for it."

Tim said, "You don't sound like the same guy."

"I'm not," Whit said. "The guy you knew before this morning is dead."

Tim laughed. "Sure," he said, "and the guy I met this morning will be dead too before the day's over if he doesn't slow down."

Whit whipped the car into the curb. "I'm going to keep going, Tim, and I don't intend to slow down. If you want to get out and walk, now's your chance. If you want to come along with me, that's good; but remember we're going at my speed."

"Hell, don't be so damned touchy. I'm with you, sure; only it's just hard to believe one guy could change so much so damned fast."

Whit grinned. "You ain't seen nothing yet." Whit knew he had to push himself; he had to keep going and he didn't dare look back.

That night he stole two more cars and committed three burglaries. Early the next morning he and Tim had breakfast in an all-night drive-in. The loot from the burglaries had been hidden at the cabin in the hills. The cash had been divided equally and was in their pockets.

"I'm going home for a while and then I'm going to meet Virginia," Whit said. "I'll take the Ford and you take the Buick, and I'll meet you here tonight around six."

"Got ya," Tim said. His voice as well as his walk had a swagger in it. "But you better watch out for Virgie. That broad is dynamite. And she's hotter than a two-dollar pistol." He was one man of the world talking to another. His fox face was animated.

Whit returned home. He hadn't any more than stepped through the front doorway, and closed the door behind him, when his dad asked him where he had been. He didn't answer the question. He walked around his dad and entered his mother's bedroom.

"Hello, Whit," she said. "You've come home." She didn't accuse him. She didn't make a scene. If she had it would have been easier. He saw her face was haggard, but she was smiling. His dad stood behind him, saying nothing, but full of things to say and waiting for the chance to say them.

"Did you find my note?" Whit asked.

"Yes," his mother said.

"Was Barbara's family here?"

"Yes."

"The cops?"

"No."

"Reverend . . . ?"

"No."

His father broke in. "Now that your mother has answered your questions," Serl said, "don't you think you owe her some explanation?"

Whit looked then at his dad. Serl was a shell of his former self; life had beaten him down.

The rebellion flared in Whit's mind and it hardened him. His dad had taught him that honesty is the best policy. His mother had taught him that they were God's children. They, his parents, were good and decent and honest beyond dispute, and yet look at them. *Oh, God, look at his parents!* At that moment Whit would have battered and smashed anyone who might have suggested to him his mother and father would be rewarded in the next world. After this, the very idea of it seemed the vilest cruelty imaginable. Why, why had they been so wantonly treated for being good and decent and honest?

Whit told himself: It's because they are good. That is the terrible truth. The good are defenseless.

"I asked you a question," Serl said.

"I know," Whit replied. "I heard you. I'm not sure how to answer or explain. I'm not sure I could. Or should."

His dad stiffened.

Whit said, "Maybe it's just that I'm fed up with poverty. Maybe I just feel like having some fun for a change."

His dad began to lecture him angrily. "I would think, at least for your mother's sake, that you would . . ."

Whit refused to listen. He would have walked out right then, but his mother stopped him. Her helplessness and her goodness stopped him. She told him she was sorry for their poverty and that she and his father would try to make him happier.

That was what Whit hated most—the vicious irony of it. His mother was willing always to take the blame, forever was she thinking only of him. Better she should hate him.

His mother continued talking to him and he almost turned back. But he couldn't and wouldn't turn back to fear. He had to prove there was no need to be afraid. He had to combat cruelty with cruelty. He had to give God a chance to destroy him, and the Devil too. Most of all he needed to be strong. Right then nothing else was important.

He began to wheeze.

9

Conquest, and the Wall

Whit paid another visit to the parsonage. "Hello, Reverend," he said. "How are you?" His smile was broad, boyish, disarming, seemingly carefree.

"Come in, son. Do come in," the minister said, and his own countenance perceptibly brightened. "It's good to see you smiling again. Can it be that my prayers for a satisfactory solution to your problem have been answered?" The minister looked optimistic.

"My problem?" Whit said. "I haven't any problem, Reverend."

A puzzled expression appeared on the man of God's face. He reminded Whit gently, "But the other day . . . you told me . . ."

Whit frowned, simulating perplexity. "Me, Reverend? *I* told you something the other day? Oh, no, Reverend; you've got me mixed up with somebody else."

The minister was patient. "Saturday morning last. You were here. You were definitely here. And you told me—" Then followed a disturbingly accurate account of what Whit had told him.

Whit's face hardened and all expression went from it. "Have you told anyone else what you just told me, Reverend?"

"Why, no. I told you I wouldn't."

Very softly, Whit spoke the question: "Reverend, do you think you could prove I was here and that I said what you *claim* I said?"

The lean frame of the minister stiffened. He took a step forward. "See here, young man: what do you mean by that? Exactly what are you getting at?"

"I'll tell you what I'm getting at, Reverend. It just happens that I don't remember coming to see you. I don't remember telling you anything. So if anyone asked me, that's exactly what I'd have to tell them. I'd have to tell them that *you* must have been dreaming. And that's a pretty bad story to be telling on somebody, Reverend. I think my folks have enough problems already without having that story of yours being added to them. So if I were you, I wouldn't tell it unless I could prove it, Reverend. I'd forget it."

Whit turned on his heel and walked out. He didn't bother to close the door behind him. He didn't bother to look back. He knew the preacher was probably standing there watching him, perhaps with his mouth agape.

Whit thought viciously: *Well, let him pray for some more guidance. He needs it more than I do now.*

Being cruel to be kind wasn't an original idea. Hamlet had heeded that same injunction. But Whit wasn't concerned with literary analogies or comparisons. He was interested in burning bridges, in being sure no avenue of retreat was left. Less than two months in the future, a kindly policeman would warn him: "Sonny boy, keep on like you're going and you'll wind up in the gas chamber."

And where was he going? Why, to Hell, of course. So to hell with the gas chamber.

Whit walked into the malt shop and looked around. Virginia was sitting in a booth on the left. Whit was disappointed because she wasn't alone. He had wanted her to be alone and waiting for him. Instead, a couple of boys were with her, and the three of them were so engrossed in their own conversation they didn't notice Whit. He sat on one of the stools at the fountain and ordered a Coke. Sipping the Coke, he started to think, but that was the last thing he wanted to do, or dared do. He swallowed the rest of the Coke with one gulp, set the glass down, spun around on the stool, and looked straight at Virginia.

She saw him. She smiled a quick, mocking smile. "Well," she said, "if it isn't the little boy!"

He walked to the booth and stood looking down at her, ignoring the two boys, not smiling, hiding the fact her words had stung. "Yesterday," he remarked, "it was little *man,* and I haven't shrunk any since."

She looked at him and laughed hilariously. The boys with her laughed too.

Whit stood there, embarrassed and angry. His face felt hot. His eyes took in every detail of the sinuous girl: the hair, the white, strong teeth, the cat's eyes, the full, red mouth, the ivory column of neck, the casually worn sweater. Too, the knowing look, worn as offhandedly as the pancake makeup, and the animal animation. A blatant advertisement of an available commodity, and a psychological cannibalism. Perhaps the male spider suspects that the female intends to eat him as soon as she has mated with him. But at least Mr. Spider has an excuse for what he does. Whit had no excuse and he wanted none. He had only a reason that was obstinate and arbitrary. So he stood still and said nothing.

Virginia stopped laughing. "Something on your mind, little boy?" she asked, but the laughter remained in her words.

"I want to talk to you," Whit said.

"You want to *talk* to me?" The incredulity was obscene and feigned.

The skinny boy who kept trying to paw Virginia snorted and played the game with her. "He wants to *talk* to you!"

"I guess he wants to give you some fatherly advice," said the other boy, the one who resembled Mortimer Snerd.

Virginia's reaction was instantaneous and savage. She turned on Mortimer Snerd. "You shut your goddam smart mouth!"

Snerd was the picture of shocked and injured innocence. He looked at his skinny friend with a now-what-did-I-say look. Skinny could only shrug.

Unsmilingly, Virginia stood up, shoved Skinny out of the way and brushed past him. She sunk her fingers into Whit's left arm and said, "I need some fresh air." Then she propelled Whit out the door of the malt shop. Under her breath she was saying some very uncomplimentary things about Snerd. Her choice of language was not judicious, and her anger amounted almost to mania.

"Have you got a car?" she asked.

Whit nodded he did have. He pointed to an immaculate tan '34 Ford coupe at the curb. "I found it last night in a used-car lot."

As he was pulling away from the curb, Virginia took a cigarette package and matches from her sweater. Out of the corner of his eye, he watched her extract the last cigarette and light it. She gave the match a flip out the window. She inhaled the smoke deeply into her lungs. Her hands were trembling slightly. Then she slowly closed her left hand on the empty cigarette pack, crushing it. This done, she threw it from the window.

"Drive fast," she said. "Drive crazy fast."

He speeded up.

"Faster! Lots faster!"

He whipped the light Ford through the city traffic, then out onto the highway, heading for the hills. He came close to killing them both several times. Neither of them cared.

Whit parked on an abandoned road high in his hills, near the cabin he and Tim had built. "Well, here we are," he said, settling back in the seat. The wild ride had left him keyed up, expectant. And one part of his mind was still trying to comprehend Virginia.

She stretched luxuriously, and yawned. A smile played at the corners of her mouth; her green eyes were boldly appraising. "You're crazy, little boy," she said.

Whit's smile lighted his young face for only an instant. Those green eyes boring into him could have been ten thousand years old. He would have to ignore them. "Thanks," he said. "Maybe it won't take me too long to be crazier."

"I don't know about you," Virginia said, "but I could go crazy a lot easier if I had a cigarette and something to drink."

Whit didn't let his smile reach his lips, but he let it radiate through him. Proud of himself he said, "In that case, you aren't going to have any trouble at all." He pushed open the door and got out. "Just a minute," he told the girl; "I'll be right back." He walked to the cabin hidden in the trees, selected three cartons of cigarettes from the loot he and Tim had hidden inside. Then he followed the trail to the reservoir; from the cold waters he extracted a green bottle, more of last night's loot. He returned to the car, indulging in a grin of pleasure. Fear was a tyrant and he was committing an act of tyrannicide.

Whit tossed the cigarettes onto the seat of the coupe. "There's something to smoke," he said casually. Then he held up the bottle so Virginia could see it. "And here's something to drink."

"What's in the bottle?" Virginia wanted to know.

"Champagne," Whit said. "The best you can buy." He popped the cork with a flourish.

Virginia accepted the bottle, examined its label, and then put it to her lips, taking a long pull. She finished and exhaled audibly. Then she asked, "What're you trying to do, little boy, buy me?"

He should have expected such a question. He was angry because he hadn't. "And what're you doing now, selling what you used to give away?"

Whit regretted the words the instant he spoke them.

"Aren't we funny today!" Virginia said.

"I'm sorry," he said, ill at ease.

"You make me laugh," she said, and did. "You think you want to be bad and you don't know how."

"Bad" had a non-dictionary meaning they both understood. The word connoted something affirmative, forceful.

"How come you know so much?" Whit asked. "You're not much older than I am."

"If I told you we'd both know."

Virginia took another long pull from the bottle. "Say, this stuff is good." She smacked her lips. "Here, little boy, have a drink."

"I don't want a drink."

"Have I made the little boy mad?"

"You're not very nice, are you, Virginia?"

"If I was nice, you wouldn't have brought me up here."

"Maybe I made a mistake."

Virginia ignored that. "You think Barbara was a nice girl, don't you, little boy?" she said slyly.

Whit's face twisted. "I *know* she was!"

"How? How do you know? Did you get her cherry?"

"Shut your dirty mouth!" Whit shouted. "Shut your dirty, filthy mouth!" He wanted to hit this tormentor, to beat the vileness out of her. "If you keep talking like that I'll kill you! I'll kill you with my bare hands!"

Again Virginia laughed, contemptuously. "Don't you talk big for such a little piss ant! Well, go ahead and kill me. Only wait till I finish this bottle." She took another drink, and the bottle was then almost half empty.

Whit gave the ignition key a twist and stabbed at the starter; the motor turned over, coughed to life.

"Where're we going now, little boy?"

"I'm taking you home," Whit said stiffly, virtuously.

"I thought you were going to kill me."

"You're not worth killing."

"I know it."

He looked at her, suddenly, and he put into words what perplexed him: "What made you like this, Virginia?"

"Like what?" she asked.

Like what? As if she didn't know!

"You know. Like you are. The dirty way you talk all the time."

She said, "If you don't like the way I talk, let's stop talking and do something else. Got any suggestions?"

He blushed. Virginia was too much for him; a girl was too much for him.

"I think I better take you home," he said, and he sounded apologetic. Slowly, he began backing the Ford to a wide spot where he could turn around.

Words can sneer; Virginia's did, when she said, "And I think you better take yourself home to mama!"

I'll make you run back home to mama, yelling for help. That was what she had told him yesterday, and today it was happening. But he would stop that from happening. Physical compliance with necessity was easy; the tough part was mental. In swift, violent movements he braked, shifted into low, slammed the Ford back into the place where they had been parked, killed the motor. That was the easy part.

"Whoops," Virginia said, as some of the contents of the bottle spilled on her. Then she giggled.

"Yeah, whoops," he said.

"How does it feel not to be afraid of the Devil?"

"Okay, Virginia," he said. "You win."

"I win what?" She giggled some more.

"Oh please shut up, won't you?"

"Why should I?"

"Because I don't want to be fighting with you all the time."

"That's because you're afraid of me," Virginia said.

"No, it isn't either."

"Then what is it?" she demanded.

"If I told you, you'd laugh. You make fun of everything I say."

"There you go again being mysterious. I suppose I'm some kind of a symbol, too." She giggled once more. "What am I, a witch or a bitch?"

"I think you're a fool," Whit said. "And I know more about you than you think I do." He had to take that gamble.

"And I think I'm cute," she said; and Whit knew he had won his gamble. She pulled her skirt above her knees. "I said I'm cute."

"All right, you're cute."

"I mean I got bow legs, stupid. When a girl has bow legs they call her cute. Look."

She stretched out her legs and pulled her skirt higher. "I said look!"

Whit looked. He looked because he didn't know what else to do. He looked because Virginia had told him she knew a short cut to Hell. He looked, and he told himself that being an animal was enough; *because that is what we all are, nothing but animals.* He looked, and the animal part of him was excited by Virginia's legs.

"That's better," Virginia said. "You know, Ace always brings me up in the hills, too."

"Who's Ace?"

"Oh, a guy I know."

"You seem to know lots of guys."

She giggled. "Most of them are bigger'n you, though."

Whit didn't answer. Virginia took another drink. "I suppose you think they call me Virgie because I'm a virgin."

"I'm not *that* stupid," he said.

"You think you're smart," she said obliquely. "You think you're real smart. But you got a whole lot to learn, little boy, and you aren't going to find it in books. Dummies like me are going to teach you, and we'll make you damned sorry you ever wanted to learn in the first place. And you know why? Because you're just like all the rest of them. You only got one thing on your mind, but you haven't got the nerve to say so. You probably think you're doing something real dangerous by bringing me up here. Well, I know what you want and you can have it. But don't try to think you're fooling me. Don't feed me a lot of talk about how much you like me. I don't want to hear anything like that. You see, little boy, I can see through you. You got a glass head. You're just another male and all you want from me is one thing."

Virginia was drunk. The champagne had loosened her tongue; it had thickened her words, but they were still her words. Having unburdened herself, she lapsed into a scowling silence. The game of baiting Whit couldn't satisfy her any longer, not when she knew he was caught in her web. Like a fog, her words hung there between them. And the fog the words produced was more pregnant with meaning than the words themselves.

"You're drunk," Whit said. "You're sloppy drunk. Besides, what makes you think you got anything I want?"

"So now you're a wise guy," Virginia said, slurring the words.

"Oh, no," he said. "I'm not a wise guy. How could I be when you just said I got so much to learn?"

"You're a damned fool," she said.

"Make up your mind. One second I'm a wise guy and the next I'm a damn fool. Which is it?"

Virginia cursed him obscenely. He grinned. With her free hand she slapped him across the face, as hard as she could. He still grinned. She struck at him with the bottle. He caught her wrist and twisted it until she dropped the bottle. They struggled fiercely, twisting and turning, breathing hard. She was like a wildcat. His hand accidentally fell on her bare thigh. She ceased struggling and went limp, again giggling.

"What're you trying to do, grab a free feel? Well, go ahead and feel all you want."

He jerked his hand away, as though from an open flame. His breath was coming in gasps.

"I told you—you're afraid of me!" Virginia's words were a taunt, a challenge.

"No. No, I'm not."

"Then prove it. Prove it, if you're man enough."

It was Whit's turn to bait her. "How?"

"How do you think, stupid? Do I have to draw you a picture?"

When Whit didn't reply immediately, Virginia said, "What's the matter—think you're a saint or something?"

"I just don't think we should," he said, not meaning it.

"You're scared," she said. "You're either scared or else you're a pansy. Maybe that's it."

She stung his pride and he laughed. "I'm not scared," he said, "and I'm not a pansy. In fact, if anybody's a little bit queer in this crowd, it's you."

She cursed him, and he made love to her, not expertly.

Virginia was like an alley cat. She scratched and bit and cursed, but wouldn't let him go.

They lay there panting. Gradually his wheezing subsided.

"I suppose now you got a guilty conscience," Virginia said. "Either that or you hate looking at me. Well, I hope I spoiled all your big ideas for you. I hope I dirtied them up. Now you're not any better than I am, and I'm no good at all. I'm just a slut. I like being a slut. I like being easy to make and after I'm made I like to make the bastard who makes me so sick he wants to throw up. I like making him hate himself and me and sex and everything about it. I like . . ."

Virginia talked on and on. She couldn't stop talking. She couldn't help passing on her contamination. She talked even after the toughness, the hardness melted, after she began to cry, softly. She revealed to Whit the ugliness that was in her, not trying to hide it or to pretty it up, knowing the truth would shock and disgust him more than anything else she could say or do. She told him that all men are animals, that she had been cuffed, cursed, and then compelled to submit to them.

So Virginia hated all males; this was her way of getting even. This was her way of fighting back.

Whit listened until he could stand no more, until he felt weak and sick. He gripped Virginia by her shoulders, his fingers biting into the bare flesh.

"You're lying!" he shouted. "You're making up that story!" And she had to be; what she was telling him was too terrible to be true. Dear God, he thought, surely You wouldn't let anything like that happen!

"It's true," Virginia said quietly. "Every word I told you is the truth."

Whit sobbed. He took Virginia in his arms and clung to her. She knew he was trying to hide and she didn't intend to let him. Right then he was feverishly building his fortress. How desperately he needed its protection! And she was finding little satisfaction in making him suffer.

"Oh," she said, "it's not as bad as all that."

"It's wrong! It's all wrong!" he sobbed.

"Sure it is," she agreed; "but what can you do about it?"

The clarity was sudden, and absolute. Until that instant they both had been inexperienced actors clumsily playing a scene from a badly written play, not even knowing why or how it had happened that they had been cast in their respective roles. Then Whit knew why, and he knew what he could do about it.

And Virginia was right. She had known a short cut to Hell and had shown it to him. Not Hell, a place; but hell, a state of mind. The worst hell of all. And probably the only one. This mental hell was still wanting to believe in something when you knew you were wrong; and it was insisting upon believing something when you had overwhelming proof that what you believed couldn't possibly be true. It was wanting to believe in what was good and right and decent yet being obliged to question the goodness, the rightness and the decency of all things. It was insisting upon believing in yourself; it was persisting in the belief you had a meaning, and yet knowing you lived in a jungle where men were capable of callously using their own daughters. Too, it was living in a jungle where the denizens either made you into one of them or found a way to torture you beyond endurance and ultimately to destroy you. It was living there, or with the bleating sheep in a pasture cleared in the middle of the jungle.

What could Whit do about it? Well, he could start by believing in Virginia, by believing in her even when she refused to believe in herself. He could take her hate for his own. He could fight for her and himself too. He could make himself a strange sort of guinea pig.

He told her so. And he said: "Don't let them make you throw your life away. Don't do that, Virginia. Don't do it. Give your hate to me. Let me have it. I need it. I'll use it against them. I'll get even for both of us. I can get even where you can only get hurt. Don't let them hurt you any more and don't hurt yourself any more. There's no reason for you to. Change, Virginia, and laugh at them. Be the kind of girl you really want to be. They can't stop you. Show them they can't. And let me do the fighting. Let me take your place in this dirty jungle. Please do me that favor. And we'll always have our secret. We'll never let anybody know about it."

"And we'll always be friends," Virginia said, fiercely. "*Always! Forever!*"

"And we'll always be friends," Whit heartily agreed.

And they always have been friends. Even after Whit was doomed.

10

"Sonny Boy, Keep on Like You're Going . . . "

Sonny boy, keep on like you're going and you'll wind up in the gas chamber.

To hell with the gas chamber!

Whit kept on. He kept on through the summer. One reckless escapade followed another.

Whit mastered the technics of his trade: how to make and use hot boxes, gadgets to start cars without keys; how to gain swift access to a locked car; how to soup up a car, make it go incredibly fast; how to do a dozen other, similar things.

He stole—"expropriated," he would say—car after car, mostly fast, sleek, new ones. With the same studied passion he had practiced playing the piano years earlier, he practiced driving or "tooling" these hot heaps. He learned to corner, to broadside, to speed and snap-shift them. He purposely rolled and crashed them. He sent them hurtling through traffic at high speeds. He sought out patrol cars and motorcycle cops and taunted them into chasing him, just for the thrill of ditching them, just for the hell of it, and for practice.

For Whit, driving was a joyous form of creative expression. Driving made him free. Driving was his personal, triumphant accomplishment. His coordination, his timing was uncanny, and nature had given him perfect depth perception. With these assets, plus an open contempt for his own safety, he had learned to drive with such astonishing skill that his uncounted exploits behind the wheel soon multiplied and became legend. An exhilarating feeling of amoral triumph swept over him. Good and bad, right and wrong, were only blurred, unheeded abstract concepts, without real meaning. He had failed at being good, at fitting in, being a contributor. Now it was different. Now he couldn't be ignored. He was only sixteen, but he was a factor.

Quit stealing? Why? "Because honesty is the best policy," they said. That made Whit laugh derisively. *Thou shalt not steal.* "Well, stop me then. Between the squares and Heaven, that shouldn't be much of a job."

But it was. He saw to that.

Whit was "only a boy," they said. Just a confused, unhappy, emotionally disturbed boy. And they were not his apologists; they were society's. They didn't try to see him, and into him; they refused to look at their society through his eyes. Oh, no. He was *per se* "wrong," and that was all there was to it.

Except that it wasn't all there was to it. "They" had stolen something from him. Perhaps even God had been a party to the theft. They had stolen his faith. So let them prove their mouthings. He would approach the problem scientifically; he would fling himself into the inferno and find out what happened. He wouldn't take anybody's word for anything. He would find out the answers for himself, in his own way, without giving a damn for consequences, by trial and error. And without fear. Fear was an intolerable sickness. Fear was a bully, too, a tyrant to be hated.

Don't steal or we'll put you in jail. We'll punish you. Don't sin or you'll burn in Hell. Don't! *Don't!* DON'T!

Whit continued stealing.

Early one morning he snapped the padlock on a private garage and removed the radio from a car inside. The car was used by a burglar-alarm company; the radio in it would receive police calls. He installed this pilfered radio successively in the various stolen cars he used. He stole license plates from wrecked cars in junkyards and put these cool plates on the cars he drove, using wing nuts for quick changes. He experimented with smoke screens, testing kerosene at first and later stealing some skywriting fluid from an airport. From a burglary he procured an old, hammerless .32 revolver, fully loaded, and tried his hand at robbery.

He was caught burglarizing a market when the lookout, another boy who had begged to go along and who had been carrying the gun, ran off and left him. Taken to the police station, Whit refused to give his name or to say a word. One of the detectives slapped him, called him a smart little punk. When Whit persisted in his refusal to say a word, the big, beefy dick who had slapped him growled, "We got ways of making you goddamed punks talk." Then the dick stood on Whit's arches, and the pain brought tears to Whit's eyes. "Well, ready to talk?" the dick demanded. Whit nodded a violent affirmative. Then the dick was all patronizing reasonableness. "I told you we had ways of making you talk," he said, "so you shouldn't've been uncooperative. Now we'll get along fine, kid. Just fine."

And, in a manner of speaking, the dick was right. He and Whit got along just fine. Whit was most cooperative. He eagerly answered all questions put to him, and the dick beamed, much pleased with himself. "Now we're getting somewhere," he said, and the questioning continued. Whit obligingly told the dick everything he wanted to know. Except for the fact that it was unabashed hokum, the cop would have gotten himself a promotion on the strength of it. Instead, he ended up with a fairy tale and no prisoner.

When they began to fingerprint Whit, he shoved over a table, ran out of the room, into another room and jumped out an open window. He got away.

That made it a game. You got away with anything you were smart enough to get away with.

Sometimes events would move too swiftly and crowd Whit, not give him time to think. When this happened he would go off by himself. He would go to the hills and stand there, looking down, thinking.

One day he had been a slave whose masters were contemptuous of him. The next he had rebelled; he had declared himself free. And the irony was that, without doubt, he soon would be enjoying his stolen freedom in jail.

What would the good people think, should they suspect for a moment that he regarded crime more as the projection of a philosophical war between ideas into physical terms than as a means of getting something for nothing?

The game of cops and robbers was the most competitive game in the world. Whit liked the rewards of that game and he gave not a damn for the penalties, but that didn't erase the fact that he was contemptuous of those rewards. Those who preached, "You can't win; you can't outsmart the law!" were nothing more than talking parrots or provocateurs; the most they could accomplish was to excite him and his kind to anger, greater defiance. To act out the disproof.

Why wasn't all this obvious? Whit knew and he didn't know. He cared and he didn't care.

Whit stood on the grass looking down. A wire fence ran around three sides of the walkway that surrounded the swimming pool. The building housing the dressing rooms was on the far side, away from him. He stood right where the grassy earth of the park sloped downward rather abruptly. He stood and looked, intently, fixedly. The anger started with a tightening in his belly, and it was not a blind anger. But it was an anger that insisted he ignore everything except the object inspiring it.

Sonny. Sonny stood at the fence enclosing the swimming pool, talking to a tall, blond girl in a two-piece bathing suit. Talking big talk, with two cohorts feeding him his lines, stooging for him. One of the two was the leering Charley. T-shirted, Sonny looked huge, brutishly huge and tanned. He was smoking a cigarette and he held it through the fence so the blonde could take a drag. She did and puffed the smoke out foolishly, in a cloud, without first having inhaled it. Then she said, addressing Sonny with her eyes as well as her voice, "You wait right here. I'll be out in a jiffy." She disappeared into the girls' dressing room with a suggestive twitch of her ample derrière. Sonny whistled appreciatively.

And Whit's anger grew much colder. The afternoon was hot and the sky cloudless but he couldn't feel the burning warmth of the summer sun. He could feel only the dry, cold anger as it writhed within him, changing him, not subtly but crudely. He had to hold himself back. He had to wait, no matter how hard waiting was. He surely could stand waiting a few more minutes. For weeks he had waited. He had seen Sonny from a distance during those weeks; but he hadn't been ready. The time hadn't been right. Now it was.

Keyed up, he waited for them at the head of the stairs. Sonny came first, with a cocky walk, with the blond girl beside him. Sonny's two pals, his two stooges, were bringing up the rear.

Whit said casually, with mock deference, "Hello, Sonny."

"Yeah, hello," Sonny said, not even bothering to glance at Whit.

Then Sonny was almost beside him, and Whit said, "It's me, Sonny. It's your old friend Whit."

Sonny stopped, abruptly. He had been hearing stories about Whit, how Whit had changed. Sonny measured Whit with his eyes, "fronting" for the blonde. "Well," he said, "if it ain't the gutless wonder. You looking for another ass-kicking, maybe?"

Whit was grinning, the way a skull grins. "No," he said, shaking his head, keeping his eyes riveted on Sonny, but seeing the others too. "No, that's not what I'm looking for. I just wanted to tell you what a vile, rotten, lying dog you are, Sonny. I just wanted you to know I knew."

For an instant Sonny's jaw fell open, and he couldn't believe his ears. Then the enormity of the words sunk in.

"Why, you . . ."

Whit held the revolver in his right hand. The blonde's eyes grew wide, round at the sight of it. She and Sonny's two stooges froze. And once more Sonny hesitated, trying to convince himself his eyes were deceiving him.

"It's loaded, Sonny. And I know how to use it."

"You ain't got the guts," Sonny said, but without conviction.

"Then take one step toward me and find out. Take that step and I'll blow you to hell."

Sonny blustered, "I got a notion to take that pop gun away from you and shove it where it'll fit." But he couldn't bring himself to take the step.

"Why don't you try to take the gun away from me, Sonny?" And then it was Whit who took that one step forward. "Please, Sonny, please try to take it away from me."

Whit's voice was faint and hoarse. Anger amounting almost to blood lust had taken hold of him. It was goading him. Sibilant words of hate were pouring from his lips without his being more than partially aware of what he was saying: that those who arbitrarily took advantage of others who were smaller were unspeakably vile. That he would happily kill all the Sonnys in the world. That he'd like to squash them as bugs are squashed.

And then, having spoken the theretofore unworded hate inside him, the cold, destructive anger left Whit.

The sun was back in the sky and its warmth could be felt. Sonny once more stood in front of him, a real, live person again. And Whit could see he had spat in Sonny's face. And that face was ugly with fear, a more terrible fear because of the degradation it imposed.

Whit felt no triumph. Disgust, revulsion, but not triumph. Rational once more, he smiled and said with an excess of politeness, "You caused me to lose Barbara, Sonny. Your filthy mouth caused that. You trampled on something I thought was sacred and your rotten mind soiled it. So now I'm getting even, Sonny. I'm taking the blonde here. She's going with me. And if you or your two stooges don't like it, or if you tell anybody about it, I'll kill all three of you. That's not a threat, that's a promise. Now scram. All of you."

He watched them go.

There followed a series of gun fights, arrests, escapes and attempted escapes from juvenile detention homes and police stations, interviews by psychologists and social workers, appearances before juvenile court referees.

Tim started it off when he was arrested in a stolen car. He was drunk, cocky and defiant when first taken to the police station, but the officers were familiar with his kind. They talked tough and shoved him around a little, not hurting him but scaring the daylights out of him. This psychology worked. In the language of the street, Tim then spilled his guts. He told everything he knew, implicating Bobby, Virginia, himself and all the others, including some who had ridden in stolen cars without knowing they were stolen.

The police called at Whit's home when he was away, and his father promised he would bring his son to the station. When Whit returned home that evening, Serl and Hallie had a talk with him. Between themselves, before Whit had returned home, they had concluded their son had fallen into bad company. They told Whit they wanted him to give himself up, to take his medicine and get a new start. They said they would stand by him.

"O.K.," Whit readily agreed, "I'll do exactly what you want."

And he did. Accompanied by his father, he walked into the police station and surrendered. "I'll make you a deal," he told the lieutenant of detectives in charge of the investigation. "I'll tell you everything I've done and that I know has been done, but not who did it, if you'll promise to let everybody go but me and my pal Tim. We're the only really guilty ones."

After asking a few questions to satisfy himself that Whit meant what he said, the lieutenant agreed and kept the bargain. None of the others involved was ever arrested. Many of them are respected citizens today, substantial young men and women without a mark against them. Three of them volunteered for military service and gave their lives to their country during World War II.

As a result of Whit's deal with the police, he and Tim were committed to a—but a different—forestry camp maintained by the county for young delinquents. Each escaped. Each was recaptured. Whit escaped again, again was taken into custody after a wild adventure. Then he was committed to reform school.

The month was September. The year, 1937.

11

A Reformation Factory

This was "reform" school. A reformation factory.

A group of buildings, some old, some new, out in the sticks. Out in rolling farm country. With the big cities far off but beckoning. Unseen, and glittering all the more because of it.

A school of industry, they called it, with its old-fashioned, ugly, brick administration building squatting on "the hill," but rising up, not proudly, and visible for miles around. A stern puritan of a building.

A school of industry, with its seven hundred odd charges. A school of industry bulging with charges, with boys, young men between fifteen and twenty-one years, of all sizes and shapes. With young rebels and young savages and young fools. With young minds, some twisted, some warped, some wounded, some confused. All thrown together. Put on the conveyor belt. Mass production correction. . . .

Whit's indoctrination began with suddenness and violence. His first day in the receiving company, he was jabbed in the ribs by the captain for getting out of step as the company marched to the dining room. Whit expressed his indignation.

"You don't like it, huh, peewee?" asked the cadet officer, a lean, red-headed youngster.

"No," Whit said; "I don't like it, huh."

"Well, you will before I get through with you," the captain assured him, "because I got a way of learning you to like it."

Still naïve in the savage ways of his new environment, Whit wondered, as he ate his meal in the huge B.D.R.—boy's dining room—how this brick-topped cadet officer would go about learning him to like it. He found out that night when, in the dressing room and after the rest of the company had undressed, pegged their clothes, and were passed to their dormitory cots, the captain started slapping him around, his two lieutenants standing nearby.

Whit fought back, and when he did all three cadet officers battered him with their fists. He was hospitalized with a broken nose and a fractured jaw. When questioned sharply by school personnel about the beating, he said it had been his fault, that he had started the fight. The statement was not prompted by fear but by the conviction that what had happened to him was his personal problem. He would look out for himself or get his brains scrambled worse than they already were.

Red, the captain, visited Whit at the hospital. "So you're no stoolie, huh, peewee?" Red said. "That's good. I been talking to some of your friends from L.A. They tell me you're an all right guy even if you are a shrimp. I heard you rode the beef for a lot of other people when your partner squealed. That made me feel bad about the other night, so I came to see you and thought maybe we could be friends, huh?"

It was difficult to speak with a swollen, fractured jaw, but Whit managed. "Sure, Red," he said, "I'd like that. And forget about the other night. I already have."

"You're O.K.," Red said. "You know, usually you shrimps are wise guys. I guess that's what fooled me, because I thought you was a smart little snitch at first. I felt like hell when I found out different."

Thinking it over later, Whit realized he had learned something extremely important from Red: Don't be a wise guy. Be tough, be "right," but not wise in the sense of thinking you know all the answers and running off at the mouth all the time. And never tell a policeman or anyone else in authority the right time.

After that, more and more, Whit aligned himself with that hard core of tough young rebels who, conscious of the fact or not, were serving their apprenticeship in crime. The reasons for their rebellion were many: a broken home, no parental supervision, poverty, feelings of antagonism or rejection, a craving for thrills, adventure, a good time, a power or sex impulse. And once they had had a taste of the false freedom of living outside the law, rebelliously, as nonconformists, their former lives seemed tame and insipid by contrast. They were young, impressionable rebels, and because such rebels must have a cause they made their cause crime.

They justified that cause—society, they believed, didn't give a damn about them personally; so why should they give a damn about society? They idealized that cause. They observed its code, its proprieties. They said you didn't squeal. They said you were fiercely loyal to one of your kind and to hell with all the rest. They said you had to be tough and able to take it. They said to hell with authority in any form; when authority got hold of you you out-toughed or out-slicked it. You'd "shoot an angle." They embraced the necessarily cynical philosophy of that cause. The squares with dough—the hoosiers, the marks, the chumps—would have to look out for themselves. The only thing you ever regretted was getting caught; and if you were caught you didn't let them con you or break you.

Unwittingly, the citizen who clamors for more and severer laws, bigger and tougher jails and prisons, harsher punishments is crime's most successful recruiting officer, for his loud voice is always heard and his heavy hand felt by the young rebel who invariably reacts against that voice and hand with increased hostility.

There must be laws and law enforcement, of course. But society must understand that the delinquent who worships toughness, and who mistakenly equates that toughness with lawlessness, will never live within the law, tractably, at peace with his fellows, simply because of a fear of consequences, however dire. Society must understand, too, that it is considerably cheaper, more humane and more practical to salvage the potential young criminal than it is to destroy his spirit or so harden it that he turns into professional badman and killer.

The months he spent at the school were memorable ones for Whit. Memorable for their savagery and violence. Memorable, too, for what they taught. Whit soon learned how cruel youth can be to its own, and how a systematized cruelty was encouraged by those in charge. Here, violence was a virtue, and rewarded accordingly. The boys were kept in line by other boys, and snitching, finking to The Man was encouraged. God help you if you were small, had any personal sense of honor and showed the least inclination to be a man.

When released from the hospital, Whit was transferred to another company where the younger inmates, who were not yet chronic disciplinary problems, were quartered. Quite a few of these were snotty brats who hadn't long been away from mama. These were especially vicious, especially quick to turn against each other and become tools of The Man. Whit noted this and considered it wrong. He had it in his head they should stick together and not be used. Custody should be The Man's worry alone. But it wasn't. The Man had his cadet officers and his detail boys, and he gave you two hundred extra credits toward release for catching another boy trying to escape. And, of course, there were the clever ones who talked or bullied other youngsters into making escape attempts and then grabbed them for the credits. Whit cheerfully hated the guts of the escape-catchers and those who made them possible.

At his own request he was made a cadet officer, thinking he could change this, that by his own example he could show the others they didn't have to prey upon each other like jungle animals. But several of the would-be tough guys mistook his actions for weakness. They reasoned that he had to be weak because he didn't swagger and pose and growl and throw Sunday punches and try to make sex perverts or "punks" out of the small and the frightened. Because he said "please" and "thank you" to everybody, not just to The Man.

So they took advantage of him and The Man asked him if he couldn't run the company "the way it's supposed to be run." The Man told him if he couldn't he would find somebody who could. And the word got around. Forced into it, Whit began to fight, reluctantly at first. He learned that another cadet officer was agitating the whole company against him because he didn't fit into the pattern. Whit and this other cadet officer tangled; they had quite a battle, and The Man got rid of Whit, had him transferred to another company, the Foreign Legion, it was called. E Company. By chance, the cadet officers in E Company all were released on parole within two weeks after Whit's transfer and the supervisor in charge made Whit captain, perhaps more as a grim joke than anything, since Whit was one of the smallest and most pleasant boys in the company.

But he ran the company. He ran it without "copping Sundays," catching any who attempted to escape or telling The Man anything, and not as a policeman. He ran it by fighting whenever he had to, which was often. There were those who wanted his job, who wanted to make a reputation as tough guys, bad dukes, at his expense. Whit was often battered to the borderline of insensibility. But he never quit. Something inside himself wouldn't let him. No matter how badly he found himself being beaten, he stood his ground and, grinning hideously, would continue fighting until his arm-weary opponent grew sick at the sight of his own gory handiwork and quit.

Once a company supervisor, who took pleasure in watching his youthful charges battle, chided one iron-fisted young stalwart for quitting under such conditions. "Dammit," was this youngster's gasped retort, "what good would it do to keep pounding on a grinning little bastard who doesn't know when he's beat?"

Sponge-like, Whit sopped up both practical and academic knowledge from correspondence courses and school classes. He read voraciously, particularly the works of the philosophers. He read of the gentle Nazarene and of the cat-faced Florentine, Niccolo Machiavelli. He read and studied and thought. He enrolled in the typing class. The teacher, an elderly, fidgety gossipy woman, seated him before an old typewriter, handed him a typing book opened to the first lesson and then, regarding her job done, walked away, back to her desk. Undismayed, he taught himself to type, and won a job in the assistant superintendent's office as an inmate clerk.

Whit worked willingly, cheerfully, keeping his brooding thoughts to himself, his eyes and ears open, determined to learn all there was to know about the school's administration and its personnel. He soon added the word "nepotism" to his vocabulary and its practical meaning became clear to him. Because, seeking, he found too much, cynicism formed an essential ingredient of his philosophy—not an affected, surface cynicism, but a cynicism that lay deep and hidden inside him.

Without suspecting it, the free personnel became his implacable enemies. The sincere and honest ones, comprising the majority, piqued him with their myopic innocence.

When you least expected it, it rose and smote you between the eyes. One Sunday Whit attended the services conducted by the Protestant chaplain, who meant well and undoubtedly did good. Holy Joe, most inmates called him. As a thundering condemnation of sin was being delivered from the pulpit, a homosexual in the back row seat slid down and committed an act of sex perversion on four boys, one after the other. Practically every inmate in the church knew what was going on; the chaplain and the supervisor present didn't. Things like that —even when you had no part in them—made you wonder. They made it temptingly easy to sneer. Or to vomit.

Release from the school on parole was granted the inmate after he earned five thousand credits, which then took an average of fourteen months. Credits were given, in varying amounts, for maintaining a satisfactory work record, for school and church attendance, turning in lost keys, being in a company that won a competitive drill, catching another inmate who attempted to escape (as mentioned earlier) and for other reasons. They were lost, also in varying amounts, for a violation of the rules. Any employee could "write-up" an inmate. The inmate was written up on a "slip" and the slips were turned in to the chief detail officer, who supervised custody and discipline.

The chief detail officer marked on the slip the number of credits to be forfeited and forwarded it to the assistant superintendent's secretary, a young woman in whose office Whit worked. These slips were kept in a locked drawer of the secretary's desk until the credit forfeitures were posted in a master book.

Whit had no difficulty in picking the lock on that desk. He had his own sense of justice. The slips of his friends and those he regarded as right he destroyed as often as he could, and with a great deal of satisfaction. The slips against the snitches, the rats, the escape-catchers and others of that breed, he left. So far as he was concerned such characters would have to look out for themselves. They were on their own.

And all the while Whit was learning his lessons, making his adjustment to the school in his own way, applying a studied "why?" to almost every situation.

He adapted and he hardened. He looked out for himself. He had the guts and the flexibility and the cunning to do that. And he didn't mind getting hurt, getting his face beaten out of shape. That was a relatively cheap price to pay to keep his entity and his integrity. But look what happened to those who were less cunning, who couldn't stand physical pain, who couldn't resist the tyranny of those who specialized in degradation. Well, if society didn't seem to care what happened to them, why should he?

Why? Because of guys like Skinny, that was why.

Skinny, the scrawny hater, became his friend. Skinny hated everybody and everything. Skinny said the gods were dead. He often raised his tortured eyes to the heavens and blasphemed his Creator until he ran out of breath. He argued with Whit—and he worshipped him, and he hated himself because he did. He was afraid of friendship; afraid because he feared he would betray it, because everything except hate and cynicism was an illusion. "They know you got brains and they'll use you," Skinny told Whit bitterly. "They'll use a lot of sweet talk to split you off. They'll tell you to look out for yourself."

Whit interrupted. "Sure they will, Skin, only they'll be wasting breath."

"They got a lot of breath to waste," Skinny said wryly, thawing out.

Whit grinned. "Social halitosis never reformed anybody."

12

I Can Kill!

Playboy they called him, and he liked the name. At twenty he was the budding personification of what he fancied himself—a pimp. A tall stringbean with rather oily good looks, he was one of those at the school who spent full time looking out for himself. If this happened to be at the expense of another or others, well—so what? It was dog eat dog. He flattered and did favors for the bad dukes and those inmates who carried any weight—and readily, neatly doublecrossed them whenever it was to his advantage and he didn't think he'd get caught doing so. He kept The Man's favor by passing along whatever he heard he thought The Man might like to know. Of course, when The Man turned his back the words came out of the other side of Playboy's mouth. With the ladies—the female employees—he was a perfect gentleman. So long as they were within seeing and hearing distance, that is. When they weren't around, he had some fantastic tales to relate how they were falling over one another in their desire to bestow their favors upon him.

To quite a few of the inmates, Playboy was a hero of no small stature. To Whit he was another question mark. How was it that characters like Playboy were such a success in this world while the Skinnys were such a failure? And what made the Playboys tick? How did they get that way in the first place?

Whit decided to find out. He decided he should know. He didn't realize at the time what certain kinds of knowledge can do to you. So he cultivated Playboy and drew him out.

This fledgling pimp usually prefaced all his conversations with an observation on womankind: "Stand 'em on their heads and they all look the same." And to Playboy every female under discussion was a bitch. (Not discussed, of course, were the listener's mother, sisters, girl friend or wife.) "When I hit the bricks this time I'm going to get me a stable of high-class bitches," Whit was told.

Then Whit learned that Playboy's idea of the good life was to acquire—this required a practiced eye—a number of voluptuous courtesans, install them in expensive "houses," put in a fix with the bulls, establish himself in a swank apartment, ride around in a Cadillac convertible, play the ponies and hobnob with others of the pimping gentry. That, man, was really living!

Playboy gave assurance he was no lunch-bucket pimp. He had no time for ordinary hustlers—women of the world who bartered their charms on street corners, in bars and other such common places. And he had connections; he knew where the right houses were and the people who ran them; in L.A. he knew pimpdom's wheels. Moreover, he was versed in the pimping arts; an old hand had perceived his potential and had taught him the tricks of the trade. If Whit was interested, Playboy could knock him down (introduce him) to those worth knowing. And when Whit feigned a polite skepticism that Playboy could be the possessor of such a useful fund of information, Playboy was so ill-advised as to name names, to give addresses, to furnish details. And Whit smiled, nodded and filed this intelligence away in his mind.

How did Playboy happen to aspire toward pimpdom's lush heights? Well, therein hung a tale. He admitted he hadn't always been big time. (This was a preliminary admission which assisted in demonstrating how unerringly his pimping genius had asserted itself at the proper time.) Seems there'd been a married broad in the district where he lived; not old, maybe twenty-five or thirty, and not bad looking, "a sexy bitch, with hot pants." Playboy and the lady hooked up. He told his friends of his find and they enjoined him to cut them in. An accommodating sort, Playboy did so—for a reasonable fee. Oh, sure, the gal had posed the question of the proprieties in having high-school boys beating a path to her door, particularly when rumors reached her of the commercial aspects of the project. But Playboy soft conned her. Didn't she love him? Well, what was wrong with doing a few friends a favor? Confident that she would succumb to such un-answerable—if not exactly Aristotelian—logic, but still a thorough campaigner, Playboy allowed as how he also "told the bitch I might not be able to keep some of the disappointed guys from letting her old man know what's been going on with us."

Flushed with success, Playboy grew more ambitious—and more ruthlessly avaricious. One bitch wasn't enough. He began casting about for more. For younger, unsuspecting ones he could break in right. He narrated, in elaborate detail, how he converted them into "two-way bitches." He recited with some satisfaction how he had broken the will of the sexy bitch and compelled her to aid him. Play-boy thought it real funny that her old man had tried to commit sui-cide when he got wise, and that she had ultimately been committed to an insane asylum. He further assured Whit that part of his enthusiasm for pimping derived from the fact that "you make the bitch do what you tell her, and like it, or you kick her teeth out."

Oh, sure, it's an attractive calling! Who can deny that? And it's an addiction, too, like a shot of "H" in the main line. You get so you got to have it. It's a lust to degrade. It's holding a whip and using it. It's power—perverted, debased, but still power. It's another part of the jungle. "You get the bitch drunk, see, and then you lay it on the line to her. You tell her what she's going to do and how. And when she tells you she's never done anything like that, you slap her a couple of times and tell her this is when she starts."

The darkness wasn't black; it was red, a red so intense and thick it blotted out sight. It was the redness of molten lava spewing from an erupting volcano.

"Hey, what's the matter?" Playboy said. "You look sick."

"I'm O.K.," Whit said. "Yeah, I'm just fine. Never felt better." He brushed his forehead with his hand; it was wet with a cold perspira-tion. One thought obscured all others. It came to him with a perfect clarity: *I can kill!*

He could be his own law: judge, prosecutor, jury, executioner. Even gravedigger, if necessary. He could grin and calmly pump slugs into the degraders, all of them. And never stop grinning. He could kill and kill and kill—but what would it prove? What did death prove? He could reach out and tear the life out of Playboy. And grin. But not know who was responsible for the world's Playboys.

Paradoxically, the realization he could kill was quieting. It brought Whit a new detachment and a satisfaction. Almost an impersonal satisfaction. And a neo-sanity from emotional bedlam. A violent calmness. The red haze receded. Slowly. Very slowly.

Playboy came back into focus, but with a new face beneath his old one—a toad's face.

Whit's voice was controlled, casual. "I just don't think I got the qualifications to be a P.I.," he said.

Playboy nodded and observed as how those qualifications were for a fact rather rigid.

One April morning in 1938 Whit was called to the detail grounds and told to go immediately to his company and get his personal property. "A court release just came through for you," he was informed.

A court release! That meant he was free, and no strings attached. He learned that the chief juvenile judge of the county from which he had been committed had ordered that he be turned loose unconditionally. His release seemed almost too good to be true.

That evening Whit was in San Francisco, walking down Market Street, looking at the sights, getting the feel of his sudden new freedom. The next day he was home, and his homecoming was a happy one. For his part, Whit was glad to be with his mother and father again, and he knew they were equally glad to have him back with them. Not a word of censure did he hear. His parents' sole concern was for his future and how it could be made a success. And they were immensely pleased at how sturdy and healthy he appeared. Although not tall, he had grown several inches and had put on weight.

"And do you know something? I never had one attack of that darned asthma the whole time I was at the school!"

How bright was the future—for a few days.

He tried to see the chief juvenile judge who had ordered his release. Did he want to see the judge on business? Not exactly. He wanted to thank the judge and discuss a personal idea with him. The judge was busy. Couldn't he come back another time? Yes, he could; and did. And the judge was busy; so couldn't he come back another time? Yes, he could; but he didn't.

He borrowed his dad's car and drove out to the juvenile hall. After waiting for almost an hour, he was permitted to see the lady juvenile court referee who originally had committed him to reform school. She appeared genuinely pleased to see him. She said she was sorry she could spare only a few minutes. Yes, he understood how jammed her calendar was. She said he was looking well—the school had been good for him, now hadn't it? She hoped that he'd learned his lesson; she was sure he had; she was glad. The trouble was that some youngsters were obstinate: they just wouldn't benefit by institutional training. (How good she was, how well-meaning, how humane, and yet how tragically innocent for all her years, degrees and position!) She simply would have to continue calling her calendar; but wouldn't he stay for the next case, a particularly troublesome one?

The boy who was brought in was a surly, angry lad with a freckled face and an air of defiance. His mother accompanied him, a tired, tried, plain-looking woman. The boy had a long record of minor offenses. Then he had been caught in a burglary. The best thing for him, said the lady judge, was a commitment to reform school. Whit was proof. The lady judge told the boy and his mother about Whit. Whit had learned his lesson. (It was very simple: you learned your lesson or you didn't, and it was entirely up to you. Only it wasn't very simple—it was very complicated—when *you* were the one learning the lesson.) Whit tried to say so; he failed, not because of a lack of words, but because of an absence of understanding. The surly, angry lad heard himself committed, glared at all the parties present and was led away.

The mother left, crying softly. The lady judge thanked Whit, told him to come back from time to time and let her know how he was doing, said goodbye and wished him luck.

Less than a week following his release from the school Whit began wheezing and grew increasingly short of breath. He lost his appetite and became thin again before his parents' eyes. They worried when he went off by himself, staying away for hours at a time. He sat in a park nearby, in a deserted spot, listening to the wind rustling the leaves of the trees, watching cloud battalions scud across the sky above him. But mostly his eyes were turned inward, and he was only vaguely conscious of the grandeur of early spring. There were devils inside him. And he knew some of their names: philosophic anarchism, pluralism, empiricism.

A society, a religion, even existence itself, when built upon fear, was false. Whit refused to concede it possessed any validity, particularly when maintained by force. But how did you demonstrate its invalidity? Whit thought of Nietzsche. The German's advocacy of forcible self-assertion as a means of achieving perfection might prove to be just the mental battering ram he needed. He could use it to batter the gates of absolutism. And how he hated the absolutists! He hated them so passionately he would emulate them. His end would justify his means. Dead these four hundred years, Machiavelli, his friend Niccolo, would vouch for the efficacy of that cynical doctrine. And the means? Why, by declaring war in the jungle, of course. Of course.

13

And He Ran Faster

"That boy's a bad one. He's about to go off the deep end again. I can tell by the funny look in his eye."

"Well, what can you expect? Surely you know his mother was abandoned on some church steps a day or two after she was born. The Cottles took the poor waif in and raised her in a God-fearing atmosphere."

"And they never knew who her parents were?"

"Why, no, they never did. But if you ask me . . ."

Ah, God; *if you ask me!* But I'm not asking you. I don't care what you think. And damn your sly insinuations! There's more than one kind of bastard.

"Mom," Whit said, "I want you to tell me every single thing you know about yourself."

Hallie told her son. She added that more than almost anything else in the world she had prayed that the mystery of her birth might one day be solved. But Mother and Dad Cottle, those stern puritans, had vigorously resisted any moves on her part to learn the truth. Trying to penetrate the mystery would be questioning God's will. And *that* could produce calamitous results. It wasn't done.

Except by the Whits, the bad ones.

He asked his grandmother about his mother. And he got a lecture instead of an answer. His grandmother warned him about Hell and told him about God. If he didn't obey God's commandments he would go to Hell; it would be there, in a kind of Dante's Inferno, he would spend eternity, burning and burning and burning. The boy shouldn't concern himself with the question of the parentage of "my little girl." God knew best. The book should remain closed.

Whit still wanted to know about his mother.

The tiny old lady talked on and said nothing. She saw herself as the chosen instrument of God's Charity. She and Dad Cottle had taken his mother in and raised her, never shirking their duty. Even so, the sins of the father had been visited upon her little girl. And wasn't it written that this should be so?

And wasn't it written that the streets of hell are paved with good intentions?

The wife of the Pasadena, California, Postmaster made an honest mistake. She parked her husband's 1937 Ford V8 sedan at the curb of a busy Pasadena street one May morning in the year 1938, leaving the ignition key in it. When she returned from a brief shopping tour the car was gone. . . .

Whit eased the Ford he was driving along at a leisurely speed. On the western outskirts of the city, he parked and inspected his acquisition. In the glove compartment he found a credit card, and it was then he learned whose car he had borrowed. He grinned. And then the violence boiled up out of him.

He put the car through the gears, viciously. He rammed it through traffic, slammed it around corners, tires screaming. "All right, you grim reaper bastard," he thought, broadsiding crazily into another corner, "here's your chance!"

He pulled into a gas station when he reached Montrose, above Glendale. "Five of your ethyl," he told the attendant.

"Yes, sir."

Whit got out. He watched the hand of the gas meter race around, listened to the bell ding five times. He had the oil checked and the windshield cleaned. He checked the tires himself. Then he handed the attendant the credit card, signed the slip with the postmaster's name, adding a "Jr.," and pocketed his copy.

He drove off.

He was a factor again.

Moose lived in a district of Los Angeles, bordered on one side by the Los Angeles River and on the opposite side by a busy truck highway.

Moose was an incorrigible romantic, and to that extent a character. He was forever falling in love with some cute young thing, tarts and chippies and good-bad girls by no means excluded. Indeed, the quantitative aspects of *l'amour* seemed wholly to have won him over, leaving no room for any qualitative considerations. Possessed of a nature as fickle as it was amorous, each week he discarded an old flame for a new and gaudier one. This catch-as-catch-can brand of romance kept Moose broke—for he was a notoriously free spender—and made him an opportunist always in search of a fast buck.

Whit braked the Ford to a stop in front of the small frame house where Moose lived. A horn blast brought Moose to the door and a shout brought him lumbering out to the car. His walk was deceptive. Actually he was agile as a cat.

Greetings exchanged, Moose asked, "Where'd ya get this crate, clout it?"

" 'Borrowed' is a nicer word," Whit said.

"Sure," Moose agreed amiably, "but they both add up to the same thing. Besides, I thought you'd got religion and turned square."

Whit didn't crack wise. He said simply, without glibness, "I guess I've backslid."

"I don't get it," Moose said, perplexed. Moose wasn't a thinker, yet he had a homely way of getting incisively to the heart of a problem.

"I don't get it at all. When you were little you were raising more hell than six other guys could. Just like that"—Moose snapped his fingers—"you changed from a mama's boy into a wild man. And when the bulls nailed Tim, damned if you didn't ride the beef for all of us. Then you get out of that place up north and you act like you got a halo around your head. Now here you are with a hot heap. So what happens next?"

"We engage in a little free enterprise," Whit said.

"Meaning we take somebody's dough?" Moose asked.

Whit nodded. "That's about it."

"Well, pal, that's O.K. with me, but are you sure that's what you want? I mean you got brains enough to amount to something. I got an idea for some screwy reason I don't understand you keep trying to throw your life away by getting into jams and I don't think that's really what you want to do. Me, I keep it simple. All I try to do is get along, have a little fun and, one way or another, keep a few nickels in my jeans. I don't try to find any hidden meanings in what happens or try to figure out what makes the world go round. But you're different. You act like a guy that's looking for something characters like me don't even know exists. And if it's like that, pal, you better be sure you're looking in the right place."

Whit's laugh was spontaneous. "Moose," he said, "whether you know it or not, the philosophers and psychologists could take some lessons from you."

Moose's brow furrowed with concentration. He looked at his big hands. Ordinarily he didn't put his nose into anyone else's business or subject their motives to a nice analysis. It made him uneasy to do so. But Whit was his friend. "Don't get me wrong, pal. I'm not trying to tell you what to do. And I know I won't get hurt by going in with you. At least not through any fault of yours. But that's the trouble. What'll probably happen is that I'll do all right for myself and you'll wind up in a jackpot."

Whit said, and meant it, "I'm willing to take my chances. Now let me tell you what I got in mind."

"Fire away, pal," Moose invited. "I'm all ears."

The next afternoon, with Moose in the front seat beside him, Whit guided the postmaster's Ford along a narrow, winding drive that meandered among the Hollywood Hills.

"That's the place," Whit said, pointing out an impressive structure of decidedly haughty architecture. High green hedges walled it off from neighboring homes.

"Classy looking joint, all right," Moose commented.

Whit nodded his agreement. He eased the Ford in toward the curb. "I'm parking a couple of doors down to reduce the chance of the car being seen. Now, have you got everything straight?"

"Sure," Moose said, full of brash confidence.

"O.K., then let's go. But remember, let me do the talking. From what I hear, getting into this place won't be easy."

The walk was flower-bordered and arced at a fish pond where marble cranes squirted water at each other, and fat goldfish swam aimlessly. With Moose beside him, Whit punched the door button. They heard the muted notes of a chimes. A coffee-complexioned young woman in a trim maid's uniform opened the door.

Whit looked at her and then dropped his eyes and squirmed, simulating a keen embarrassment. He stammered, "I was wondering—I, I mean—well, my friend and I, we . . ."

The maid couldn't resist a knowing grin. She invited them in. Inside, in a sumptuously decorated parlor, they were met by a woman, perhaps forty, of the type the French would call *très chic*. This woman made no effort to conceal her amusement at the sight of the fuzzy-cheeked Whit then eyeing her boldly.

"You're a little young to be coming here, aren't you, junior," she asked in a voice that purred.

Whit had dropped all pretense of being the gauche young innocent. "Ah, madam," he replied, "surely you realize how impetuous even tender youth can be."

"Give the word, Stella," said an oily masculine voice, "and I'll toss this smart-cracking punk out on his ear."

Whit turned to its source. Lolling in an easy chair in a corner of the

room was a tall, slim, exquisite dandy who bore the conspicuous stamp
of the pimp.

"Well, listen to this lap dog, will you," Whit said, not bothering to
make his words exclamatory.

The dandy muttered an oath and started to push himself up from
the chair when the woman called Stella spoke sharply.

"It's all right, Frank. Sit still." Then she asked Whit, "Did you
have any particular girl in mind?"

"To tell you the truth," Whit told her, "I've got all your girls in
mind."

Stella became excusably suspicious. "Just exactly what do you mean
by that?" she demanded.

"This," Whit said. He drew a snub-nosed gun from a pocket of his
sport jacket and held it casually in his right hand. At the same time
Moose produced a larger-calibered, long-barreled revolver, a horse
pistol. Whit had Moose stay with Stella, the maid and the pimp while
he rounded up the girls.

He found four of them chatting in a sun porch at the rear of the
house. These he turned over to the custody of Moose before vaulting
up the stairs. He walked in, unannounced, on a fifth abed with a customer in a bedroom on the second floor. This one was an outraged
spitfire with a small, feline face and the pungent vocabulary of a mule-
skinner. While throwing her ample self into a near-diaphanous housecoat, she discoursed on the subject of "half-pint, two-bit hoodlums
with guns who come busting into a working girl's boudoir."

Whit apologized for the intrusion, and tried with indifferent success to be grave while doing so.

Meanwhile, the customer, a bald, paunchy individual, resignedly
put on his clothes. His moon face, at first disorganized by this sudden
and untoward turn of events, gradually assumed an expression of acute
disenchantment.

At the point of his snub-nosed gun, Whit induced Moonface and
Spitfire to descend the stairs and join the others.

One of the girls was cooing suggestively at Moose who, forever susceptible to feminine blandishment, appeared on the verge of forgetting the original and exclusive purpose of their invasion.

"All right, you big ox, get your mind back on your business," Whit said, and Moose grinned sheepishly.

At Whit's urging, Stella reluctantly opened a hidden wall safe. He stuffed its cash contents into a jacket pocket, ignoring all else in the safe except the inevitable little black book which he palmed gingerly. "Well, well," he said, looking knowingly at the madam of the place.

"My book," Stella said. Her statement implied a question.

"Sure," Whit said. "Your book." He tossed it to her. "No good to me unless I wanted to make trouble. And neither one of us wants trouble, do we, Stella?"

Stella quickly agreed they did not.

"All right," he said. "Then you don't squawk to anybody about getting hijacked. You just write it off as an occupational hazard. And in return, I forget all about your place here. I don't make any anonymous calls, say, to a certain crusading newspaper that's hot to expose houses like yours. Deal?"

"Deal," Stella said, adding, "You know, junior, for a sprout you seem damn clever. But watch out you don't outsmart yourself."

Whit grinned. "I'll try real hard, Stella," he said. "I'll try real hard just for your sake."

Then he sent Moose upstairs to make a fast search of the girls' rooms. "No jewelry," he emphasized. "Nothing but cash."

Moose was gone several minutes. He returned with a fistful of bills clutched in one hand and his large gun still held in the other one. Spying the money, Spitfire squalled bitter protest, screaming she had worked hard for that dough.

"Don't take it so rough, baby," Moose said placatingly, his big homely face splashed with humor. "There's plenty more where that came from."

Spitfire sputtered something fierce. Then she subsided, rendered speechless by the immensity of her own righteous indignation.

Apparently of the opinion it was high time his authoritative male voice be heard, the dandy declared, "I guess you know you won't get away with this."

"No kidding," Whit said. He walked over to confront the dandy. He stripped off the dandy's fancy wristwatch and ground it under his heel. He jerked a diamond ring from one of the dandy's fingers and had Moose go flush it down a toilet. All the time he held his gun aimed at the dandy's midsection, and his eyes dared the dandy to resist. He frisked the dandy, memorizing the name and address on a driver's license found in the latter's wallet. A man of discretion, the dandy suffered these numerous indignities in silence, including the removal of several bills from his wallet.

"Maybe next time," Whit said, "you'll have sense enough to keep your fat pimp mouth shut. If you don't, you're apt to have your tiny pimp brains blown out."

The dandy had no comment.

"How about the old gink here," Moose asked, "do we shake him down too?"

Whit shook his head. "No, we leave him strictly alone and we apologize for interrupting his party. Now put that cannon away and let's get out of here."

They strode quickly to the Ford, got in and drove off. Moose counted and divided the loot. After relaxing expansively in the seat, he gazed fondly at the roll of bills he held in a big hand. "Nothing to it," he said. Then he looked at Whit and saw more than a skinny adolescent with a rather large head and an odd way of grinning.

In less than a week following their initial foray into the Hollywood Hills, employing the same *modus operandi,* they robbed eight more bordellos. Moose was jubilant with his sudden riches. "Man, we're really riding a gravy train," he exalted. "I take it away from one tomato and then turn right around and blow it on another. Broads're gonna be the death of me yet."

Whit had to grin. He said, "You know, Moose, there's a lot more truth than poetry in what you just said."

Moose sobered. "What makes you say that?" he asked.

"Well, mainly because I got wind the P.I.'s and some other people are all riled up over what we've been doing. I got reason to believe there'll be a hot reception party waiting for us at the next place we walk into."

Moose got the point. "Meaning, then, we stop walking into those kind of places?"

"That's what I mean."

Moose reacted to the news philosophically. "Well, I guess nobody should expect a good thing to last forever," he said with a shrug. "Got anything else in mind?"

"Not anything that'll pay off in the kind of coin you're looking for. Just three or four miscellaneous projects. Besides, I think we better split up for a while, hot as we are. If I'm not nailed in the meantime I'll be back to see you in three or four weeks, maybe sooner."

Moose didn't ask any questions. "Okay, pal, take it easy."

"Sure, Moose," Whit said. "And you do the same."

The private detective agency was located in the heart of Los Angeles, on the fifth floor of a building that had seen better times. Whit walked in and confronted a mousey-looking receptionist.

"Yes?" she said. "What is it you want? If you're selling subscriptions we don't want any."

"Quit trying to scare off a cash customer before he gets a chance to talk with your boss," Whit said.

The private dick was a seedy-appearing, middle-aged guy with alert eyes. "You want to see me about something?" he asked.

Whit said he did, privately.

"Come into my office then."

Whit got right down to business. He told the private dick all he knew about where, when and how his mother had been found.

"You want to find the girl—I mean that woman?"

"No, I want to find out who her parents were."

"That'd be a tough job. It might cost a lot of money and even then I couldn't guarantee results."

"Never mind the build-up," Whit said. "Just tell me how much money is a lot of money."

"Well, fifteen bucks a day, expenses, and train or plane fare both ways."

Whit produced a thick roll of bills. The money was every last dollar he had netted from the houses. He gave the roll a little toss into the air, caught it, surveyed it critically, looked at the private dick, whose eyes had opened wider and grown considerably more interested with the appearance of the roll, and then Whit threw the roll.

"Catch," he said, and the private dick caught, with both hands. "There's enough money to pay your expenses and keep you looking for a helluva lot of days. But I'm not going to ask for a refund, not even if you have the answer for me tomorrow. All I want is results."

"Sure," the private dick said, "all you want is results, and that's what you'll get."

"Now you *could* go south with my money," Whit observed, "because I don't intend to try to check on you, and I'm not even asking for a receipt. And if you did go south, I wouldn't yell copper. I wouldn't say a word to anybody. But . . ."

The private dick interrupted with protestations of his honesty. "I guarantee value received," he said, with just the right amount of injured professional pride.

"Sure, sure," Whit said. "I know. But I still think I should make it plain that I wouldn't be happy if you got scientific with me, figuring maybe you were just dealing with a dumb kid."

Whit heard elaborate assurances there was no chance this would happen.

"All right," Whit said. "Now that we understand each other let's

work out the details. You take the money and you go look for the answer. While you're looking, you make reports of everybody you talk to and everything you do. I want a complete record. When you find the answer, you come back here. You put all the reports in a file and seal them up. One of these days I walk in and get them. Then I walk out and we both forget we ever saw each other."

The private dick nodded and said, "That sounds like a most satisfactory arrangement." He buzzed for the mousey-looking receptionist
who doubled as his secretary. "I want you to take down every word
this young man has to say."

Whit repeated what he had told the private dick about how, when
and where his mother had been abandoned. Leaving, he gently reminded the dick, "Remember, we got a gentleman's agreement."

Whit spent the night at his mother's bedside, slowly rocking back
and forth in a rocking chair. This was an old habit they had, softly
talking the night away, for sleep was a luxury the pain-ridden Hallie
seldom enjoyed without the aid of drugs and she far preferred the
company of her son to a drugged sleep. They talked happily of everything bright and warm under the sun—of writers and artists and poets
and books and paintings and poetry and happenings both new and
old and other people and other times—and yet they did not once mention their dark and unhappy personal world, nor did Whit tell his
mother of his visit to the private detective agency. And she, of course,
knew nothing of his money-gathering activities, or of the fact that he
had taken the postmaster's car.

Their night was calm and peaceful; the dark and disruptive violence
touching their lives was remote.

During the ensuing two weeks Whit kept the Ford on the road almost day and night. Later, checking back on him, the police learned
he had used the credit card to put as much as twenty gallons of gas
in the car daily.

Whit was on the run, and traveling fast. He was in a hurry and
yet not too certain of where he was going.

He tried and failed to find a lead to Barbara, who had never written
his mother. He looked up one of Barbara's former girl friends and
asked for Barbara's address.

"If I knew it, I wouldn't give it to you," the girl said and looked at
him with loathing. She knew he had been in reform school.

"I loved Barbara," Whit said simply. But there was no explaining to this girl. He sensed that.

"I know what love means to your kind," the girl said.

"You fool!" Whit said, the anger rising in him suddenly. "You goddam virtuous fool!"

He jammed the Ford in gear and roared off, still on the run. Still in a hurry.

He didn't want to find Barbara any longer. He no longer needed to find her. He had loved an ideal and not a girl, and now he hated the ideal because it still had the power to torment him. And he couldn't bring Barbara's face into focus in his mind, try as he might—at least not with the sharp, clear perfection he desperately desired. So he rejected the face. He had to, urgently. And he apologized. He said, "I'm sorry, Barbara. I'm sorry."

And he ran faster.

Whit looked up some reform-school graduates who lived in a tough section of the city, a slum quarter. That night they had a "tea party." Even in those days marijuana was plentiful, although Whit "blasted" his first "stick," and his last, that night. He got so high he had to get down on his hands and knees to get off the curbs. Everything was hilariously funny and when he started coming off the kick he was ravenously hungry. "No more of that stuff," he said, "I don't have too much sense on the natural, so I can't afford to give up what I do have." They assured him it would be different next time. But he shook his head, no next time.

Where was the stuff coming from? He found out, paid a visit to the upstanding citizen who was masterminding its distribution. A violent argument developed and was resolved suddenly and decisively by Whit, who then buried his snub-nosed gun where it would never be found. Later he told a friend, "But don't go jumping to the conclusion I murdered the sonofabitch, because I didn't."

Whit was arrested in the early morning hours of his seventeenth birthday. Two radio-car officers spotted him in front of a Glendale,

California, drugstore. Investigating, these officers found a crowbar and jimmie marks on the establishment's front door. Parked nearby was the postmaster's missing auto. At the police station Whit told one glib lie after another in accounting for his presence near the drugstore at that early hour of the morning. His conduct developed into a foolproof technique: tell near-truths, half-truths, but never the whole truth. Throw in a few outrageous fabrications and the police will give up in disgust. They'll become convinced you're a fraud and won't look too far.

• *14* •

"Apparently You Didn't Learn Your Lesson."

Whit was recommitted to reform school—for vehicle theft and forgery—by the same chief juvenile judge who had ordered his unconditional release but a few weeks earlier. The hearing was in chambers and brief. That Whit had stolen the Pasadena postmaster's car and used the credit card by forging a name and creating a fictitious identity appeared reasonably certain. That he had been involved in other and more serious offenses could only be strongly suspected. Physical or tangible proof was lacking, and Whit had declined to implicate himself beyond leading the officers on several wild goose chases.

Near the conclusion of the hearing, the judge fixed his gaze upon Whit and said sternly, "Apparently you didn't learn your lesson, and certainly this report shows you haven't been cooperative with the investigating officers. I see no alternative but to commit you to the industrial school in the hope further training there will prove beneficial."

Whit's eyes met and held the judge's, and they were squinting with appraisal. *Apparently you didn't learn your lesson . . . haven't been cooperative . . . further training . . .* The same old words. The same meaningless mumbo jumbo. The same complete lack of rapport.

Whit smiled faintly—or did he sneer? And he, then being judged, passed judgment.

What did he have to say for himself?

Nothing.

Whit was returned to the overcrowded juvenile tank at the jail to

113

await transfer to the school. Another folly, jamming all these young-sters in together—the dumb ones and the bright ones, the lions and the lambs, the romantics and the psychotics—and then leaving them that way for weeks at a time, while their cases were being processed through the courts. Leaving them to fight and gamble and agitate and scheme and dream and brag and bully and pervert. Establishing a hierarchy of cunning and brute force. A nice place for a sixteen- or seventeen-year-old—unless he happens to be your son.

Whit was self-reliant. He got along. Nobody tried to hoosier him out of his money. Nobody bothered him. He didn't bother the others. He did his own time, minded his own business. Then he was on his way.

While being driven north, he and another boy to whom he was manacled escaped by a ruse from the two officers transporting them. For a hectic hour the two boys ran, hid and ran. Then, still manacled together, they were recaptured by a posse of high-school students who had volunteered to aid the police and the juvenile officers in the search for them. On arrival at the school, both boys were ordered to the iso-lated two-story building where the most rebellious of the institution's wards were quartered. The other boy's mind and body proved less durable than Whit's. He lost his reason. He deliberately infected his hand and then, after transfer to the school's hospital, where he per-sisted in sticking wire and pins into the infected area and tearing off the bandages, he was sent to a mental hospital. He had failed to benefit by the training program.

This disciplinary unit was called G Company. Here Whit's room was a cell, with a steel door and bars and heavy mesh screening on the window which kept out most of the sunlight. A low-watt bulb fur-nished illumination and was turned off at nine in the evening. Whit spent sixteen hours a day behind the locked steel door and sixteen times a day a supervisor, making a check of the cells, would peer in at him through a rectangular opening in the door. One of the supervisors, who clomped heavily when he walked on his rounds, invariably would ask, "Still in there?" Whit never answered but many of the other boys did. An excitable youngster quartered next door to Whit listened to the question for a couple of weeks and then, one evening, shouted back, "Yeah, and I got your peg-legged, syphilitic mama in here with me, you bastard!" This malefactor was, of course, appropriately disciplined.

A Bible was kept in each cell and was the only reading material permitted. Whit knew many of the inmates used the thin pages to roll smuggled tobacco in. He discovered, however, that no pages were missing from the Bible in his cell. He read the book through from cover to cover. He reread it. Particularly was his mind provoked by Ecclesiastes:

To every thing there is a season, and a time to every purpose under the heaven: . . . a time to die . . . a time to kill . . . a time to cast away . . . a time to hate . . . a time of war.

Out of context? Admitted. But no more so than this place was out of social context.

It was midsummer of the year 1938. The school's brick yard, where its segregated disciplinary offenders worked, was a veritable hell hole. There, shirtless, his face caked with sweat and brick dust, his hands blistered and raw before the thick calluses formed, his body being bronzed by the burning sun's rays, Whit labored each weekday with a kind of maniacal fury, ruthlessly driving himself to the very limit of his endurance. One of the many supervisors, seated close by in the shade, marveled at Whit's astonishing industry and grew curious.

"Hey, kid, come here a minute. . . . Yeah, you there."

Whit set his wheelbarrow down and approached the supervisor, a large man turned flabby and sour, with watery eyes and numerous chins.

"What're you trying to do, kid, impress somebody?"

Whit smiled, and his face was more masked than ever. "Maybe you could call it that," he replied, amiably insolent. "I just wanted you people to know that the tougher it gets the better I like it."

"Oh, a tough guy, huh?" the supervisor snapped, his fleshy, sagging face crimsoning with sudden anger. "Well, we got ways of teaching you tough guys some respect for authority."

"Have you?" Whit said. "I never would have guessed it."

The supervisor bit off an angry retort, clamping his jaws shut. A vein near his Adam's apple throbbed. His thin lips parted in a travesty of a smile, and he said, "Now, now; there's no reason for you to feel like that. Here, have a drink." He offered Whit his canteen.

Whit contemptuously matched the other's surface change of attitude. "Sure, be glad to," he said, unsuspecting. He should have known better. He knew he had been working for two hours under a broiling sun; he knew supervisors carried ice water in their canteens. But he didn't stop to think. He filled his belly with ice water, drinking greedily, and promptly became violently sick.

The supervisor laughed mirthlessly. "Now, tough guy, get back to work."

Whit retched, worked and cursed himself for a fool.

Two days later he was caught whispering to another youngster and put on light rations, the standard punishment for those seen or heard violating the strictly enforced no-talking rule—strictly enforced, that is, unless you were one of The Man's pets or finks. For breakfast light rations meant some prune juice, three or four prunes, a scoop of mush; for the noon and night meal, one soggy slice of bread, some bean juice, a few beans and a cup of milk. The boys on light rations were fed in their cells, but they were worked the same as those on the regular diet. This latter group ate in a small mess hall on the first floor; they filed in and stood at their assigned places. When The Man clapped his hands they seated themselves and began to eat. When he clapped again they got up and filed out. If you bolted the food you got enough. Sometimes.

A blind anger he did not attempt to control took possession of Whit one evening when another of the supervisors accompanied the inmate waiter to his cell with the light rations and made a smart crack.

"You pus-gutted bastard," Whit said, "take those goddam beans

and . . ." He took a step toward the supervisor, his fists clenched
tightly.

The supervisor slapped him across the face with a beefy hand that
held the cell door keys. He struck back. The supervisor slammed the
door shut in his face, locking it, and minutes later returned with two
other supervisors. Whit was forcibly taken from his cell and marched
to a special, empty cell. He knew what was coming. When the door
banged shut on him, the supervisor said through the slot, "Here's
something to keep you company." Then they shot a cartridge of tear
gas into the cell.

The next several minutes of Whit's life were not pleasant ones.

They were didactic minutes. They taught him the folly, the futility
of open, unbending defiance against such embodiments of authority
as the world's Supervisors. Whit perceived that the social function of
The Supervisors was a relatively simple one—they were the agency
through which the rebel, if goaded to self-destruction by an ugly, un-
reasoning hate, quickly achieved his unnatural purpose.

The Supervisors were vise-turners. But they didn't put you in the
vise; they waited for you to do it. And when you did, they would keep
turning until you told them—politely, hoarsely, shudderingly, however you were able—that you had had enough. Then they released you
to the custody of gentler hands, if not less inflexible minds. Yet should
the pain of the vise so enrage you that you defied them to turn and be
damned, they would accede to your masochistic demand. Refusing to
bend, you broke.

Jackie broke. One day at work he tried to run a pick through his
head and only failed when another boy grabbed him. Back in his cell,
Jackie became hysterical. He cursed the supervisors. That was his
mistake. They gassed Jackie. Whit listened to him alternately continue
to scream obscene defiance and beg for a drink of water after he was
brought from the gas cell and put into a stripped cell. They tried to
shut Jackie up; they slapped him around, but this only made him
worse. So they took him to the hospital and when he failed to improve
they shipped him to the "bug house." They used a lot of big words to

describe what was wrong with Jackie and to explain why it was he had reacted so adversely to the school's training program.

After his enlightening experience with the tear gas, after observing what happened to the Jackies and the others, Whit grinned and fought back in more cunningly subtle ways. The brick yard baked almost all traces of his asthma out of him. Simultaneously, he let the brick yard bake Hate into him. He made Hate his friend and counsellor. Hate told him to grin. To be wily. He heeded the advice. It won him release from the disciplinary company into the school's general population and a short while later reassignment to his former job in the assistant superintendent's office.

First he was hospitalized, but not because he had become a "bug." The physical machine he owned simply had been subjected to too great a strain. His pulse was irregular; he had developed a heart murmur, a rapid pulse; he ran a fever; he had night sweats. They had him in a private room and for a week he didn't think he would make it. But he did, and here again Hate helped him when medicine and medical care couldn't. One of the attendants used his bathroom to sneak a smoke every day. And one morning this boy had just walked out when Table Legs, one of the nurses, walked in, smelled smoke and accused Whit of malingering, of just pretending to be sick, of himself sneaking into the bathroom and smoking. Table Legs ranted at him for ten solid minutes. And he just grinned, denying nothing, and thereby agitated this bombastic female all the more.

Sure he was sick—he was so sick he had thought he was going to die—but Table Legs would never know it. She and the rest of them could think what they pleased. In time he recovered, with Hate's help, by simply getting out of bed and ignoring what was wrong with him; by getting back up when he fell on his face; by refilling his belly when he threw up what he had eaten; by paying no attention to the black dizziness, and acting as though it weren't there.

Back at his job in the assistant superintendent's office, a friendly grin and a willingness and ability to carry an enormous work load offered the protective coloration he needed while he sought an early release. Again he was made a cadet officer, but his enthusiasm to help the weak ones was gone, put on cold storage. And he didn't fight as often; slugging it out with the big-mouthed tigers was no longer a pleasure. It was simply a job to be done when they got in his face and that was the only way to get them out. He knew what he was doing—withdrawing. Reform school had taught him all it could; truly he had learned his lessons. Not singular; plural. He was nearing his eighteenth birthday—he felt as though it might be his eightieth—and he knew he had a choice to make. It was a very simple choice. He either had to go out, go home, settle down, get a job, get married, have kids, forget everything he had seen and had started out to learn, becoming a washer in a barrel, or he had to go on living in the jungle until he destroyed it or it destroyed him.

A square, a John, with its effete, futile, burlesque connotations. A blindly believing, wholly obedient, ineffectual, unthinking square. That was the safe thing to become. Safe until he started to think. Until he recalled what happened to the weak and the meek. Until the Hate rose up in him and his trigger finger began to itch.

An employee of the school had drawn Whit to one side, covertly sympathized with his mistrust of his society. His capitalist society. Blame your plight on that society and its cancerous economics, he had been told. Its degradation, its enslavement of the masses. Look you that Marx and Lenin and the other comrades have conceived how the perfect society may be achieved. So put your Hate to work, consecrate it. Become one of us.

Of course this proposition had not been made suddenly or crudely. First there had been the build-up, the winning of confidence, the offered friendship, the doing of small favors, the idea planting. But in vain. "No thanks," Whit had said. "I don't think I'm interested." Why not? "Let's say I just don't think I'd make a very good comrade and let it go at that."

Why not? Because the Hate inside him didn't deserve consecration. Because it was a disease with a peculiar pathology of its own, not a noble weapon. Whit had traded fear for it, and for guile.

And that was his trouble. He had allowed Hate and Guile to serve him too well. He had contracted with them to do his bidding, and their devotion to him had become fanatic. They clamored to aid him in everything he did. Their loyalty to him was so fierce, so unwavering, they made him believe he could not get along without them. They made him believe they were the only friends he had whose loyalty was absolute. They had persuasive ways of convincing him even against his will.

For example, Whit's work brought him into daily contact with an attractive female administrative employee. Whit liked Miss Turner —as we shall call her—because she was never superior or highhanded with the inmates, and particularly because she wasn't forever lecturing or scolding them. Being totally human, she refused to take offense because others were human too. Her evident friendliness to the school's charges assigned to do clerical or cleanup work in the administration building set prudish tongues to wagging and prompted one prim lady to warn her that "I think it's only fair I tell you what 'they' are saying."

Miss Turner responded to this warning by laughing heartily in the prim lady's face.

"Well, I never!" huffed the prim lady indignantly before marching off. The prim lady saw her duty and set out to do it. She pumped a sneaky boy who did house-squad work on the top floor of the administration building where Miss Turner and other employees had rooms, learning from the sneaky one that the friendly lady now and then had a bottle of beer in her room, which was strictly *verboten* by the rules. By promising a rich reward of extra credits, the prim lady exacted an assurance from the sneaky one that he would keep his eyes open and promptly report to her the next time he located a bottle of the brew in the friendly lady's room.

From another house-squad worker Whit learned that the sneaky one was prowling Miss Turner's room and that the prim lady was evincing an unusual interest in the sneaky one's activities. Whit cornered the sneaky one at the first opportunity and said, "I hear stuff has been missing from the rooms upstairs and that they've got you under suspicion because you've been seen sneaking into them."

"I ain't been taking nothing," the sneaky one whined. "I just been looking."

"For what?" Whit demanded. To emphasize his demand, he said, "You think that old bag is going to stick her neck out for you when they put you in the brick yard?"

"They ain't gonna put me there," the sneaky one said. "They're gonna give me a parole if I let 'em know when I find a bottle of beer in Miss Turner's room."

Whit fought the impulse to smash the sneaky one in his face. "So that's it," he said.

"Sure," the sneaky one said. "I'm just trying to help myself."

I'm just trying to help myself! More famous last words. A new kind of Brazen Age—when commissary punks would betray their mothers for a price, for any slight advantage.

"Then go right ahead," Whit said, as if the fact the sneaky one was simply trying to help himself explained and justified all. "By all means, go right ahead."

"And you ain't gonna say nothing to Miss Turner?"

"Why, no," Whit said. "Why should I?"

It took a couple of days for the sneaky one to get his nerve back. Whit, in the meantime, connived a bottle of root beer and waited, saying nothing to the friendly lady, Miss Turner, because his code declared he could not. When he got the signal from his friend assigned to the upstairs house squad, he snitched the door key to Miss Turner's room from her purse, grabbed the bottle of root beer from where he had hidden it and raced unobserved up the back stairs. His friend had gone up the front stairs. Reaching the top floor, this youngster had kicked up a diversionary fuss, thus enabling Whit to duck unseen into Miss Turner's room, remove from a tiny ice chest the bottle in question (it was discreetly wrapped in a wet towel), put the bottle of root beer in its place, dash down the back stairs and cache the beer. On his way to Miss Turner's office he observed the prim lady closeted with the assistant superintendent in the latter's office, and he grinned.

He found the friendly lady busy at a filing cabinet. "You know, Miss Turner, I have a funny feeling that in about another minute or two you will be called in by the assistant superintendent and asked if there isn't a bottle of beer in your room."

The friendly lady blanched.

"Naturally," Whit continued, "since there isn't, you'll laugh when he asks you. You'll tell him what is there is a bottle of *root* beer. You'll become mildly indignant that anyone thinks otherwise, and you will insist he go with you to your room and see for himself."

Then Whit handed the friendly lady her door key, turned and walked away. Moments later the friendly lady was informed the assistant superintendent wanted to speak to her.

For a considerable time thereafter the prim lady was conspicuously red of face, and the sneaky one, needless to add, did not get his parole.

And so it was that a grin became Whit's trade-mark, and hate and guile the tools of his trade. Whit was still grinning the day of his release on parole. He was grinning when, a few days prior to leaving the school, he delivered the final speech at the supper held for those scheduled for parole release during the next thirty days. He glowingly lauded all the school had done for him. He warmly thanked its personnel for what they had taught him, particularly singling out for praise the important lessons learned from The Supervisors regarding a "respect for authority," and the necessity for "high moral standards" as exemplified in the person and daily life of the prim lady. He assured them all that the training he had received, coupled with his experiences at the school, would stay with him and influence him throughout his life. And he hoped one day to repay them for all they had done for him.

Miss Turner alone, of all those present, recognized the real meaning of Whit's glittering words. The prim lady, accepting those words at face value, preened herself. "Wasn't that simply the nicest talk! I'm just positive now, after listening to him, the boy will make good. And I feel ever so proud, to know we are rendering such a worth-while service to society by helping these unfortunate, misguided young men and showing them the right way."

One supervisor did not share the prim lady's enthusiasm. If anything, he then appeared more dour than ever. "Don't be too sure about that one," he said glumly. "He's too smart for his own good. And don't let that grin or those words of his fool you. He's not grinning inside, unless it's *at* us. He talks nice. But when he doesn't know he's being watched, he looks as mean and deadly as a cobra. Mark my words. We'll be hearing more about that one. He'll come to no good end."

And, seemingly, the prophecy has been proved correct. The man now confined to Cell 2455 quite clearly has "come to no good end." After nine years of criminal violence and penal servitude following his release from reform school, he has come to the Condemned Row at California's San Quentin Prison—twice sentenced to death, fifteen times to terms of imprisonment ranging from a life sentence without possibility of parole on down to an indeterminate sentence of from one to ten years. And on top of that, his present discharge date on prior, unexpired commitments to prison is December 10, 2009. Of course, he will not have to worry about serving all that time if and when the state's professional technicians of death once manage to strap him down in one of the gas cell's two chairs.

But, being keenly aware of the infallible efficiency of that squat, ugly, green chamber, he has exhibited a conspicuously obstinate disinclination to go near it. Patently, however, disinclination alone is not enough to thwart the will of the state; for if it were, the executioner's art would soon become a lost one. Yet add to disinclination ruthless self-discipline, bulldog tenacity, the knack of using words, a willingness to gamble boldly, a calculating mind impervious to defeat after defeat, and a mobilized triumvirate of legal skill, imaginative opportunism and intellectual craft—do that and you have the materials from which may be fashioned weapons with which, in the judicial arena, you can wage lively battle for survival, asking no quarter and giving none.

Singlehandedly, for the last more than five years of his life, the beleaguered man in Cell 2455 has stood alone in the cold shadow of the state's gas chamber. By tirelessly wielding legal bludgeon and rapier, he has so far defied the Grim Reaper, stubbornly refusing to acquiesce to California's demand that he forfeit his life, the only possession he has left. Each time the net has been drawn tightly around him he has found a hole in it or a way to slash his way through it. Time after time he has taken the offensive and sought from one court or another a finding that he was, in the legal sense, wrongly and unconstitutionally convicted; time after time he has sought to have the sentences of death and imprisonment vacated and a new trial ordered. Rebuffed, he has retreated, trading space for time, to borrow the language of the military tactician, and figured out another angle of attack. Not long ago he came within three days of being executed, and at the time this book is being written he is engaged in what undoubtedly is a final and decisive court battle. He must win or die.

In answering a recent collateral legal action he instituted against prison officials to test the area and extent of his legal rights in representing himself, an assistant to the California Attorney General characterized Cell 2455's present occupant as "a man who regards the law as a plaything" and, further, one who has made a "mockery of the law." Bay Area dailies have branded him a "chronic troublemaker" on the Row. The San Francisco *Chronicle,* in reporting his filing of an earlier petition for habeas corpus in a federal court, wrote: "He has led riots and participated in fights and other infractions of prison rules during his tenure in death row and has kept his case almost continually before the courts." In a feature story the San Francisco *Examiner* has profiled him as a "hunching 190 pound man . . . brilliant, but absolutely ruthless and callous." The Los Angeles *Daily News* was the first to tag him a "criminal genius."

The majority opinion of the California Supreme Court affirming the death and other judgments pronounced against him stated the evidence adduced at his trial indicates he is a "clever professional criminal" with a "self-admitted violent criminal past and [a] present dangerous, antisocial state of mind."

The foregoing is not, to be sure, a pretty or a flattering sketch, but a harsh and a shocking one. Inevitably the time came when society was obliged, in the judgment of its servants, to test decisively his right to survive.

That time came unexpectedly. A curious, incredible set of circumstances brought him to the Row, psychically a mighty grim place, and it is here he has waged a long, relentless battle for survival against almost hopeless odds.

This account of his life and probable death could be brought to abrupt conclusion by trumpeting an obvious and oft-trumpeted moral —CRIME DOESN'T PAY!—and then letting it go at that. But law-abiding citizens already know this and a large segment of the so-called criminal element (those apprehended for their penal misdeeds) have heard these resounding words so often they have become wholly meaningless.

So let us try a new tack. At least tentatively, let us accept the thought that the only thing the execution of the man in Cell 2455 will prove is that he will be dead. And then let us ask: What will his being dead prove?

The problem of dealing with crime and criminals obviously will not die with him. The harsh fact is that society can execute him and his kind until it wallows neck deep in their blood and still there will be crime. Still there will be "criminals."

Social vengeance—disguised as justice—is therefore a monumentally futile thing and society needlessly confounds itself by exacting it.

This writer knows.

He, you see, is himself the occupant of Cell 2455!

This is his own story, told in his own words, written while he waits to die.

PART TWO

CUILIBET IN ARTE SUA PERITO
EST CREDENDUM

A Peculiar Art

Yes, the Whit in Part One of our book is I—Caryl Whittier Chessman—San Quentin #66565—status, condemned. Or, as some would say, *Doomed!*

And, yes, there is much more of Whit's—my—story to be told.

It is the story of a grinning, brooding young criminal psychopath in defiantly willing bondage to his psychopathy, and is thus an account of a war that is fought too often, too violently, too purposelessly and at too staggering a cost to its thousands upon thousands of combatants and casualties and victims.

It is time we recognized this war for what it is: An externalized, sometimes nicely subtle and oftentimes crudely savage Armageddon of an embattled personality that uncompromisingly seeks either its destruction or its liberation from an internal horror.

Factual truth can equal reality in a way that is an ugly, damning indictment of those responsible for it. Such is the case with this war that is fought in the jungle, under jungle law. And this being so, it undoubtedly explains why most of you cling so tenaciously to those dangerous, crime-perpetuating fictions we hear at every turn. They're so neat and comforting and plausible—and *wrong*.

You can't win! Get that through your thick skull! You can't win! Crime doesn't pay!

But who's kidding whom?

". . . often crime *does* pay. According to an FBI report, only 13% of the nation's criminals ever end up in jail." So states *Time* Magazine in its March 9, 1953 issue (p. 62). The staggering implications of that statistic are driven home when one pauses to consider the appalling number of major crimes committed within the nation each year.

Two million crimes committed in the United States in 1952, according to J. Edgar Hoover, and only 13 per cent of the nation's criminals ever end up in jail! Think of that for a moment. Think of what it means to you.

I personally know of one busy commercial gentleman to whom the crime rate meant nothing until his shiny new car was stolen (used in a series of robberies, then driven into a mountain lake and hence never recovered). Waxing more indignant with each passing day that the police were unable to find *his* car, he confronted the chief of the auto-theft detail and querulously demanded, "If Dick Tracy can catch 'em, why can't you?"

"Mister," said the patient chief, "that's a long story."

"Well, it seems to me," announced the outraged citizen, "that we are entitled to some protection. We taxpayers, that is. Here we pay you perfectly good money to protect us and now you can't even catch the man who stole my car."

"We're doing all we can," said the chief.

The busy commercial gentleman humphed suspiciously at this. "And I suppose if you do catch him, all he'll get is a slap on the wrist and then be turned loose."

"What punishment he gets," explained the chief, "is up to the judge."

"Well, if you ask me, he should be taught a lesson he won't forget. I say lock him up and throw away the key!"

Most people experience no difficulty at all in shrugging off the crime problem—until they are the victim of a crime. Then it's an entirely different story. Then they want to know what's the matter with the police and everyone else concerned with dealing with the problem in one capacity or another. Without putting forth the least effort to try to see the problem in context or to grasp the most rudimentary facts about it, they are willing to hurl indictments, hand down summary judgments and adopt a "lock 'em up and throw away the key" philosophy.

As a result, the uninformed, the cynical, and political opportunists are forever clamoring for law enforcement to "declare war on the underworld."

Crack down! Go into action! Get tough! Move in! Smash!

Words.

Today the country's jails and prisons are bursting at their penal seams—and with but 13% of those who commit major crimes!

It has apparently never occurred to those who loudly argue for an aggressive, ruthless, warlike, put-'em-behind-bars-and-let-'em-rot-there policy to combat crime that not only is law enforcement able to apprehend but a small fraction of the men who commit major crimes— even with the miracle aids of modern scientific crime detecting methods—but that if all those who committed major crimes were somehow caught it would be literally impossible to jail them after arrest, try them and then imprison them.

It would be impossible, that is, unless we built and maintained *eight times* the number of jails, criminal courtrooms and prisons we have today!

Thus, in final analysis, it may well be to our ultimate advantage that law enforcement catches so relatively few criminals.

Austin MacCormick, one of this country's most respected criminologists, has noted that thousands of professional criminals live in luxury and safety, and ". . . you and I and the police do not know who they are."

But, in many instances, *I do.* I have known many of these professionals, men who robbed, forged, burgled or killed for a living, men, too, mixed up in the rackets, in organized gambling, prostitution, dope-dealing.

I know, as well, how often pure chance has led to one man's capture, while it has kept another man out of jail. I know that, in many cities, "juice" as well as chance and cunning can keep you out of jail. "Juice" is money paid the police for protection. And I know, too, about the fix and how it works. I know that the right kind of money and knowing the right people, having the proper connections, can often square the beef against you, whether it's petty theft or murder. I know that organized crime can't exist without at least tacit approval from some members of law enforcement in the area where its calculating practitioners attempt to carry on their parasitic operations.

Those best equipped to know have time and again exposed as dangerous nonsense the theory that crime may be controlled by conducting a lawless, reign-of-terror campaign against those suspected of being criminals. Such "wars" don't solve social problems; they create them.

The main reason we continue to be plagued by our crime problem is that we perversely refuse to see it for what it is and persist in deluding ourselves by clinging to dangerous fictions about it!

We have the intestinal fortitude and the sense, so let us face a few blunt facts. Let us stop being so neurotically moral and so indignantly righteous that we dare not be honest. We should cease worrying that our virtue will flee out the back door if we open the front door to factual reality. Instead of denying there is such a thing as a dishonest or brutal cop, let's get rid of him and his kind. And let's recognize that often crime does pay, handsomely. The professional criminal knows this, so why should you, the honest citizen, foolishly deny it? And should any self-appointed guardian of your morals insist that it is necessary to keep whooping it up that *Crime doesn't pay!* on the ground that to discontinue doing so would result in our young people turning in mass to crime, tell that foolish worthy to go climb a tree, because it just isn't so. Besides, things will have reached a sorry pass indeed when society claims that it can protect itself from itself only by force, fear *and* hypocrisy.

Let us reject such sinister nonsense.

Let us open our eyes to reality. A lawless administration of the law can beget only more lawlessness. And here again the proof is not lacking. One need look no further than the transcript of testimony before that Senate investigating group popularly known as the Kefauver Committee.

Prisoners are people, and so are those accused of crime, and police-men and district attorneys and judges and jailers and criminologists and penologists and ordinary and extraordinary citizens.

All are human. All are capable of erring, of being both cruel and kind, of being just and unjust. Honest and dishonest.

What makes one man a policeman, another a criminal?

Is it not largely a matter of training and education—and even chance?

Why does one man succeed and another fail?

Because of character, you say. And I agree wholeheartedly. But what molds character or whence does it come?

And what are the ingredients of character? Courage? Intelligence? Decency? Humanity? What more?

Have *you* ever considered committing a crime? If so, why didn't you?

Why do you think the other man did?

What do you really know about the crime problem? What do you really know about those who commit crimes?

I expect one day soon to be marched into the execution chamber. When that happens, do you think it is possible the thought will occur to you that "There, but for the grace of God, go I!"

Make no mistake. I don't blame my plight on you or on society generally. I blame myself and I accept full responsibility for what has happened to me. I realize that what has happened to me probably never can and never will happen to you. And when I am dead I am perfectly willing that you say, "Well, he asked for it. He had plenty of warning, but he kept right on. He had only himself to blame."

So be it. I am prepared to accept both death and that convenient judgment.

But first I shall try to make certain that you see through those fic-tions which surround the crime problem like a deadly fog. A problem cannot be solved until it is understood. I know there is no neat, for-mula solution to the crime problem. Still there is a solution, and half o it is recognizing the problem for what it is. The problem is one criminal multiplied by the total number of criminals. The problem is what that criminal does and, when and if it catches him, what society does about him. The problem is how he got that way in the first place. The problem is convincing him that it is in his best interests not to commit crimes, and this often entails equipping him to take a useful and productive place in his community.

And thus viewed, the problem is Caryl Whittier Chessman. It is *why* Caryl Whittier Chessman. But it is more than a clinical, psychopathologically definitive, inanimate, out-of-context *why*. It is more than finding some way to hustle Caryl Whittier Chessman, the assertedly "dangerous psychopath," into the gas chamber.

It is why, dynamically, in terms of both society *and* Chessman. It isn't a one-sided why.

Of course, there is an anomaly here, but it is not a consequential one. Granted that it is hardly the normal thing for this particular kind of problem to be articulate, to be able to stand off and survey itself and society alike with critically objective detachment. But whether such detachment is normal or ordinarily encountered is irrelevant. Certainly it would be inexcusable to refuse to accept the fruits of that detachment if those fruits can help us solve the problem. I submit that I, better than anyone else, know what I have done, and that I have as well a functionally sound idea of the crucial why.

That's all very well, you may say—but what qualifies me as an authority on the subject? I'm certain that's a question you also feel should be answered. Well, let me reframe the question and pose it more bluntly: What makes me think I have something to say that you should listen to?

Cuilibet in arte sua perito est credendum, declares a maxim of the law. "Credence should be given to one skilled in his peculiar art."

• *16* •

"A Being Darkly Wise, and Rudely Great"

I lay on my Reformatory bunk and thought about the future.

Here at last was the day I had been waiting for, the day I would leave the reformation factory behind me—forever. Appropriately I was departing on a Saturday, Saturn's day. Irony's day. June, 1939.

Ahead lay freedom. Ahead lay the inferno.

My name was Caryl Chessman, not Don Quixote, and I would tilt with dragons, not windmills. I was eighteen. In the eyes of the law I was an adult. Things juvenile were in the past, and the past had decided the future. The past had contained the reformation factory. I had been reformed. Now I was being released.

The reformation factory belonged to you—society. So it must have been what you wanted. And you must have wanted its product too. . . .

Today you're turning me loose. I'm being released on parole, three years of it. Of course there's a chance I won't get out the front gate. But taking that chance is part of the game.

We're playing a game, society. You against me. And the object of the game is very simple: I do what I damned well please and you see if you can stop me.

If you wish, see if you can destroy me. That apparently is the only thing you know how to do with guys like me. Fair enough. I'll give you plenty of chances, just as I gave you plenty of warning.

But you ignored the warnings. You're huge, you possess huge power, and this gives you the idea that you can coerce or crush, that you can mentally or physically beat or scare guys like me back into line, into submissive conformity. Your servants taught me "some respect for authority" and then soft words and a grin lulled you. You're sure I've "learned my lesson." Well, I have.

"The fool is happy that he knows no more," said Pope. That's true, and you and I are both fools. So we must play a fool's game. We must play a violent and deadly game. A game of winner take all—and nothing. You tell me that I can't win. What you don't realize is that neither can you. . . .

See this fine suit and this expensive shirt, necktie and pair of shoes I'm wearing? There's a story behind them. They're not regular issue. I came to the receiving and discharge room the other day and the man threw me a cheap ready-made suit and a pair of mismatched block-toed shoes made at the school. I asked him courteously enough if I couldn't get something a little better to go out in.

"Think because you work in the assistant superintendent's office that you're better than anybody else? Take 'em and like 'em!"

What did I say? Nothing; just grinned. I had no difficulty conniving another outfit and a friend stole the shoes for me. By an odd coincidence that clothing-room gentleman and I wore the same size shoes. Also it happened that he was off that day. A relief man was working in his place who did not know one pair of shoes or suit from another.

"You better not try to smuggle out any letters for your friends," the Snake had warned me. "I'll have your parole if you do."

Thinking the matter over, I concluded the Snake should be given an opportunity to get my parole. It wasn't my fault he couldn't find all those letters I had hidden in my property—or was it?

At the administration building, just before I was checked out, and while I was waiting to be handed train fare to Los Angeles and ten dollars, the assistant superintendent's wife had a word with me. "You'll have no excuse for getting into trouble again," she said. "If you haven't learned your lesson by now you never will. And remember, we can run these places without your help."

I grinned and assured this good lady that I doubted if she ever would appreciate the full extent of my assistance. She looked at me strangely before being called to the phone.

The friendly lady, Miss Turner, was there to wish me luck. She offered me her hand. I shook it, and when I did, I felt the wadded paper and closed my fingers around it. Neither of us said a word about the paper.

"Goodbye, Caryl, and good luck."

"No lecture, pep talk or good advice?" I asked quietly.

She shook her head and smiled. Then she walked away, briskly. I had seen the friendly lady for the last time in my life.

"All right, Chessman," the superintendent's secretary said, "here's your release money."

A supervisor drove me to the sleepy little village of Ione, where I would take a bus to Stockton and then a train to Los Angeles. On the way I was told, "Next time you won't be sent back here. Next time you'll go to San Quentin. So you better use your head and stay out of trouble."

Why? What's wrong with dear old San Quentin? What's wrong with trying it out for size? Maybe running a loom in the Jute Mill is worth looking forward to. That's what the school's charges told each other. "Go to the joint and learn a trade with a future in it," they said. "Learn how to turn out that hundred yards a day for The Man." They'd heard that a task on the looms was an even hundred yards and such talk gave them a chance to show how knowledgeable they were and how casually contemptuous of the fate that probably awaited them.

I stood on the sidewalk and watched the supervisor's car disappear around a corner. Gone was my last tie to the reformation factory. I was free. I was on my way. Where didn't matter.

My fingers closed around the wadded paper in my pants pocket. I withdrew my hand and, palm up, slowly opened those fingers. I unwadded the crinkly paper. I looked thoughtfully at the two twenty-dollar bills. I thought, "Thanks, Miss Turner. Thanks for this and for skipping the lecture—and for being human."

I had been waiting and then, suddenly, the wait was over. I returned to the jungle—or the jungle returned to me. Perhaps in our zeal for reunion we met each other halfway, the jungle and I.

I had been vaguely aware that a squirming little boy of four or five, his mother and his grandfather were seated across from me. The mother had been having something of a time keeping little Georgie on her lap. "How much longer will it be, mama?" he kept asking. The grandfather was dozing and little Georgie's patient mother said that he should be a good boy and not wake the old man. "Remember, Georgie, grandfather doesn't feel well," she said. And Georgie nodded gravely.

I had heard the sniffing too, but hadn't at first paid much attention to it. The sniffer was seated just in front of me, a skinny old female with a hatchet-sharp face, porcine eyes and a nose aimed at the roof of the car. Next to her sat her spouse, a small, withdrawn man who reminded me of a harassed rabbit.

It hadn't taken me long to associate the sniffs with Georgie, since every time the little boy had said a word—actually his voice had been neither loud nor distracting—the sniffer had sniffed, and a couple of times she had half turned and shot a venomous look in Georgie's direction. When she had done so, Georgie had smiled at her engagingly, and she in turn had sniffed all the louder, thoroughly outraged. Innocently amused, Georgie had laughed gleefully, and his embarrassed mother had tried to shush him.

Obviously little Georgie had yet to learn that there were white folks in the world who sniffed at a black skin.

When a vendor came by with cold drinks, candy and sandwiches Georgie looked appealingly at his mother. Sadly, I thought, she shook her head and I could see the keen disappointment in the little boy's eyes. But he didn't protest.

I looked closely at the three of them then: Georgie, his mother and his grandfather. They were dressed in their Sunday best, and it was neat and clean—and inexpensive and worn.

And the day was hot and the coach wasn't air conditioned and little Georgie was going to have some pop, candy and sandwiches.

I waited. Another mile or so of fertile farmland was passed. Then Georgie's mother stood up and placed him on the seat. "I'll be right back, Georgie, so be a good boy and sit still beside grandfather until I return."

"All right, mama," Georgie said.

But Georgie just couldn't sit still. He looked over at me and I nodded a greeting.

"Hi, Georgie," I said (and heard a sniff).

Georgie climbed off the seat, stood in the aisle and surveyed me solemnly. Then the man with the cold drinks, candy and sandwiches returned. I ordered some of each, had the man put the candy and sandwiches on the seat beside Georgie's dozing grandfather and offered a paper cup full of cold grape-ade to Georgie.

"How about it, Georgie, thirsty?"

The little boy's head shook up and down in an emphatic affirmative. He accepted the cup and held it gingerly, broadly smiling his thanks. (A rash of sniffing took place up ahead.) Georgie's mother returned and looked crossly at her son.

"Please," I said, "I'm sure it won't spoil his dinner."

For a moment the mother looked at me searchingly, then she smiled and nodded that it was all right.

We were entering a station along the way. Georgie, who had wandered a few steps ahead while sipping his drink, was thrown against the seat when the train unexpectedly lurched. The paper cup flew from his small hands and what was left of its contents spilled on the sniffer and her rabbity spouse. The sniffer slapped Georgie across the face, sent him reeling. She called him a name. Georgie's mother jumped to her feet and snatched her son into her arms, protectively. The mother was trying desperately to apologize but hatchet-face would have none of it. "That," she shrieked, "is what comes from not keeping you niggers in your place! Now who's going to pay for this?" She indicated a few negligible spots on her dress.

Time stopped with a lurch, as did the train. Hatchet-face could send her dress and her husband's suit to the cleaners; a couple of dollars would cover the bill. But you can't send a little boy's scarred soul to the cleaners and the cost is incalculable.

I thrust myself between hatchet-face and little Georgie and his mother. I had heard Georgie sob; I had seen the stricken look on his mother's face. I practically threw the two twenty-dollar bills at the shrieking sniffer. I must not have been a pleasant sight, for this gentle-bred creature clamped her thin mouth shut and retreated a step, clutching the two bills.

"The money will cover your cleaning bill, madam," I said very quietly. "So shut your obscene mouth and get out of here, *quickly!* You're not fit to ride with human beings."

Hatchet-face immediately found voice. "How dare you speak to me like this!" she exclaimed in a sickening parody of offended gentility and virtue. "Who do you think you are, anyway, sticking up for these . . ."

"I'm the Devil," I said in a whisper, grinning my best grin. "But I hardly thought I'd have to introduce myself to *you*, madam."

The rabbit touched his mate's elbow and whispered in her ear, "He's mad! Come, dear, before he becomes violent."

Hatchet-face snatched up a satchel and they scurried off down the aisle. I watched them go. Then I turned and smiled reassuringly at Georgie.

The little boy's eyes were very wide. "Are you really the Devil?" he asked.

"Only, Georgie, to those righteous, holier-than-thou citizens who want to believe I am."

"Oh," Georgie said.

To the little boy's mother and grandfather, I said: "I'm sorry this had to happen. As God is my judge, I'm sorry."

It was the grandfather who spoke. "You only meant to be kind to us," he said. "Don't blame yourself."

"Yes," I agreed, "I meant only to be kind."

And I failed.

I turned, walked down the aisle and stepped from the train, stifling

an impulse to throw my traveling bag as far as I could see it. I walked
briskly from the train depot. I was in a hurry to get nowhere. In four
or five minutes I reached the outskirts of the city. There, on the main
highway, I stuck out my thumb. The first car that came along pulled
over and stopped, almost standing on end. When I ran up to the car
the driver asked me, "Can you drive?"

I nodded. "Sure."

"Then drive," he said, and slid over.

I climbed in behind the wheel, threw my bag at the back seat and
in a couple of seconds had the car, an almost new Pontiac two-door,
on its way again. My host wore a rumpled suit and a tired look. Still
I could see the tiredness was superficial, something he could ignore if
he chose.

"I'm a salesman," he told me. "Oil supplies. Been driving steady
from Portland. In a damned big hurry to get to Bakersfield. Big deal
if I can get there in time. So drive like hell. I'll take the tickets." He
threw his wallet onto the seat between us. "Money in there for gas.
Anything else. Wake me up when we get to Bakersfield."

I grinned. "You're sure a trusting Joe with strangers."

He yawned, closed his eyes, stretched out in the seat and grunted
sleepily, "You got an honest face."

I laughed out loud and the tired salesman began to snore, very
softly. I didn't even wonder how he knew I was going as far as
Bakersfield.

I drove. I drove "like hell," as I had been enjoined. Doing so was a
therapeutic pleasure. I was driving right to the center of the universe.
Everything else whirled around but I stood quite still. The egoist *I*
was the only stable thing in the whole of infinity, in time or space or
thought.

In Bakersfield I pulled in to the curb in the middle of the business
district. The salesman continued to sleep the sleep of the righteous. His
wallet still lay on the seat between us. The nest egg it contained, while
no fortune, was not to be sneezed at. All I had to do was pocket it,
wipe the wheel of prints, grab my bag, walk off.

But I didn't take a second look at the wallet. A good hoodlum doesn't beat his friends or those who do him a favor. Bag in hand, I alighted and walked around to the passenger side of the car. I reached in and tapped the salesman on the shoulder. "All right, sleeping beauty," I said, "wake up."

The salesman came awake instantly. He looked at me and then at his wristwatch and then back at me. He whistled. "What the hell did we do, fly?"

"In a way," I said. "Thanks for the ride." I pointed at his wallet. "We made one stop for gas. I thought you might be on an expense account, so I got a receipt. You'll find it and the change in the wallet."

"Smart boy," he said. "Can't I give you something for the chauffeuring?" He reached for his wallet.

I shook my head. "No. But you can check your wallet to be sure all your money's still there."

He pocketed the wallet without looking inside it. "Why? I told you before, you got an honest face."

"All right, all right," I said. "Don't rub it in."

The salesman handed me one of his cards. "Here," he said. "The next time you want to drill for oil, let me sell you the rig." He added, "By the way, I didn't get the name."

"That's right," I said, "you didn't." I grinned, thanked him for the ride and walked away.

The afternoon shadows were lengthening.

A few minutes later I thumbed another ride, and was wide-eyed and silent the remainder of the trip in an old Lincoln, listening to a constant stream of what Aunt Elsie (my loquacious chauffeur) had said to Henry (her husband) and what Henry had said to Aunt Elsie, what Aunt Elsie had said to Henry . . . *ad infinitum.*

I got out on Brand Boulevard in Glendale.

"Mind your P's and Q's," Aunt Elsie admonished. Then, with a loud clashing and clanking of gears, she drove off.

I waved her on her way. Then I looked around—at the traffic, the familiar buildings, the dimly seen mountains in the distance, the tall, elderly uniformed cop standing on the corner across from me. Once again I was almost home.

The curtain was about to rise on another act of an ironic, violent farce. And the show must go on.

So hurry! Don't miss your cue! Run, fool, run!

Perversely, I paused.

A skinny youngster of twelve or thirteen was hustling papers on the corner. I called him and he came on the double. "Paper, mister?" he asked eagerly.

Paper, mister? Mister Eighteen-Year-Old. Mister Wise Guy. Mister Dreamer. Mr. Nonconformist. Mr. Fledgling Psychopath.

"Just a paper," I said. "Not a paper, mister."

I took the paper and handed the kid a dollar bill. (The young sharpies invariably look at the bill, fumble in their jeans or with their coin changer, which they keep almost empty, tell you to wait a minute while they run for change and then hesitate, hoping you'll be in a hurry and tell them to keep the bill. This dodge often works.) The kid didn't go into any routine; he immediately began to make change. I told him I didn't want it.

"Gee, mister, thanks!" the kid said. He sounded sincere.

I set my bag down and glanced at the headlines under a street light. A couple of hammy performers were posturing, raising all kinds of hell in Europe. Their names were Adolf and Benito and, from all reports, they were sinister characters indeed, full of righteous snatch-and-grab ideas.

I laughed. There were buffoons, buffoons filled with an overweening urge to trifle with things cataclysmic and infernal. And Humanity talked gravely of its destiny.

I picked up my bag and walked briskly until I came to the stucco house with the porch lamp burning. I paused. This was to be home.

I didn't knock. I simply pushed open the front door and walked in, striding through the living room, the kitchen and into my mother's bedroom. I found her propped up in bed; she had aged, her face was drawn and her arms were as thin as sticks. My sudden appearance had taken her by surprise and for two or three seconds it appeared she was having difficulty believing her eyes. Then she smiled, and her blue eyes misted.

"Hi, Mom."

My mother embraced me almost with desperation. My return **was** her personal triumph. "You're home," she said. "Thank God!"

17

The Fool and the Madman Were One

I was home.

Here was a healthy, happy, loving atmosphere, not cloying or smothering, not calculating or possessive. Life had treated my mother and father ruthlessly and I had been anything but a model son. Yet they still retained a quiet, unaggressive courage and a pervasive faith in me. Here was no whimpering self-pity, no secret, smoldering resentments, no cunningly disguised hostility. Here was no bitterness for what had been, no sly projection of felt blame or guilt from one to another. Here, indeed, was home; home was peace.

And peace was a vacuum and a threat to one who had seen and lived for so long in the jungle. For peace tempted one to drop his guard. And those who lived in the jungle feared it.

My father had gone into the window shade and venetian blind business for himself. He took me out to the big two-car garage and showed me his tables and equipment. He explained how the shades were made and the blinds assembled. "We can work together," he said, and I agreed we could. He was glad. Perhaps he could be a pal to his son now. That is what he had always wanted, and he had held himself largely to blame for my conflicts with the law. For he believed that somehow he had failed to stay close to me and to help me and guide me when I had needed help and guidance most. My father had failed to grasp the real reasons for my many clashes with authority. He never would understand what drove me. He would never be fully aware of the jungle.

When we returned to the house, my mother told me, "Dad's fixed you a nice room on the back porch."

As gently as possible, I explained that I preferred to fix a place for myself in a corner of the garage. "Some nights I'll want to work and study and if I'm out there I won't disturb anyone."

"Whatever you want, Hon," my mother said. "Dad and I just want you to be happy."

My father nodded his head in agreement. He looked at me and chuckled. "Looks to me, Mom, like he's too big to argue with."

We set up a cot in an unused portion of the garage and within a few days, with my dad's help, I had converted half of one side of the garage into a bedroom and study. Here was my castle—the quiet place where I could be alone and think and study and write and dream— and for the present, at least, I asked none better.

Later that first night home I took a long walk, thinking. Returning home at a few minutes past three, I thrust my head through the doorway of my mother's bedroom. The room was very dark, very quiet, and then my mother spoke. "Hello," she whispered softly. "I'm awake; so come in."

I felt my way to the chair near her bed. "I was hoping I'd find you awake."

"You've had a long day, Hon. You must be awfully tired."

"I've had a long day, all right, and a strange one. But, oddly enough, I'm not very tired."

We talked cheerful small talk for a while and then my mother said, "My portable typewriter is in the closet and I had Dad buy some typing paper, which you will find with it. I want you to take the portable out with you, Hon. I think you may want to use it."

"Mom," I said, "I'm convinced you're a mind reader."

"Then you do want to write?"

"More than anything in the world. But I'm afraid I want to do something I cannot do."

"But you can. You should and you must."

"I've tried. I always fail." It was best I speak the blunt truth. "You think I've changed, Mom, and I have—only not the way you think. Now I'm wearing a mask and the world is wearing a mask and we're grinning at each other, leering at each other, like gargoyles, and waiting. Waiting for the other to make the first false move; waiting to leap at the other's throat.

"Yes, I want desperately to write. But I refuse to write madness or to pay lip service to pious hypocrisy. A writer must have a faith. He must believe in more than the harsh, terrible, final reality of a jungle and his own ability to survive in that jungle."

What could be said so long as one was threatened, challenged, mocked by this jungle enemy? What could be written so long as "good citizens" made the jungle itself a continuing reality? Beauty and form were at the mercy still of a monster named Force. If what was good and creative within constantly had to be defended against the savage attacks of this monster, then goodness and creativity were not assets but liabilities which punished and invited disaster. One could not give, freely and gladly, when one was under attack both from within and without; one could only fight, defend and question whether what is called creative really matters.

"And once you are free you must write!" my mother stated, understandingly.

"Once I am free I'll write—or I'll be dead."

"You won't be dead," my mother insisted. "Not then. Not until the creative part of you has fulfilled its mission."

I laughed. "I wish I had one-tenth the faith in myself that you have in me, Mom. But I can't have. I know what has happened to me. The son you once had has been banished to a spiritual limbo, and a jungle-bred stranger has taken his place, a self-excusing, hating, rationalizing, ambiguous, violent, psychopathic stranger with a glib tongue and a grinning, battered mask for a face."

"If that is true," my mother said quietly, "then my son will find a way to return and depose this stranger. I only pray to God that he doesn't wait too long."

Doubtless that also should have been my prayer. But I was at a disadvantage. I had no God.

I reported to my parole officer in downtown Los Angeles the first thing Monday morning. This servant of the sovereign, a tall, bony individual, eyed me suspiciously. Yes, my name was Chessman, Caryl Chessman. How did I pronounce my first name? "Carol, as in Christmas Carol."

"Your record doesn't read like one," I was told with a frown.

"Appearances are often deceptive," I replied politely—with a grin.

What did I mean by that, Chessman? Nothing. Nothing in particular. I was just trying to hold up my conversational end.

Well, my record of gross antisocial conduct was no joking matter. It was time I realized that. It was time I grew up, acted the part of a man and accepted responsibility. I knew about the provision in the law that permitted the juvenile authorities to turn me over to the courts for sentence to San Quentin if I perversely refused to adjust, didn't I? It seemed to me I'd heard something about it. Well, it would be a good idea if I kept that law in mind.

"Why?"

"Yes, why?"

Because, sputtered the parole officer, I wouldn't find San Quentin a very nice place. Because . . . well . . . because I knew very well why. I wouldn't ask any more silly questions; instead, I would listen, respectfully. And the first thing I would listen to were the terms and conditions of my parole. There were rules, rules, rules and more rules. Violating any one of them or otherwise failing to "cooperate" with the parole officer could land me in San Quentin.

"Is that clear?"

"Sure, that's perfectly clear."

"Hereafter, Chessman, I don't want slangy answers. After this you will answer me 'Yes, sir,' or 'No, sir.'"

"Yes, *sir!*" I said, snapping to attention.

And that instant my parole officer became Authority, and Author-

ity turned beet red in the face. "Chessman," Authority snapped, "it appears to me that you have an extremely poor attitude."

"Toward what, *sir?*" inquired a Chessman who appeared a picture
of bewildered innocence.

"Toward me, toward parole, toward society," was the angry retort.
"It's obvious that you need supervision, close supervision. Unfortunately my case load is so heavy, I won't be able to watch you as closely
as I'd like." To this, Authority added ominously, if somewhat illogi-
cally: "But don't let that put any ideas in your head you can get away
with anything. You can't. The minute you pull any of your old stunts
again I'll hear about it." Authority paused to let this coercive intelligence sink in.

I thought wryly: What big ears you have, Grandma! I was sorely
tempted to inquire if Authority would hear of new stunts with equal
speed and dispatch. Already Authority had lost his standing with me
as a human being; he had become one of those absurd, plethoric per-
sonifications of a society which too often mistook its vices for its
virtues.

So tell me, Cerberus, why aren't you wearing your other two heads
today?

"Chessman, let me give you some good advice. Don't get the idea
that you're bigger than society and its laws. You're not and you
never can be. Get that through your head. Stop being a square peg in
a round hole. Take advantage of the training you received at the
school. We know what's best for you. Start following our directions.
Be man enough to admit you've been wrong. Cooperate with us. Get
the right attitude and keep it. Prove to us you're worthy of belonging
to our society!"

Sure, conform—blindly, abjectly, through fear. Seek faceless anonymity. Arbitrarily reject all subjective criteria. Society (which in
Authority's eyes means *Authority*) is right, wholly. Chessman is wrong,
completely. Chessman is an irresponsible social sinner. Make way!
Unclean! Unclean!

Comprehend nothing of your own dichotomous self, Cerberus.

What is, is only what platitudinously appears to be. Be charmed by this assurance. Hark to the beguiling music of it, and let pass unseen an Orpheus who lost his Eurydice before he found her and who was yet to find himself.

I drew myself up with a fine show of resolution. You're right, Mr. Parole Officer. I must do what you say. I must straighten up. I must settle down. I must fit in. I must . . . ad nauseam . . . be a man (without manhood, spineless, drab and gray and sickeningly meek and meaningless, with a malleable blob of a personality).

That's better. That's more like it. That's being sensible.

And slippery. And deceptive. And sly.

I didn't ordinarily drink, but I felt that the occasion of such a momentous meeting called for a drink. So I walked into a bar and had one. Just one. Just enough to violate parole.

Then I paid a visit to a friend—also an ex-inmate of the reformation factory—and acquired a revolver, plus a handful of extra shells. I got the gun for the asking. All I told my friend was, "I need a gun. Have you got one?"

He had more than one. He gave me my choice from a small arsenal. "Take yer pick," he said, and I did.

Acquiring a gun was an old stunt. Still, my parole officer failed to hear of this acquisition (or my taking that drink or doing business with a former inmate of the school of industry where we both had learned our lesson(s) so well). Apparently Authority's radar ears weren't so hypersensitive after all.

That afternoon, after a year's absence, I returned alone to my hills, and Authority, for a time, was an unopened tin can. The echoing and re-echoing roar was deafening as I blasted that tin-can personage full of holes with an inspired and deadly accuracy. Puree of tomato gushed forth from him. In no time at all he had bled to death. Then, methodically, I reloaded the gun and six more times in swift succession squeezed the trigger, watching Authority's bloodless cadaver dance and roll and jump. And then lie still, quite still, battered beyond recognition. Let that be a lesson to Authority.

In a deliberate parody of the Wild West, I uptilted the barrel of the gun and blew away the wisps of gunsmoke. The acrid odor of gunpowder filled my nostrils and I grinned with satisfaction. Once more I could hear the cadenced throbbing of the drums. Once again, Hate and Guile were standing at my side, counseling, advising, eager to leap into battle with me.

Prophetically, they told me, "You'll be needing us."

"Then stick around," I replied. "By all means, stick around."

What was it Skinny had bitterly said of his society? "They got a gun pointed at us and they're going to keep it there. If you show up with a bigger gun, then they'll listen, not before."

Well, I had a bigger gun and it wasn't the one in my hand. My bigger gun was really a flame thrower. It was fashioned of lessons learned and a peculiar jungle ideology, and it was capable of feeding a conflagration until it reached such heaven-scorching magnitude that even the most confirmed social pyromaniac would be forced to turn and flee in terror.

The question was: Did I want to use that bigger gun? Did I want to snatch it up and shout, "All right, you righteous bastards, let me have your attention!"

Hate nodded emphatically and, first swearing its undying fealty, Guile argued passionately for use of the weapon, a sly, plausible advocate.

First, *think!* With violent clarity. Satirically. Yes, and contemptuously.

Knowledge is power. Power corrupts, and absolute power corrupts absolutely. (Thank you, Lord Acton.) But even absolute power can't corrupt Authority. Indeed, not! The proof: Authority, society's benevolent Big Brothers, its pontifical patriarchs, its righteous vise-turners, all say so, by necessary implication. And what they say simply *must* be true, every last word of it. Why? Because it is they who say it, that's why.

So let them think for you; don't think for yourself. ("We know what is best for you. Start following our directions.") Stay safely within the orbit. Climb into the social womb. ("Cooperate with us.

Conform.") Blindly, passively accept its limitations, its inanities and hypocrisies, its platitudinous truths. ("Get the right attitude and keep it.") Let yourself be supervised, regulated, ordered around, manipulated. (And thereby "Prove to us that you are worthy of belonging to our society!") And feel crowded and smothered and chained.

Or take the weapon in your hand and declare yourself free. Pursue freedom and flee from it simultaneously, paradoxically. Do what the mad dog does, knowing that his conduct is animally, belligerently reflexive and but rarely guided by any critical faculty within himself. Knowing that he tries futilely to steal freedom. But only with a snarling animal violence, with roars. By coveting disease. And without realizing that imposed or invited social hydrophobia, as well as the medical kind, is not a possession to be prized for its own sake, or a condition without cause.

Hesitate no longer: continue this journey that leads both into darkness and away from darkness. Seek the prize and slay the many dragons you encounter along the way. Be grateful for their ferocity and the sustenance they offer. And keep on the march. Find that place of unbroken peace that is beyond the reach of Authority and Authority's bullets and vises and cages and mouthings and pious villainies. Fight your way to that place. Defy Authority to try to stop you. Prove that you can't be stopped. While Authority is teaching you more lessons, you in turn will be teaching Authority some lessons. And what pontifical denunciations your pedagogy will inspire! Perhaps one day in the distant future, with all dragons slain, all psychopathic battles fought, all prizes won, you will find the time to pen a whimsical report to society.

"Dear Society [the report will begin]: Once upon a time there was a markedly pathological social organism who was voraciously feeding upon the hyperpathological conditions in his environment. It seems that this particular organism entertained the quaint notion that he could thus, by the psychopathological process of introjection, destroy such conditions. Instead, he succeeded only in giving himself a grievous psychical bellyache until he discovered how to regurgitate. Then . . ."

Then.

But first *now,* the Here-and-Now in relation to a real Big Time Operator with exactly three pennies in his pockets, a smoking gun in his hand, and much on his alleged mind. And, contradictorily, this relationship between geography, time and the individual in practical, hedonistic, psychopathic terms, for the contradictions are essential ingredients. Not only within but without.

You're free, aren't you? And you know where and how to get the folding stuff the easy way, don't you? Damn right you do. Besides, what legitimate racket, what profession, offers the unlimited opportunities, the intellectual stimulation, the prestige, the power that crime does? Hell, if you want, you can be another Saint, another Simon Templar, a suave, smooth article. Look at the ego satisfaction you can get from outsmarting the slickers and the sharpers and Authority, and from being your own law and dispensing your own brand of justice. *Justice!* What an intriguing word.

And if your Herostratus complex is nagging you, then ponder the chance for immortality that crime offers. All you have to do is be a violent, robbing, murderous bastard and your fame is assured. One of the peculiarities of squares is their screwy propensity to glorify rogues and scoundrels.

So why lay that pistol down? Why be a hoosier, a chump? Your culture emphasizes material gain. You've arrived if you drive that new Cad convertible, have a closet full of sharp clothes, a swank apartment and a pocketful of dough. And it doesn't matter where the money came from; it doesn't matter if you shot poor old grandma to get it, not so long as you can get away with it. Just don't get caught; don't take a bad fall. And don't waste your time worrying about a little thing called a creative urge. Nobody gives a damn whether you put words in a string or not. Sublimate with a blonde instead of with a typewriter.

And keep in mind what the smart boys say. Die young and have a good-looking corpse. Or (you can add, acidly) be a criminal Alexander the Great and weep as you approach your majority because there are no more worlds left to be conquered. None worth conquering, that is.

"Look then to be well edified when the fool delivers the madman."

In the case of Caryl Chessman, the fool and the madman were one. And neither was content to deliver the other.

18

But This Wasn't Fiction

The private detective had moved to new and plushier quarters. When I paid him a visit, he took me into his private office, handed me a thick report and said, "Here's some sad news, I'm afraid."

The report informed me, graphically and in detail, how long and hard he had looked for my mother's parents. Still, he had been unable to find any trace of them. Their identity remained a dark mystery.

I stared at the last page of the report. "Damn!" I said very softly.

The private detective put an arm on my shoulder. "Believe me, I did everything humanly possible to find those two people."

It was obvious he had. But that didn't make my disappointment any less keen.

The idea of having to admit defeat galled. "Do you think you could find them with more money?" I asked.

"I'll be honest with you. I don't think I could find them with all the gold at Fort Knox. While I've still got two or three feelers out, I don't believe they can be found."

I stood up. "Well, I guess that's that, then."

"I'm sorry."

"Yeah. So am I."

I walked for a long time, until I was physically weary. I thought about the report, mulled it over and over. Bitterly I realized that it would have been different in fiction. The private detective would have found my mother's parents, or at least one of them, and there would have been a joyous reunion followed by a compelling explanation why my mother had been abandoned as an infant. Surely, too, the fictionist would have revealed these two—my maternal grandparents—as people of refinement and substance, tragic people perhaps, and somehow my learning their identities would have favorably altered the course of my life, and given it direction, purpose.

But this wasn't fiction.

Only life itself would have the temerity to create—for its own perverse entertainment—such a mockery: a juvenile delinquent who had turned bagnio bandit to finance a search for unknown grandparents and who, as a consequence of his banditry, served a second savage term in a reformation factory that he might be conditioned for God alone knew what sort of unbelievable future.

Clearly, Chessman at eighteen was a character much too improbable for fiction. Well, life had something to learn—that the mocked could mock.

The days passed. I talked the nights away at my mother's bedside. I worked with my father. I spent many of my evenings at a local branch of the public library, reading, studying. We traded the family sedan for a little Ford convertible which I hopped up, put in faultless running order. The Ford became my pride, my sparkling little black jewel. Two friends from grammar-school days began dropping around. Sometimes my father would join us and we'd play cards. Sometimes we'd just sit around and shoot the breeze. Other times we would go roller skating at a small rink in Glendale or to the beach, or perhaps we'd take in a show. And late at night, alone, I would feed a piece of paper into my mother's portable typewriter and write, only to tear up and write some more, as a discipline and an index, a barometer—of that which writhed and burned and glowed unnaturally within, of a warder named Hate, of a tall, broken-nosed, sardonic young man who found it so ridiculously easy to be profound, profoundly wrong. How incredible that, on his father's side, this violent young man should be a direct descendant of that gentle and quaint old Quaker, John Greenleaf Whittier!

"And the Rebel rides on his raids no more."

I was marking time and knew it.

Word had gotten around that I was home. Youngsters from the reformation factory came to see me, full of tough talk and ideas. "We got a big score lined up," they'd say. "Wanta get cut in?"

I'd shake my head. "No, not right now. I feel like taking it easy for a while."

And then I'd read in the papers that they'd been caught and shot up and killed. Sometimes they'd come to see me after a wild adventure and relate it. Then, "You sure you don't want to join us?" as though flying bullets, wild rides, gun fights and near death were irresistible inducements to "caper." These youngsters—and I was one with them psychologically—were anomalies. They committed crimes, often senselessly violent crimes, and so were criminals; but they stubbornly refused to accept crime's cynical and harsh disciplines. For the most part, they genuinely scorned those who regarded crime as a business, unspectacularly. Crime was an adventure, kicks, glamor; crime was rebellion, a psychopathic crusade, an inviting, deadly pilgrimage; crime was getting even and forcing recognition of identity—but certainly it was nothing so utterly unalluring as an unheralded, workaday means of obtaining a livelihood.

The police got into the habit of scooping me up every time they needed a suspect. I'd be given a ride to the police station, marched to the detective quarters and grilled by impatient, large-sized dicks. The more they rousted me around the more I needled them, gave them smart answers. What had I been doing, smart guy? Oh, just the usual stuff, robbing banks, kidnaping millionaires and that sort of thing.

Angrily, they'd warn me, "Don't let your foot slip."

I'd laugh. "You flat-footed clowns couldn't catch a cold."

To me it didn't make sense—or it made too much sense. The whorehouses and the gambling joints were going full blast and not getting so much as a rumble from law enforcement. But eighteen-year-old Chessman was constantly being grilled, rousted. He was the guy to watch, not the big-time pimps and madams and gamblers and fixers.

Tim put in an appearance—the same old Tim, still full of bold, bad ideas, still shifty-eyed, still with his tough-guy complex, a short, husky eighteen-year-old with a fox face and a swagger in his walk. And a Tim in trouble.

"Jeez, Chess, you gotta help me. These guys are after me and they mean business."

"These guys" meant business for a fact. They were a couple of mean characters from Burbank and Tim had gotten himself into deadly serious trouble with them. They were gunning for him. I served notice that I was taking over Tim's beef and was promptly invited to the hills to settle accounts. "And you better come ready!" I was warned. Luckily I did. Even more luckily, running into a sort of ambush, I received nothing more than a superficial flesh wound and then raised a little hell of my own.

There were other adventures and misadventures too numerous to mention. I loaned my gun to a friend and it bought him a bunk at San Quentin. A mincing homosexual, big enough to fight grizzly bears with his bare hands, punched a tough friend and myself groggy when this friend got it into his head to try to roll him. There was a wild ride in a hot car through Hollywood, with the cops in hot pursuit and shooting. Seated beside me were two gay young things who squealed with fear and delight. Today, one of them is an internationally famous movie star. I arranged to spring a young hoodlum confederate from the courtroom. At the last instant he lost his nerve and, in getting away, I very nearly lost my life.

Then it happened, perhaps inevitably, the ridiculous thing. One evening Tim and I drove onto the parking lot of a department store in Glendale, with a five-gallon can and a hose on the floor of the car. Tim got out with can and hose and walked to a nearby car. Suddenly, the vicinity was alive with people. They grabbed Tim. They had been lying in wait for burglars who had been regularly looting the premises, and they figured the hose and can were a stall, a front. Tim pointed to my Ford and said he was with me. They jerked and shoved him over to the car. "Do you know this guy?" they asked.

"Never saw him before in my life," I assured them.

They marched Tim away and I drove off. Tim was quite a boy. He couldn't keep his mouth shut. I went home. Anger mounted. If Tim talked, this penny-ante, spur-of-the-moment caper could cost me too much time in jail. I put a recently acquired little .32 revolver under my pillow and lay down, thinking, waiting. I didn't have long to wait. Within minutes someone knocked loudly on the garage door and a gruff voice said:

"All right, Chessman, we know you're in there. Open up!"

• *19* •

The Dark Night's Children

My impulse was to snatch the gun and blow the cop (or cops) away from the door. Tim was a fool; cops were fools. Tim and the cops were crowding me. Damn them!

I unlocked the garage door, pushed it open.

"Yeah," I said, glaring at the cop, a big man in a chalk-striped, double-breasted suit, "what the hell do you want?"

"You," the cop said. He walked in, uninvited, his service revolver in his right hand.

"What for?" I demanded.

The cop told me, not delicately. For petty theft; for stealing a gas cap. (When they had brought Tim over to my Ford he had got rid of the gas cap by dropping it onto the floor of the car without anyone's knowledge. Taken to the station, Tim had told them about it and who I was. He had led the cops here to get me. That hurt.)

The cop frisked me. Then he began looking around, in things, under things, at my personal papers, my writings.

"You got a search warrant?" I asked.

The cop laughed and waved his gun. "I don't need a search warrant," he said. He turned his back on me, jerking open desk drawers, spilling everything in them.

I grabbed the gun from under my pillow and savagely pulled the trigger. I'd show the smart sonofabitch whether he needed a search warrant or not! But the sliver of metal used as a substitute for the firing pin, which had been broken a couple of days before, went flying.

The only result was an audible click, nearly drowned by the cop's enthusiastic desk-searching activities. Instantly I reburied the useless gun under the pillow.

Alerted, the cop spun around. He thought I had been reaching for something; that was a break. He snatched at the pillow, then grabbed the gun. "So you got toys, huh?"

I smiled, ever so politely.

"All right," he said. "Let's go."

Tim and I didn't speak on the way to the station. The big cop sat between us, humming tunelessly. Tim huddled sullenly in one corner of the back seat, staring fixedly ahead, hating his weakness.

The cops had a gun. They had Chessman. They had their own ideas about what Chessman had been doing. They had leads that didn't pan out. Victims of a string of robberies said the car used by the two young hood perpetrators generally fitted the description of the Chessman Ford. These same victims said Tim "looked like" one of the bandits, but they were unable to identify him for sure, and Tim vehemently denied any complicity in any robberies. No one could identify Chessman, who denied everything. Chessman and Tim were put together in a bugged room; and this produced an ear-blistering opinion by Chessman of certain segments of law enforcement and a certain juvenile parole officer who was working with the police.

So the cops fell back on their prize piece of evidence—*one gas cap*. Tim and I were charged with the theft of said cap, value seventy-odd cents "lawful money of the United States." We pled guilty on the assurance that we would only be given a few days. And we were sentenced to ten days in jail. Then we were transferred from the Glendale station to the Los Angeles County Jail and were lodged in a crowded misdemeanor tank occupied mostly by old "winos" serving a few days for drunkenness. They were a pitiful, bedraggled lot, these ancient wine drinkers, and many of them had the shakes so bad they couldn't have rolled a cigarette if they had had the price of a sack of makings. Tim and I spent all the money the jail had permitted us to bring in on tailor-mades and passed them around. The old guys were really grateful; they were used to getting kicked around and couldn't quite get over it when a couple of youngsters spoke to them civilly and went broke buying them tobacco.

My parole officer came to see me. "Don't think you're going to get out when your ten days are up, Chessman, because you're not. You're a menace to society."

"Thanks," I said.

"Don't thank me; thank yourself. I warned you but you wouldn't listen. You wouldn't cooperate."

"Yeah, that's right. I wouldn't cooperate. And that makes me a menace to society, a real honest-to-God public enemy. But one thing bothers me: What does that make you?"

I didn't wait for an answer. I got up and walked out of the Attorney Room, where such interviews were held.

Those jail nights were long. And noisy. My elderly wine-imbibing friends, an odoriferous crew, industriously scratched, snored and hacked the night away. I found such a milieu a novel one, to say the least, and there were times when my sense of humor had to rush to the rescue. Somehow I had to shoot an angle and get myself released. But how? I cudgeled my brains, paced the floor of the tank and did some checking; then I had the answer.

My parole officer had failed to file a formal hold order against me; his intentions were to wait for me at the booking office and personally have me re-booked as a parole violator. But he got a surprise. I wangled an early release and was long gone when he put in an appearance.

My first stop was at the house of my gun-collecting friend, where I acquired another gun, one that wouldn't fail to fire. Then I went home. I fully intended to resist any attempts to return me to jail. Similarly, I had no intention of accepting any invitation to visit a police station.

Finding I was gone, the parole officer made a dash for my place. He came alone and I met him in the back yard. He stormed, fumed, threatened. He told me I had no business being released without his permission.

"I'm out," I said.

"And I think I should take you right back," he snapped.

"Don't," I told him very quietly. "As a favor to both of us, don't!"

He glowered at me, trying to make up his mind what to do. I said a silent prayer that he didn't try to take me in, that he didn't put his hands on me. The seconds passed. I waited; the next move was his. *Dear God, save this honorable gentleman from his own folly!*

"I'm giving you this one last chance," he finally said. Then he lectured me some more, finding increasing strength and assurance from his own rotund platitudes. "Remember, Chessman, this is your last chance. There won't be any next times."

I agreed there indeed would not be.

And I fixed a secret back way out of my garage apartment.

It was night. We—my girl and I—were parked high in my hills. We had the world to ourselves, an enchanted, shadowy, moonlit world. I held her in my arms; I kissed her. Her full lips clung hungrily to mine. I was alive once more, and whole. Here, I was then convinced, was the ultimate and the only reality worth knowing or possessing.

We made love, joyously, gladly.

And then we drifted and, for a time, were contentedly one with the night and the moon and the stars.

Gradually the stars faded from the night sky.

"It's beginning to get light," she said. "You'd better take me home."

I held her more tightly than ever. "I don't want to take you home. I'm almost afraid to take you home, afraid you'll not be there when I come for you again."

Later, she and I got into an argument. It was one of those silly things that started over nothing. It soon, however, grew heated and bitter. I learned I was just an ordinary, cheap thief; I was no good; I never would be any good. In reply, I did the ungentlemanly thing by assuring her that as far as I was concerned her only virtues were biological. She slapped me.

Irrational anger boiled up inside me. "Damn you!" I whispered. "I've got a notion to kill us both."

"Go ahead! I don't care!"

She apparently didn't. We had been driving. I slammed down on the accelerator and jerked the steering wheel to the right; my little Ford careened and headed to an unguarded place where I could send us hurtling down almost two hundred feet. She stared straight ahead, saying nothing. At the last instant I decided I wasn't yet ready to destroy myself and my defiant, voluptuous darling. I slammed on the brakes, barely stopping in time. She coolly appraised me and smiled mockingly. I pulled her to me and kissed her fiercely. Her arms encircled my neck, fingernails digging into my back like talons.

"There are other ways of killing us," she whispered.

Slower, subtler, more terrible ways.

Friday, October 13, 1939, wasn't my day. I stepped into a stolen car the Glendale police had staked out and was promptly arrested by two detectives with drawn guns. Handcuffed, I was placed in the front seat of a radio car parked nearby. One detective drove, gun in hand, while the other went ahead on foot, hoping to capture a confederate of mine they believed had entered an auto agency up the street. I lashed out with the handcuffs, striking the detective. The gun flew from his right hand; the horn honked; the radio car swerved. I elbowed the door open, jumped, stumbled, caught my balance and ran down a side street. The detective who had been walking ahead ran back, took careful aim and squeezed the trigger. The gun failed to fire. I ducked down an alley. Several minutes and some distance later, a slight, male citizen leaped on my back when I lost my balance vaulting a fence. Still handcuffed, I was unable to dislodge him. He clung like grim death and shouted mightily for help. Assorted citizens and the two detectives came on the run.

Each detective seized me with a free hand. "Run now!" growled one of them. "Come on, let's see you run now!" A gun waved under my nose.

A lady dashed forward. "Don't you dare hurt that poor boy!" she scolded. "And put those awful guns away this instant!"

Again, custody, jail, a cell, interrogation, suspicion, interminable back-room sessions, tough talk. "Next time we'll shoot first and ask questions afterward. Next time my gun won't fail to fire. Next time you'll wind up in the morgue." "All right, Chessman, if you know what's good for you, you'll come clean, and no funny business. We know what you've been doing, but we want the story from you."

Again, a visit from the parole officer with the radar ears. "We've got you this time!" Smug triumph. "You're on your way to San Quentin without fail!"

We've got you this time!

But for what? I insisted I hadn't done anything. I claimed they—the cops—were just trying to roust me.

The police were convinced that I was guilty of committing any number of felonies—but all they had was smoke and suspicion, plus scraps and fragments of evidence and some hearsay that wouldn't be admissible in a court of law. All they could definitely pin on me was the fact they had caught me in a stolen car. However, I actually hadn't stolen that particular car and could prove I hadn't. That left the lesser offense of driving the vehicle without the owner's permission.

Would the arresting officers testify I had been driving the car? I knew they would. They stated in the arrest report that I had started to pull away from the curb and had driven the machine two or three feet. I flatly denied even being behind the wheel; but assuming the statement of the detectives was accepted over mine, and that the "two or three feet" constituted "driving" within the meaning of the law, the prosecution still would have to prove with some kind of credible evidence that I had driven those thirty-six inches with the intent of depriving the owner of possession, which in turn would require proof that I had known the car was stolen. That was where they might run into a snag.

But what if I beat that charge? Then the police were sure to charge me with escape from the lawful custody of an officer. The escape carried a ten-year maximum sentence and if I was convicted, San Quentin was a certainty. The police would see to that. But a driving-without-the-owner's-consent conviction carried only a five year top and I very probably could get off with probation and a few months in the county jail if I "cooperated" with the authorities by pleading guilty to the charge and thus saving the county the time, trouble and expense of a trial. That way I would be quietly taking myself out of circulation and it appeared a solution that would satisfy all concerned—except, of course, my parole officer. He had his heart set on seeing me behind San Quentin's grim, gray walls.

I got hold of some money and hired the attorney I wanted. Through him, I entered a plea of guilty to the charge and filed an application for probation. The attorney had a talk with the judge who would sentence me. When I stood before him, the judge lectured me scathingly; he warned me that if I got into trouble again he would throw the book at me. Then he ordered me on three years' probation, the first year to be served in the county jail, with six months suspended. Next case.

Thus I exchanged three years of juvenile parole for an equal amount of adult probation, and was then wholly beyond the reach of my former parole officer, whose control over me terminated the instant the probation order was made. The Fates indeed were kind. And they became kinder still. Not more than three or four days later, I happened to be in the Attorney Room of the jail when, much to my delight, Cerberus put in an appearance. He was seated not far from me and in a couple of minutes he had some scared kid seated across from him, giving the youngster the benefit of his righteous social indignation. As I was leaving I paused briefly in front of him, grinned and proceeded to tell him exactly what I thought of him. When I got through the air was blue.

I did my time in Road Camp No. 7 in the mountains high above the fabled Malibu Colony. The food was good, the mountain air was a tonic, and the feel of the sixteen-pound sledge hammer as it smashed into rocks was pure joy.

The personnel at the camp were decent people with one notable exception, the head man himself, a soured, cranky, too tough old character who had a nasty way of making things miserable for all of us in a hundred petty ways. I vowed to find some way to give the old boy a good time of it when I was released, and I did.

Sometimes, in the evenings, talk in the barracks would get around to crime. Mostly I listened. Did I have any ideas on the subject?

"Yeah, I do. I've discovered that all my trouble always begins in a police station. So I don't think after this I'll be paying any police stations a visit."

Those listening understood what I meant.

Night counts weren't made too often in the barracks and on several occasions I had business elsewhere. I would slip off to Santa Monica or even Los Angeles. Once the California Highway Patrol mistook me for a burglar who had been prowling the area, and the pursuit was lively. I spent over an hour in a rough ocean, dodging bullets, spotlights, rocks, seaweed. It was a miracle I got back to camp before the morning check.

The months passed swiftly. I was taken to the County Jail in downtown Los Angeles and released on a Sunday morning. The date, I believe, was June 30, 1940.

Where do I go from here? I asked myself. That depended, I decided. It depended on many things. . . .

"Go away," my voluptuous darling said, after I had scratched on the window screen to wake her. But I wanted to talk to her. "There's nothing to talk about." It was all over between us; she insisted it was no more. I should go away. Yes, there *was* another. So would I *please* leave.

A baffled, angry young villain left. Suddenly, she had become a hideous sickness. *Yes, there was another!* Perhaps a casual succession

of others. I could see them all, these lovers; I could see her giving herself to them, casually, indifferently. And I suffered.

I knew that her father had learned about us shortly after my arrest,
and that he had wrathfully taken his daughter to court. I knew he
had gone so far as to have her put on probation and threatened with
being placed in an institution for incorrigible girls if she so much as
saw me. But this should have strengthened, not destroyed, our need
and desire for each other.

And it would have but for one fact—she and I were the dark night's
children.

Ding an sich—ultimate reality. Where was it? Where was it to be
found? Certainly not at the wild, drunken parties I attended. Nor in
the eager arms of young matrons with sophisticated ideas about the
institution of marriage. Nor in free-swinging brawls with jokers who,
for one reason or another, threw their weight around. Nor at a typewriter, capable only of suggesting to its operator that the sole goal of
life was to distract oneself by furious, reckless activity of one sort or
another and thus prevent recognition of life's meaninglessness.

I didn't fit. I tried to join the Army, but the Army wanted no part
of me. I attempted to get a job at one of the booming aircraft plants
and was turned down cold. My record made them shudder. So I kept
on working for my father, and marking time.

Crawling, walking, staggering, running, I had come a long way. But
all the while I had been traveling in a circle. Now I was back where I
started. I had completed my own odd Metonic cycle, and I felt as old
as though I had been born in Meton the Athenian's time. I felt as old
as time itself. Yet I was only nineteen. Nineteen *winters.*

I marveled at the fact, for I also was a man, a very old man, whose
life had been lived. My youth surely was a lie, a mockery. It existed,
had entity, persisted still, only to please a mordant Fate with its capacity for torment.

Then Judy entered my life and I thanked the gods for my youth. A
truly beautiful girl, Judy was all I could ask for in a young woman.

Indeed, with her unaffected innocence, her tinkling laughter, and her warm, fresh beauty, she was a dream come true. I told her so and we fell in love, wholly and we thought for all time. My past, she assured me, made no difference to her; all that counted was our future together. First we would be married, and as soon as possible; then we would finish school together. When I graduated, I would go to work —and really *work*. Ultimately I would establish myself as a creative writer. Meanwhile we would raise a family; there would be babies. And, of course, we would live happily ever after in a world without menacing shadows.

Everything appeared perfect. At last I had found myself; at last I had regained my sense of balance. Then one afternoon I called on Judy and she told me there could be no marriage.

I begged her to tell me what had happened.

"I . . . I can't tell you," Judy faltered, avoiding my eyes.

"But you must," I insisted.

And finally, after much urging, she did tell me. She was visiting at a girl friend's one evening, approximately two weeks earlier, when two boys called, one of whom was the boy friend of Judy's chum and the other a boy she had been out with two or three times. Judy's girl friend talked her into going for a ride with the two boys, who were drinking. Over Judy's strenuous protests, they drove to a local lover's lane and parked. Judy jumped from the car and ran, pursued by the boy she had dated in the past. Panting, he caught up with her, seized her roughly. The drink and her attempt at flight made him ugly.

"What's the matter, think you're too good for me?"

He tried to kiss her, to fondle her.

"Let me go!"

She wrenched an arm free and slapped him. He cursed her, struck her, once, twice, three times. She fell to the ground, only half conscious. He tore off her undergarments and attempted to rape her, possibly succeeding. . . .

Now my poor Judy burned with shame. She feared she might be pregnant (she wasn't, it developed), and she believed, in any event, that she had been horribly soiled, forever rendered unfit for marriage. She felt I would recoil at the sight of her if I were to learn what had happened.

I swam in a red haze, and some voice within screamed soundlessly in anguish. I wanted to kill, to smash. Never again would the malignant gods get a chance to hurt me or those I loved. For I would put them to rout; I would make them flee in terror. I would build a bastion. Hate and Guile would help me. God have mercy on the next "good" one, the next "righteous" one to inflict his goodness or his righteousness on me or mine. I was holding Judy in my arms, and at the same time planning how I would beat the life out of the vile animal who had ravaged her.

"I love you, Judy! I love you more than life! And all the fiends in Hell aren't going to stop me from marrying you!"

One Thursday, we drove to Las Vegas, and were married.

I do no more than faithfully relate the simple, if violent and bizarre, truth.

With diabolic cunning, my mind synthesized and plotted, waiting, watching, a cold, coiled, venomous thing biding its time. First the stage had to be set; the dramatis personae had to be selected and groomed for their roles.

An idyllic summer had passed, and its exquisite, intimate perfection was ours, Judy's and mine; it could never be taken from us. Here was the fall of the year, a golden autumn. We had begun school together but I had clashed with Pompous Officiousness and had been obliged to check out. Now I was attending another high school in the morning and a university in the afternoon. Judy and I were living in a luxurious third floor front apartment in Glendale, and I had acquired a new Ford coupe. As the saying goes, I was doing all right for myself.

Then an article in the back pages of a newspaper set off a chain reaction. The article told of recent advances made in neurosurgery and mentioned the name of a famous neurosurgeon. I arranged for this surgeon to visit and examine my mother. Then I had a talk with him privately.

Was there a chance, any possibility at all, surgically, to give my mother the use of her legs? Yes, there was a chance, the surgeon said. It would take at least one and more probably a series of delicate operations. The cost of hospitalization and the operations would be almost prohibitive. The specialist quoted a figure in the thousands. And he warned there was grave danger the operations might prove fatal.

I told my mother what the surgeon had told me.

"Do you think, Mom, you should risk your life against a chance to walk again?"

My mother nodded her head emphatically. "Yes," she told me. She was positive she should. All these years she had prayed for such a miracle.

But a question troubled her. Where would the money come from?

I had anticipated the question. "I believe I know where I can borrow it, Mom." My smile reassured her. And it forestalled the asking of a second and more embarrassing question, touching where I could possibly borrow such a large sum of money.

Adolf was pounding London to bits. The R.C.A.F. had set up an unofficial recruiting office in Hollywood, and was crying for skilled pilots. I made arrangements to go to Canada within sixty days and join that country's air arm. (Later, circumstances obliged me to extend the time another sixty days.) I was assured that if I had sufficient flying experience I would be promptly transferred to England. I began taking flying lessons.

I intended to let society pay for my mother's operation. Then I would pay society back in my own way—not by going to jail, but by going to England and fighting hell out of Adolf's Luftwaffe, until I found myself blown into eternity's tomorrow. Right then I wanted from life (and death) two things above all else: to see my mother walk again, and to give her, my father and Judy a reason to be proud of me. Never knowing the meaning of it, never truly possessing it, I nevertheless wanted to fight and was willing to die for what men call freedom. My motives were personal, arbitrary, and selfish.

I wanted peace and I unhesitatingly declared war to find it. I wanted to get even, to have one last defiant fling, and then to go out in a blaze of ironically stolen glory. The dialectics of psychopathy are subtle and romantic indeed. When driven, confused and acutely dissatisfied, find some reason or excuse to fight. *Raise hell!* Cunningly charge off in three or four different directions simultaneously.

20

A Game of Cops and Robbers

I was back in business again, the opportunistic business of taking people's money at the point of a pistol. Pimps, gamblers and others of similar persuasion I regarded as targets as legitimate as any to be found, and their cries of anguish at being "beat" were sweet music to my ears. Most often during the first few weeks I worked alone but occasionally I would team up with one or more other guys laboring in the same perilous vineyard.

From the start I was determined to forge an outfit that could and would get the work at hand done swiftly and efficiently, even artistically. This scheme involved recruiting a fearless soldiery, planning, specialization, and the acquisition of the requisite materiel—no small task. Still, life was not all work and no play. With the aid of tough, loyal Little Andy and his burglarious South Side crew I stocked an arsenal. I cultivated the acquaintance of a vain, snake-eyed comer in the local rackets, the Duke. Through Bob and Rabbit, a couple of boosters, I contacted a fence willing and eager to handle hijacked merchandise. Gabriella (so I'll call her), a girl with a penchant for gambling and a fancy charmer who felt she owed me herself and her life because I had extricated her from some really bad jams with an ugly element, did some fronting and fingering for me.

My friend Bill had been released from camp and we found the time to return, unseen, one Sunday afternoon and sabotage the road-building machinery on the grade near camp and drain off hundreds of gallons of gas. We were sure that would make our old friend, the lemon-faced captain, very happy. The bastard who had mistreated Judy had an accident. Tim showed up; he had just been released after serving a one-year jolt at another camp and had a suspended one to five San Quentin sentence hanging over his head. I had been willing to overlook if not entirely forgive his snitching but, nonetheless, would have run him off except for Judy, who felt sorry for this weak, brooding boyhood pal. So I told him straight, "You're welcome to stick around, Tim. But don't ever betray either of us, and especially Judy. God help you if you do."

Tim introduced me to Tuffy, an amiable, sandy-haired young giant he had met at camp. In no time at all, Tuffy and I became fast friends. Through me, Tuffy met a school chum of Judy's, a vivacious young lady as full of the joy of life as he was. They wasted no time in falling in love. Today they are happily married and have two fine sons. But thanks to Chessman, as we shall see, they faced many trials and tribulations before marriage was possible, and even now, more than a decade later, Tuffy is still paying dearly for that friendship and for being loyal.

My glib tongue talked Tuffy (and Bill) into the ways of banditry. The three of us—Tuffy, Bill and myself—formed the nucleus of a bandit gang, a gang for which I accept full responsibility, since I dreamed it angrily into existence. I brought its principals together; I stole most of its getaway cars; I procured its guns; I encouraged its operations.

Our efforts were not crowned with conspicuous economic success. Almost from the beginning we ran into more trouble than money, even though clicking perfectly as a team.

For weeks we tailed, studied and timed the manager of a large chain store who, every Saturday night, took a week's receipts from the store and deposited them in a bank chute. He invariably followed a fixed routine—until the night we were ready to rob him. This inconsiderate and unsuspecting change of routine, plus one large, mean dog, which obstinately refused to be intimidated by an impressive display of fire power, hopelessly frustrated our robbery attempt. Instead of making off with a sack containing several thousand dollars, we were left holding the sack. We wound up robbing liquor stores and gas stations that night, whatever came along. And for the money we got out of it, our robbing could just as well have been for practice.

Another time, after a thorough study of the place, we had a liquor store, which did a huge volume of business, all set up for the taking. Arriving on the scene, we observed what appeared to be a customer in the store and decided to give him a chance to leave. We drove around the block. When we returned the customer was gone. I parked in front of the place, cradling a shotgun. Tuffy and Bill walked in and, displaying revolvers, got right down to business. The proprietor laughed in their faces and invited them to rob away to their hearts' content. The customer, it developed, had been a collector; he had driven off with a whole week's receipts! And brainy boys that we were, we'd made sure he got safely away.

On still another occasion, Tuffy and Bill took a place where I was known, thus excluding me from direct participation. Most of the money wasn't kept in the cash register but was hidden near it. I knew approximately where and, after my briefing, so did Tuffy and Bill when they walked in. But just as they started to rob this particular place there was one of those spectacular automobile accidents out front. Thus they were obliged to leave hastily—and without the several hundred dollars we knew to be in the "plant." All they got was about eighty dollars from the cash register.

When you encounter a dozen or so such incidents in a row you begin to feel frustrated. "Hell," you comment drily, "it's getting so an honest bandit hasn't got a chance any more."

So you cowboy it; you rob everything and anything in the way of business establishments that you happen to find open for business. You try to make up in quantity what's lacking in quality. You knock over six, eight, ten or twelve places in a night. You get as little as nothing, as much as a hundred or so dollars. You're angry, and not very proud of yourself—your ego is taking a beating—and so you're just a whole lot harder to handle if the bulls happen to get in your way. And you can be sure the bulls will get in your way, not once or twice, not every now and then, but regularly until they nail you.

The serious heat, for us, was generated a few days after the new year began. At a few minutes past midnight. Tuffy, Bill and I were seated in a stolen Buick sedan, a new, torpedo-bodied one. We were parked in the Flintridge Hills, off the road. We were waiting, impatiently now, for Tim and Whitey. I had loaned them my Ford on the condition that they meet us here at exactly 11:30. The Buick we occupied was hot, very hot. We had used it in a series of robberies; then the bulls had been in uncomfortably close pursuit and had gotten a good look at it. Now, here we were sitting in it, fuming at Tim and Whitey.

Impatiently, I lit another cigarette. "What the hell happened to those two clowns?" I demanded.

As if in reply to my question, the twin beams of a car's headlights cut a path through the darkness and struck the Buick—and us.

"This must be them now," Bill said.

Then a third blaze of white light burned into the interior of the Buick. A spotlight, with a beam as searching as an angry conscience.

Blinded, Tuffy growled, "What's the matter with those fools?"

I blinked, shielded my eyes and shouted, "Turn that damned thing off!"

The spotlight died. We heard a door open. We saw, dimly, a shape coming toward us. A uniformed shape! John Law again!

"Bulls!" I whispered, warningly.

The radio-car officer was tall. He bent down to look in at us. The head I saw a few inches from my face was large, with a bulging forehead and a receding hairline. There was a craggy strength in the face, and more curiosity than suspicion in the alert eyes.

"What are you fellows doing up here at this time of night?" the cop asked.

"Waiting," I replied, noting that the cop's brother officer had remained in the police car.

"Yes?"

I drew in a breath, said, "It's like this," and then launched on a long-winded, plausible account of how we happened to be parked here in the hills at midnight. I concluded, "The girls said they'd be right back but that's been almost an hour ago and I don't think they're coming. I guess we may as well go on home to bed. What do you think?"

"I think I'd better take a look at your driver's license," the cop said.

"Sure thing," I replied smilingly. I promptly reached for my wallet, felt it and then contrived an expression of puzzled annoyance. "What the heck happened to my wallet?" I thought about this for a moment. I frowningly pondered the question. "Maybe I put it in the glove compartment."

I reached across Bill and punched open the glove compartment and looked studiously at the barrel of my gun, which, from where he stood, the cop couldn't see. I was hoping Tuffy and Bill would take the hint. "Not in there." I glanced at my two companions. "Either one of you two guys know what happened to it?" They both shook their heads. "Looks like I lost the darned thing," I told the cop. "However," I added innocently, "if all you want is my name and address I can give that to you. I live right down there on Linda Vista, not far from the school."

"Is this your car?"

Cops can ask the damnedest questions!

"Not exactly," I said. "I've been thinking about buying the equity in it." I proceeded to narrate the facts surrounding my prospective purchase.

"Where's the registration slip?" the cop then wanted to know. He held a flashlight in his hand and played its beam up and down the steering column.

"Isn't it right here?" I said, looking at the column.

"Just a minute," the cop said, and then he stepped over to the police car.

"We better take 'em," I whispered. Tuffy and Bill nodded.

"Say," I called out, "is there any law against people parking up here?"

"What's that?"

I repeated the question. I received no direct answer. The cop who had been doing the questioning came to the driver's side, the other cop went around to the passenger side. We were told to get out of the car, to keep our hands in sight.

The cops began to search us. Tuffy and Bill were ready, but they hesitated because I was gunless and on the wrong side of the car. So I did the only thing I could do under the circumstances. I just walked away from the cop who was searching me, around the front of the Buick to the other side.

"Hey," said the cop, surprised, "come back here!"

"No," I said, "you come around here."

And that's what the cop did, walking into the trap.

Tuffy and Bill immediately stepped back, whipped out their guns. "All right, coppers," Bill said, "up with your hands!"

Both cops hesitated. One went so far as to make a grab for his holstered gun. I shouted a warning and sprang forward, hearing Tuffy say, very quietly, "Don't do it, copper! *Don't do it!*" Then I was beside the cops; I snatched their guns and audibly cocked them. "Now get 'em up—high!" I barked. "And no more heroics!" The cops complied; they had no alternative.

I told Tuffy and Bill, "I'll take the radio car. You two guys follow in the Buick."

Tuffy waved his gun at the two cops. "What about them?"

I grinned. "They can walk. The exercise'll do 'em good."

The motor of the radio car was running. I climbed in behind the wheel, threw the two guns on the seat beside me, and backed out onto the road. Tuffy and Bill pulled out behind me, Bill driving. With a whine of motors, we sped off.

We abandoned the Buick in Roscoe, first wiping it clean of fingerprints. While doing this, a man came running from a house nearby. "What's going on out here?" this individual demanded officiously.

Bill and I kept wiping. Tuffy displayed a gun and said, "I really don't think that's any of your business. So get back in that house where it's nice and warm." He added, "And safe."

We drove off. The police radio kept barking out an urgent summons for this particular radio car to call in. Tuffy, who was occupying the passenger side of the front seat, looked at me quizzically. I nodded and he grinned. First fiddling with buttons and knobs, Tuffy took the microphone in hand and spoke ever so gently into it. Receiving a reply, he beamed triumphantly. Whereupon he proceeded to unburden himself, unpoetically but feelingly, on the subject of this radio car in particular and all radio cars in general. It was a stirring little speech and Bill and I both roundly applauded when he signed off. It also moved the radio broadcaster, but in a different direction. Coded signals began to pour forth.

We were speeding along a main drag out in San Fernando Valley when we ran into thick fog. The fog slowed us down to a crawl. We crept along for perhaps a mile when suddenly the fog cleared—and there were the cops! Luckily, we spotted them first, parked at the curb not five feet from us. Bill had been cradling the riot gun—a twelve-gauge shotgun—we had found in the radio car. He instantly shoved its long menacing snout out the window, right into the astonished faces of the two uniformed bulls seated in the parked police car. With magical speed, Tuffy also produced a pistol in each fist, barrels pointed at the cops. "Sit still!" Bill shouted. They did. They had no choice.

We got out of there fast, disappearing back into the fog. "I make a motion that we dump this crate," I said, turning off onto a side street. "It's getting too hot to handle." Tuffy and Bill agreed. The coded signals kept coming.

We were closest to Hollywood and Bill's, so I drove to his place first, keeping to the side streets as much as possible. On the way I explained, "We'll drop you off first, Bill, and then make a run for my place. That way we'll save a trip, and I can dump this clunker as soon as we can get hold of my car."

"You don't think you're apt to run into any more cops? I wouldn't want to be left out of the fun."

This, I knew, was Bill's way of assuring us that if we expected any more trouble he felt he should share it with us.

I shook my head and laughed. "No, I think the evening's fun is all over. Now it's just a matter of abandoning this heap, finding Tim and Whitey and then going on home to bed."

After letting Bill off, Tuffy and I proceeded without incident to my Glendale apartment.

I found the apartment dark and Judy gone. She'd left no note and there was no sign of Whitey, Tim or my Ford. That was strange. It obliged me to admit the possibility that somehow Judy had become involved, and I became coldly angry. I cursed softly. *If anything had happened to Judy* . . .

"Tuff," I said, "I've got to go back where we came from. I intend to find Judy and that's the first place I know to look."

Tuffy understood. "Let's go," he said.

We went—on two wheels. We flew like homing pigeons to the exact spot where we had taken this car from the cops, fully expecting trouble, ready for it. But the hills were dark, deserted. No cops; no Judy; no Whitey and Tim. I raced next to my parents' house, waking my mother. Judy, I was told, hadn't been there. I put through half a dozen phone calls at an all-night drugstore. Still no trace of Judy. I even phoned the Glendale, Pasadena and Los Angeles police departments, gave her maiden name and asked if she had been arrested on a drunk charge. I said I had heard she had, that I was a friend and that I wanted to bail her out if she had been jailed. In each instance I was told, "Our records don't show anyone by that name having been arrested." The search continued. My anxiety drove me. I was ready to storm the gates of Hell if need be to get my Judy back.

We ran out of places to look. Then we ran out of cigarettes. On sighting a cocktail lounge, I jerked the police car in to the curb. We were still getting the code over the radio, and I was getting fed up listening to it.

"Wait in the car," I told Tuffy. "I'm going to run in here and get us some cigarettes." I exited from the cocktail lounge not only with the cigarettes but with the contents of two cash registers. Speeding away from the scene, I told Tuffy, "That'll give 'em something to 23-Z about," referring to the coded broadcasts.

And it did.

We pulled two more robberies on the way back to my apartment—

because we were angry; because nothing was going right; because Judy had been swallowed up by the night; and perhaps even because we were unwilling to pass up an opportunity to add needed dollars to the coffers. It must have been something of a shock to the victims when they watched the robbers making their getaway in a police car.

The instant I turned off Glendale Avenue, I spied my Ford at the curb across the street from the apartment house, facing me. "There they are," I told Tuffy. I speeded up, then braked to a quick stop beside the Ford, startling its three occupants. They were even more startled when I shined the red light directly into their faces and thrust the barrel of the riot gun out the window at them. Tim and Whitey, I decided, needed an object lesson, one they wouldn't soon forget. "All right," I growled, disguising my voice, "you're the two guys we've been looking for. Get out of that car and come over here!"

White-faced and confused, Tim and Whitey fumbled with a bottle of whisky from which they had been drinking. Judy was the cool one of the trio. She faced the red light—and us—and smiled, prettily. Then, calmly she turned to Tim and Whitey, spoke to them sharply, took the bottle, replaced the cap and dropped it to the floor. The three of them alighted.

My object lesson had gone far enough, I decided. I snapped off the red light, threw the shotgun onto the back seat of the radio car and said to Tim and Whitey, "You know something. You're a couple of sorry-looking specimens."

They recognized my voice and ran over to the car, full of exclamations, questions.

"Get in," I told them, dead-panned. "The back seat."

"Yeah," Tuffy said, "and make it quick."

They hastened to comply. Tuffy grabbed the shotgun.

I told Judy, "Follow me, Honey. But not too close. And if any trouble starts, you come on home."

Judy followed at about a hundred yards. I drove unhurriedly along side streets for roughly a mile. Tuffy had turned the radio completely off. We were no longer interested in what the cops might have to say.

It was a few minutes past two. Only two hours had passed since we had acquired the police car; it seemed more like a couple of years or decades.

"Jeez," Tim said, marveling at the idea, "a goddamed squad car! I thought you guys were up to something big." Tim was half drunk and the tough-guy talk welled up out of him. This was big stuff. He, Tim, was in with an outfit that took police cars away from the bulls! He savored the idea, built it up in his mind. Then he asked, "Did you have to shoot any bulls when you took this crate?"

That was the wrong question. It didn't sit well with either Tuffy or me. "No," I said, making no effort to veil the sarcasm the question deserved, "all we did was explain to the cops we were having a tough time finding a couple of guys who didn't know what it meant to keep a promise and they insisted we take their car and use it until we found those two guys."

"Hell," Tim said, going on the defensive, "you got no reason to be sore. We got hung up."

"Yeah, you got hung up. And I know where." I laughed. "You got hung up in some whorehouse. You got so busy fronting for some two-dollar hustler that you either forgot or didn't give a damn about your promise to meet us."

That stung. Tim grew sullen. He had been brooding for a long time about being left in the fringes, in the dark, and it hurt him to be chewed out in front of easy-going, non-violent Whitey. He sought refuge in demanding, irrationally, "Well, ain't you supposed to be smart guys who know how to take care of yourselves?"

"Oh, sure," Tuffy said, answering for both of us, "we're supposed to be smarter and tougher than all the bulls in southern California."

Then Tim exploded—vocally. "If you don't think I got guts just gimme a gun and I'll show you! I'll shoot it out with you or cops or anybody! Just gimme a gun!" He snarled the words, seething with hate against the whole world, because he thought the world was laughing at him.

I parked, selecting a dark and deserted residential street. We didn't give Tim a gun. Instead we gave him a talking to. We felt sorry for him. We knew what a terrible, punishing thing was the sense of inadequacy that writhed constantly inside him. Whitey said it was probably his fault that he and Tim had failed to meet us. We knew better but didn't contradict him.

Tim finally calmed down. He still wanted and needed his front, and he wanted me to believe in him, to be his pal and trust him. His voice was raw-edged when he whispered, "I'll be there next time, goddamit. Believe me, Chess, I'll be there!"

I told Tim I believed him.

Judy had parked half a block away. After wiping the interior of the police car, we strode swiftly and silently to my Ford—bringing the riot gun along with us—got in and drove off, unseen, undetected. I let Tim and Whitey off at Tim's, telling them, "You two guys come on around to the apartment after you've got some sleep." They said they would. Then I chauffeured Tuffy to his home in Pasadena. "Give me a call, Tuff, when you're ready for me to make the run back over here and pick you up." He nodded and waved Judy and me on our way.

We reached the apartment and I parked. I took Judy in my arms, held her, kissed her. "Judy," I whispered, "I love you—so much that I don't want what I'm doing to touch you, not in any way." So I asked her to promise me that she would forget all about this night and that hereafter she never would come looking for me again, that, unless I personally told her, she never would even think about what I might be doing.

"I promise," Judy said, adding: "But I only wanted to help, Daddy. I was afraid I'd lose you. And I can't stand that feeling. I can't!"

I kissed Judy again.

"Darling! Darling!" Judy whispered. "Don't go away!"

Later, still holding her in my arms, I said, "I'm a fool, Judy Baby. But I've got to gamble. I've got to gamble everything, even our love."

And that's what I did.

21

The Game Grows Grimmer

We were continually on the move.

Incident piled upon incident.

I drove myself and my friends toward a mirage, an impossible goal. If you knew your way around, if you knew how to look out for yourself, nothing was impossible, I insisted.

You had to know, though, what you wanted and then you had to have the guts and the savvy to go after it. You took the violent, the savage, the macabre, the humorous, the fantastic in stride. Soon you would go off to war and you didn't expect to return; you didn't give a damn if you returned. So you occupied yourself with cramming a lifetime into a few months.

You got around. You robbed. You hijacked. You snatched a pimp here; you knocked over a bookie or gambling joint there. You sat at your paralyzed mother's bedside and talked the night away. You saved.

You had friends. And enemies. You loved one girl—your wife—more than life. But you knew that for you, love and life were exquisite instruments of torture.

You met gay, sophisticated young things who bestowed their favors liberally, who, for a moment, shared their physical selves with you. And you knew that they were as lost as you were. Behind their laughter was not a tearful melancholy but a terrifying emptiness. Unable to fill the void, they fled from it. They made flight their goal. Briefly you fled with them.

Occasionally you dreamed still, and laughed mightily at yourself when you did. For you knew that only hopelessly innocent fools dared dream.

And you were beyond innocence. You had convinced yourself that you were a knowledgeable young cynic who knew all the answers, all the angles. And you were so positive that only the impossible, and the unattainable, would satisfy you.

Oh, you were a clever young man, all right.

No doubt of that.

A clever young man and a busy one. . . .

That brings us to the evening of January 16, 1941, and a violent prelude of things to come.

In swank San Marino Tuffy and I stole an expensive Packard club convertible. Ten minutes later we walked into a liquor store. "Two quarts of beer," Tuffy said, naming the brand. The clerk was getting us the beer when a tiny old lady came from a back room and looked at us with sharp appraisal.

"You boys are too young to be buying beer," she said.

Tuffy and I exchanged glances. I nodded. We displayed our guns. There was no age limit on banditry.

"Pardon me, ma'am," Tuffy said, "but this is a robbery."

"It's nothing of the sort," the old lady snapped back.

"But it *is*," Tuffy insisted, as gently as possible.

"Your guns don't scare me, young man," Tuffy was told. "And you can't have our money. We need it. You ought to be ashamed of yourselves for trying to take it."

This spirited little old lady—she must have been at least seventy and couldn't possibly have been five feet tall or weighed a hundred pounds—gave us an inspired scolding. She wagged a finger at us and told us what we needed was a good tanning. She continued to lay down the law for a good five minutes, until a customer walked in. Then she smiled sweetly at us.

"Now you be good boys and be on your way," she said. "And think about what I've told you."

"Yes, ma'am," Tuffy said. But he picked up the two quarts of beer, and was rewarded with a scowl. Sheepishly he dug into his pants pockets and brought out a couple of half dollars, which he laid on the counter.

"Thank you, ma'am," Tuffy said, "and good night."

"Good night, boys," the little old lady said.

Whereupon we got out as fast as we respectably could.

"Whew!" Tuffy said, as we drove off.

"Yeah," I concurred. "And I see we're off to a flying start."

We didn't run into any more tiny old ladies but we did encounter something considerably more violent. After four or five quick robberies I got to thinking about that old Nemesis at road camp. Our travels had brought us out to Santa Monica and by then—it was near midnight—the police radio was crackling with a description of us and the Packard.

"Tuff," I said, "I'm in the mood to mix in a little pleasure with business." Then I told Tuffy about old bad eye at the road camp. "I feel like driving out there and blowing the roof off his shack as a token of my esteem."

"Let's go," Tuffy said without an instant's hesitation.

The trouble started when we turned out onto the Roosevelt Highway. A couple of cops in a patrol car spotted us.

Tuffy was looking back. "They're following."

"Let's see how good they are at following," I said. I speeded up, began weaving in and out through relatively heavy traffic.

"They're catching up," Tuffy said.

So I rammed the gas pedal to the floorboard and the Packard leaped ahead. Tuffy climbed over into the back seat, got his guns ready, knowing what to expect if John Law got within range.

The wind shrieked in my ears. According to the speedometer needle, we were doing over a hundred miles an hour. But John was still gaining, closing the gap between us.

Then came the bullets, whizzing, zinging, thudding. And at that precise point it became a very elemental proposition: escape, kill or be killed. We had no intention of being captured.

Up ahead was an S-turn and after that the highway straightened out for a couple of miles. On the straightaway we would be sitting ducks. Well, I had a surprise for John. Theoretically what I had in mind was possible. Actually I wasn't so sure, but I had an inquiring mind. I was willing to find out. We were approaching the slow turn. I shouted to Tuffy to hold on.

Then I took the wraps off my dubious surprise. I savagely jerked the steering wheel to the right, hit the brake. The tiniest fraction of a second before we rammed into the cliff face we lost traction and went into a dizzy spin. The rear end whipped around. And around. And around. I fought the wheel, cursed, prayed and used the brake sparingly. We missed passing cars by inches. We missed plowing into the cliff or diving into the ocean by inches. But inches were all we needed. We slid, lurched sideways to a stop. The patrol car whizzed by, unable to stop. Miraculously my surprise had worked.

The motor had died, a bad break. By the time I had it going again the cops had got stopped and turned. They were sitting down the highway using the Packard for target practice. We got underway again, in the opposite direction. John continued shooting. One shot got the right rear tire. The spin had got the right front one. I zigged and zagged like mad to throw both tires, finally succeeded. Sparks flew. The screech of the rims on the pavement was something awful. Other cars along the way were frantically heading for the wide open spaces, out of the line of fire. Bullets kept smacking into the Packard.

Tuffy said, "I think it's time I was heard from."

I heartily endorsed this idea and he began to fire at John. The speedometer needle climbed to eighty before it and half the instrument panel were blown away. I heard strange sounds coming from the back seat, darted a glance around in time to see Tuffy flying to the floor, heels up and kicking. I thought John had got him and began to curse. Then I heard grumbling. Up rose Tuffy from the floor, wiping the blood from his face. "Those bastards can't do this to me," he said, whereupon he snatched up the shotgun and began booming away until it jammed. Then he emptied two pistols simultaneously, all the while voicing his indignations. What had happened was that a bullet had struck him on the forehead and deflected through the fabric top. The impact had slammed him to the floor and then another slug had blown off the heel of one shoe, which explained why he had kicked and jerked so.

Going through the Santa Monica tunnels John sneaked up—while Tuffy was reloading—and let go a burst at us. A furious burst. And Tuffy shouted, "The damn gas tank's on fire!" Sure enough, it was; flame was shooting out of it as it does from a flame thrower. "Will she blow up on us?" Tuffy asked, and I said I didn't think so. "Then we got nothing to worry about," Tuffy said. "Just keep going. You're doing fine."

We got run down a dead-end street and had to turn around and go back the way we'd come. We passed John at a literal distance of not more than ten feet. Again shots roared and metal ripped—but no one was hit. Not long thereafter, John's car conked out; Tuffy had blown half of its motor into kingdom come.

So we limped away to freedom.

Tuffy asked, "How much farther do you think this crate will go?"

I had no more than said "Not much farther" when the right front wheel crumpled. We climbed out and took one last look at the Packard. It was a smoking, burning, bullet-riddled wreck.

"We'll leave the shotgun behind," I said. "It'd draw too much heat if we took it. Can't tell how far we may have to walk or who'll be looking."

Tuffy nodded agreement, wiping blood from his face. He took precisely one step, stumbled and winced in pain.

"What's wrong?"

"My ankle. It must be sprained." He lifted his foot and we saw then what the cop's bullet had done.

"Let that be a lesson to you for getting in the way of bullets," I admonished. "Here, I'll help you."

A couple of blocks away we encountered a man and his wife getting into their Ford sedan. I stepped around to the street side, pulled my gun and covered the man. "Get out," I said. "We want your car." The woman screamed, leaped from the car and ran, shouting "Help! Help!" at the top of her lungs. We ignored her. The man froze, speechless. (He was so frightened, we learned later, that he reported to the police the two bandits had stolen his Plymouth, a second car he owned, rather than his Ford.) I reached out and took the car keys from him, then said, "Start walking and keep walking!" With an effort, he did, jerkily, like an automaton. Sometimes the sight of a gun will have that effect.

We beat it for my place and got there without incident. Tuffy followed in my coupe while I drove the hot Ford to upper Glendale, where I left it.

Back at my apartment I treated Tuffy's scalp wound. "You got a hard head," I told him. "Otherwise you wouldn't have a head."

Tuffy grinned. "People been tellin' me how hard my head is for a long time. But this's the first time I realized having a hard head can be such an advantage."

With my help Tuffy hobbled down to the car. "Take the Ford home and come on back this afternoon." I handed him the car keys.

Then Tuffy remembered. "Hey," he said, "I still got all the money."

"Keep it. We can split later."

"All right. Take it easy."

"That's all I ever do is take it easy."

When I went back upstairs, Judy didn't ask any questions, perhaps for fear of the answers she would get. But the worry, the fear was in her eyes, in the tight, strained lines of her face.

When I kissed her she clung to me for a long time. I knew then, holding her, what a prize heel I was. Judy loved me so much she trusted me absolutely. I could do no wrong. But she knew—although I had never told her—what I was doing. I was breaking her heart. Still she fiercely loved me; still she fiercely wanted to believe in me.

Her slim fingers explored some holes she'd found in my coat— neat, round holes. Her eyes grew large with a terror that suddenly assumed tangible shape, chilling meaning.

"Must have ripped my coat," I said, grinning. Then I took off the coat and looked closely at those holes—four of them. And I hadn't been scratched! I was almost ready to believe I had a guardian angel. Perhaps Judy's unwavering love was keeping me from getting killed. What else could explain my incredible luck?

Judy looked up into my face, searchingly. "How much longer, Daddy?"

"Not much longer, Judy Honey," I reassured her. "Just a little while and then everything will be fine."

The next day's papers devoted considerable space to the gun fight. One account began: "Police of the metropolitan area loosened revolvers in their holsters and removed the safety on shotguns today as they followed a trail of armed robbery and screaming bullets, a trail which has been punctuated by a series of robberies and automobile thefts and which always leads back to Glendale. Detective Captain W. E. Hegi of the Glendale police said he is convinced that at least one of the gang of armed desperadoes who held up and robbed two deputy sheriffs early this month in Flintridge and who have since terrorized the entire southland lives in this city."

I thought of Judy and her question—*How much longer, Daddy?* I could hear her stirring around in the kitchen, humming as she prepared dinner. My presence, and the daylight, had driven off her fears. But I would have to leave; the darkness would return. All the night long Judy had slept fretfully and even as she slept she had held me tightly, as though if she clung to me physically I couldn't get away, nothing could happen to me. But much that was ugly and sudden and violent could happen to me. In the closet there was a coat with four bullet holes in it. I lit a cigarette, walked over to the front windows and looked down at the street three stories below. It was a dark, gray, gloomy day, but children were happily at play. I thought again of my beloved Judy and how much she had wanted to have a baby—"A teeny, weeny little Chessman, Daddy," she had coaxed. I thought how I had insisted we wait. Surely that had been wise, for now the end was near, and it might not be a pleasant end.

• 22 •

The Beginning of the End

Perhaps the malignant gods had worked out the denouement in advance, in a moment of inspired malice. Again, perhaps Saint Nick, the patron saint of thieves, had withdrawn his patronage, just to see what would happen.

We knew how hot we were. Our luck in escaping capture had been consistently, incredibly good. Every time we had turned around we had run into cops but, amazingly, we always had managed to fight our way out of their attempted custodial embrace, their traps. At the same time we had contrived to stay out of the morgue—no small feat. But we realized such luck couldn't last forever. If nothing else, the law of averages would catch up with us if we kept on recklessly pulling such heavy stuff. And when that happened we would find ourselves permanently buried either in some cemetery or in some penitentiary, some joint. "And there's no future in that," Tuffy pointed out, with irresistible logic.

So, after holding council, after debating the pros and cons of our future in the business of organized banditry, we called it quits. Just like that. I gathered up the guns and put them away. All except my own gun, that is. "We let the town cool off," I said. "From this day on we're out of business." Unfortunately, Fate wasn't content with such a simple, direct decision.

There were complications, dramatic and violent ones. For long, unquiet months—through the summer, the fall, most of the winter— I had been living a Jekyll-Hyde life. Student by day, bandit by night.

Hijacker and gunfighter on occasion. I had been, of necessity and yet by choice, many things to many people, and to myself as well. Now—this was late January of the year 1941—there was promise that these many Chessmans soon would find it possible to fuse into one. The R.C.A.F. was but days away. I had logged all the flying time I needed or wanted. In not more than two or three weeks I planned to be in Canada—all arrangements had been made and I expected no difficulties to arise with my probation officer—and within a couple of months after going to Canada I would be in England. Instead of shooting it out with cops I would be shooting it out with Jerry.

I had saved and saved for my mother's operation. Unhappily, the joint venture with Tuffy, Bill and the others had brought us only modest financial return—and a million dollars' worth of heat. For a time, however, we—or at least I—had gotten bullheaded. An unbelievable run of bad luck, and having cops always getting in our way, had only made us rashly angry. Repeatedly, we had had it impressed upon us that the road we followed led not to riches but to prison or the grave. Soon we reached the point where we were unable to justify a continuation of our collective effort without frankly admitting that our goal was merely to raise as much irrational, violent, dramatic, suicidal hell as possible for as long as possible, and that wasn't our goal. It never had been, notwithstanding my own proclivities.

Later I was asked why I had got into such serious trouble. What had been my "reason"? When I attempted to explain, I was told, "Why, that's not a good reason at all!" Maybe not, but it was a good enough reason. Such virtuous belittling of motivation, moreover, proves nothing. I doubt if, by accepted social standards, the youngster who clashes with the law ever has a "good reason" for doing so. But the indubitable fact remains that delinquency rates continue to rise alarmingly. And they will continue to do so until society itself, in turn, is able to give the delinquent boy or girl a positive and compelling "reason" why he or she should abstain at all costs from turning to crime. Certainly menacing or belittling the delinquent won't turn him away from crime, as my own case demonstrates.

The end was near. My worlds, the revealed and some of the hidden ones, were about to collide. My bold dreams would soon go up in a puff of smoke—gunsmoke. Sensing this, I checked out of school a few days before the end of the semester. The next day the Duke double-crossed me. However, I virtually invited this doublecross. My business relations with the Duke, who was becoming a big wheel in the local rackets, had been truly lucrative, but we were far from palsy-walsy. The Duke knew I had acquired a pile of money and that I was ever anxious to increase the size of that pile. In a moment of apparent magnanimity, he offered to cut me in on a deal which would permit me to double whatever I was willing to invest. I asked for details. All I had to do, I was told, was go to a certain place, purchase a certain something, return to Hollywood, park in a certain parking lot, walk away, leaving what I had purchased in my car, and then return in a specified time and find a certain amount of money in the glove compartment. "Of course," said the Duke, "there's a helluva risk involved. Me, I don't want no personal connection with the deal. Too dangerous." I snapped at the bait, investing almost every dime I possessed.

From the start, I ran into trouble—all kinds of trouble. And all kinds of human vultures, hyenas, jackals. It was a dirty, tough piece of business. I didn't like it, but once I started I saw it through. I got back to Hollywood. I made a phone call. Then I waited the half hour I'd been instructed before I returned to my car. I looked in the glove compartment. There was the money, a large bundle of it—operation money, bill money, R.C.A.F. money. And when I looked up there were three mean-looking jokers with equally mean-looking guns. They took the money and a gun from my shoulder holster and walked off without so much as saying thanks. I jerked out the little .25 automatic I kept hidden in the car and emptied it at them, into them, but futilely. They got away.

In a rage, I drove to the apartment at top speed. I grabbed and loaded the two largest calibered revolvers I could find in our former arsenal and went hunting for the Duke. I finally ran across one of his stooges. This individual swore he had no idea where I could find his double-crossing boss until I had massaged his head with a pistol butt for the third time. Then, suddenly, his memory returned. I took him along with me. We walked in on the Duke and a bodyguard, taking them both by surprise. I disarmed the bodyguard and made him and the stooge get down on their hands and knees against the wall.

Without saying a word, I began to give my friend a vicious pistol whipping. All the while he kept pleading with me to tell him what this was all about and begging me not to beat him any more. I beat him bloodily insensible before I quit. Then I kicked him back to consciousness. I took what money I found in his wallet. I told him, speaking softly, "You made a mistake, Duke. You used me as long as I was useful and then you tried to doublecross me. But it isn't going to work. I get my money back or you don't leave this room alive."

The Duke swore he had had nothing to do with my being hijacked. I whacked him some more for fibbing. He wasn't a very pretty sight when I got through with him. "Do I get my money back or don't I, Duke? I'm giving you a minute to make up your mind."

The Duke lay on the floor, bleeding, moaning. Thirty seconds passed. I cocked the gun in my right hand. "All right," the Duke whispered, "you get the money. How much do you want?"

"Only what your boys took me for." I named the figure and then let him put through a phone call to make arrangements for one of his runners to come with the money on the double. When he hung up I said, "That's using your head, Duke."

"You made a mistake, Chess," the Duke said, dabbing at his bloody face with a handkerchief. "You shouldn't have done this to me."

"You made a mistake too, Duke. You shouldn't have tried that doublecross."

Then I got the least bit careless and my carelessness almost cost me my life. The Duke's bodyguard and his stooge jumped me when I gave them permission to do what they could for their too-smart boss. The bodyguard, a muscular ape, almost broke my arm with a sap. The stooge threw a chair. When the fight started the Duke made a run for it. He got away. The bodyguard got hold of his gun and we broke a couple of caps at each other. Somebody yelled cops. I ducked out a back way and took off. All night long I looked vainly for the Duke.

He was one lucky gangster I didn't find him. Every place I stopped at I left word that I wanted my money or his life.

Friday night an unctuous emissary of his phoned. Would I forget the whole thing if I got the money I believed I had coming? Yes, I would. All right, I'd get it. When? It would be mailed to me, not later than Monday. Why not today? Because the Duke was in a pretty bad way. He had been put to bed in a private sanatarium. His doctor had given him a strong sedative and wouldn't allow him to discuss business affairs with anyone, and it was the Duke who would have to approve release of the money.

I said, warningly, "If this is some kind of stall or run around, I guarantee you . . ."

The emissary interrupted. "We're on the up and up. These kind of beefs are bad for business. We don't want trouble. We . . ."

Then I interrupted. "O.K., O.K. You're all just a lot of honest businessmen who want to do right. Fine. And all I want's my money and when I get it that's the last you hear of me unless you people decide you want to play some more. So now you've got until next Monday night to phone and tell me the money's in the mail. If I don't get it by then I promise you I'll try to run every last one of you scummy animals out of town."

I hung up. My promise wasn't an empty one and I didn't throw out that weight just because I liked to play tough. It was the only language these big shot "businessmen" understood. They would push you around unless they were convinced you couldn't be pushed and that you would start shooting if they tried to push. I had the reputation for being a wild, crazy kid with a gun, and I wanted them to think I was willing to live up to that reputation.

The first thing we needed was money, so we went after it. We robbed seven or eight places of business in quick succession. Liquor stores. Markets. Gas stations. We did very well using this approach to the monetary problem until a prowl car happened to drive up on us *in flagrante delicto*. Bullets began to fly almost immediately. Tuffy, obstinately refusing to leave until he obtained the money, didn't return to the car for a good fifteen seconds after I had honked the horn in warning. That gave John Law an excellent opportunity to move into firing position. And John showed us he wasn't one to pass any bets. Nevertheless, we got under way unscathed, with John panting eagerly in hot pursuit. A solitary bullet slammed harmlessly into the car.

"I think I can shake 'em," I said. "If I can't, knock out the back window and we'll blow the bastards back where they came from."

I rammed the Ford into corner after corner and was succeeding in giving our quick-triggered pursuers the slip when, on a sliding turn, apparently from too much stress, a right front tire blew. The Ford banged into the curb, I heard something snap and the steering wheel shuddered and jerked violently.

What happened next belonged in a nightmare. Suspecting the worst, I spun the wheel. It turned and the Ford didn't. Of its own accord, the Ford straightened out after a fashion and, since my foot still rested heavily on the accelerator, picked up speed. We were wobbling and bouncing along in what most appropriately can be described as a remarkable rendition of a vehicular kootch dance. In the process we grazed several parked cars. And all the while I was turning the steering wheel in one direction while the Ford proceeded in another.

We came suddenly to a cross street and the unbelievable occurred. Strictly of its own volition, the Ford made a perfect right-hand turn —but not out of the goodness of its black, vengeful heart. Indeed, no! For after making the turn the Ford aimed itself with diabolic accuracy—and, I am convinced, with malice aforethought—at a thick, squat palm tree. Doing at least fifty, we rammed the palm tree head on.

All three of us were involuntarily ejected from the Ford in a highly unconventional and extremely rapid fashion. I never have been quite sure about the precise routes taken by Tuffy and Little Andy. I missed going through the windshield when I caromed off the steering wheel and other unknown objects, and flew out an open window on the driver's side of the car. I then plowed, face first, into a front lawn and eventually came to a leisurely stop.

There was a burst of gunfire. Tuffy jerked me to my feet. One of the cops in the prowl car had let go at us as they bore down on us. We ran (I staggered) to a back yard. I remember seeing a fence. It shimmered and swam before my eyes. I felt myself start to float.

"You guys get going," I muttered. "I can't make it."

They both wanted to stay. I shouted, "Goddamit, get going or we'll all get killed!"

Clutching my gun, I turned and began to stumble in what I thought was the direction of the cops. I wobbled. My head spun. I couldn't track. I hardly knew up from down. A gun roared; then another. (One of the cops, I was later to learn, had blown Little Andy's gun out of his hand in true wild West style.) I fired back in the direction of the flashes. "Come on, you dirty bastards," I screamed hoarsely, "let's play!"

I lurched forward and the whole world turned blacker. I stumbled sideways, against a wall of a house right at a point where a chimney jutted out. I began to sink to the ground. The whole universe was spinning crazily.

Down the driveway came a cop, gun in hand, advancing cautiously. He passed not three feet from me and I couldn't even raise the hand that held my gun. My arms just wouldn't work. Even Hate couldn't make them work. The cop should have seen me. He didn't!

"They got away!" a voice shouted. Both cops ran back to their prowl car and sped off. I grinned. I was down on my knees and still sinking. "Pray, Chessman!" I said, and then flopped over, awkwardly. Still I didn't pass out. A tiny part of my mind remained conscious.

I stuck my tongue out, tasting the wet grass between the cement. Perhaps a minute passed. I managed to get to my feet on the third try.

Concussion is like being on a cheap binge, with something special added. You're high in more ways than one and you're not sure whether all those roaring noises are originating outside or inside your head.

A three-foot fence separated the yard I was in from the adjoining one. I walked into it full speed ahead, jackknifed, and let the law of gravity deposit me in a heap on the other side. I crossed a street. I made my way incautiously and erratically through several more back yards. Two or three (or four?) blocks from where I'd started I came to a school and entered its play yard through an unlocked gate, in search of a drinking fountain. I found one. Just as I did, I heard gunfire, vicious bursts of it, and ran in the direction from which I thought it had come. I collided with the high wire fence surrounding the school grounds, tried to climb the fence and couldn't. I wept with frustration, certain there was no time to go back to the gate. Tuffy and Little Andy needed help right then. I was sure of that.

But they already were beyond immediate help. They had got away clean but they'd made a mistake, almost a fatal one. Little Andy had a useless hand; a cop's bullet had ripped through it. Tuffy was holding a match, cupping it to Andy's cigarette, when a prowl car whizzed around a corner. Flashlight in one hand, gun in the other, a cop jumped from the car and ordered both of them to put up their hands. Tuffy didn't comply. He reached for his gun. The cop unloaded his revolver into him at point-blank range. Tuffy went down, still clawing for his gun. He managed to get it out only to have the cop step on his hand, then kick the gun away. Tuffy tried to get up and fight—fight bullets with his bare hands. He got to his knees before he collapsed and was handcuffed. The cops also handcuffed Little Andy, who had tried to help Tuffy, and shoved him into the back seat of the police car.

Waiting for the ambulance, Tuffy lay where he had fallen, ringed by a crowd of curious which had quickly gathered. It was reasonable to conclude he was dying. The cop asked him if there was anything he wanted to say. "Yeah," Tuffy said, "how about a drink of water and a cigarette?"

A woman in the crowd said, "Don't give the dirty rat nothin'."

Tuffy grinned. The cop gave him a cigarette, lit it for him and Tuffy said, "Thanks." Then the cop said he didn't think Tuffy should drink anything because the water might not be good for him, what with his belly full of holes.

And I stood at the school fence and wept and pounded the wire and cursed. Some sixth sense told me what had happened. I promised myself that if Tuffy and Little Andy lived, I would get them out. I would

storm Hell itself to get them. They were my friends and that explained everything. But then I remembered and I sneered at myself;
here I was promising I would get them out and I couldn't even climb
a fence.

I was on the wrong side of the fence! "You're on the wrong side
of the fence." How many times had I been told that? Now here I
was, literally on the wrong side of the fence, half goofy with concussion.

I called myself some unflattering names. Tuffy had never belonged
in this business in the first place. I'd brought him in. Then, sensibly,
he'd been ready to call it quits and I'd talked him into accompanying
us on that last senseless shoplifting tour. "Hell," I'd said, "come on
along for the ride." Unwittingly I'd sealed his fate. And you couldn't
explain to the cops or a judge that Tuffy really wasn't at fault. Tuffy
wouldn't want you to try. He'd insist on riding the beef with you. The
same was true of Little Andy. They didn't offer any excuses for themselves and they didn't want anybody offering any for them.

Well, I had to act and quickly. Tim's place wouldn't be safe any
longer, not as soon as they started tying us together, and that was
something the cops would succeed in doing in a hurry. I pocketed the
gun and washed the blood and mud from my face and hair at the
drinking fountain.

I staggered from the school yard. I dodged prowl cars. My head
cleared a little and I spotted a parked car. I formulated a plan when
I saw its tail-light wink.

I jerked open the door on the driver's side and displayed the gun.
Two youngsters, around sixteen, were seated inside. "Start the car,"
I told the one behind the wheel.

"I can't," he said, and explained why: no car keys. The car belonged
to his parents. His parents were inside *that* house, visiting the other
boy's parents.

I marched the two boys down the driveway ahead of me and into
the house. Two couples were playing bridge, intently bidding their
hands. "Go sit down on that divan," I told the boys. Then I said,
"Pardon the interruption." When the foursome looked up, under-

standably startled at being suddenly confronted by a gun-wielding, bloody-faced intruder, I tried to put them at ease. "Please sit still. There's no need for alarm. No one is going to get hurt." I watched their reactions as I wiped the blood away from my left eye; the cut above the eye was bleeding again. My words seemed to be having a relaxing effect on the two couples. That was good. Maybe they would cooperate. Maybe there would be no trouble. "Who owns the Chevvy coupe out front?" I asked.

One of the men at the card table said he did.

"I want it. Throw me the keys." I held out my left hand.

The man stood up, hesitated. He looked at me, not belligerently but with something bothering him.

"Well?"

"I use the car in my work," he told me. "There are some maps and other papers in it I would hate to lose. May I get them?"

The request was reasonable enough. "Sure. Sure you can get them. But no tricks." I told the others, "The rest of you stay seated," and they nodded they would. I apologized for my intrusion and then marched the owner out to his Chevvy. He removed the maps and papers he wanted.

"Long as you're out here, start it up for me, will you?"

He started the Chevvy, then got out. I got in.

He said, "Take good care of it, won't you?"

"Mister," I assured him, "I'll treat your car like a brother. And as soon as you get back in the house you phone the cops and report this. They'll see that you get your car back almost before you know it's gone. Of course don't blame me if they get all excited and shoot it full of holes. I really hope, for your sake, that doesn't happen."

I drove off, leaving the owner of the Chevrolet standing at the curb, holding his maps and papers and wondering, I imagine, what strange sort of bird it was who had clouted his car. Sure, it would be a shame if the cops used his shiny new car for target practice, now wouldn't it?

Again I wiped the blood away from my left eye and thought about the box score for the day.

And not a dime to show for it, only a concussion and various contusions, abrasions and complications. The money we'd taken had been scattered from hell to breakfast when the Ford rammed the palm tree.

Crime doesn't pay. You're on the wrong side of the fence. Sonny boy, keep on like you're going and you'll wind up in the gas chamber.

Or the morgue.

No R.C.A.F.

Just the usual dime-novel ending.

I wanted a cigarette and cigarettes were obtainable if the contents of dreams weren't. I wanted a cigarette and I didn't have one, so I jerked the Chevvy into the curb in front of a supermarket that was still open. I entered the store on rubber legs.

"Coupla packs of Camels," I told the clerk, who eyed me strangely.

"Little accident," I said. The clerk handed me the two packs of cigarettes and I reached into a pocket of my pants for change. None. Irritating. Embarrassing. So I opened my coat and exposed the gun. "Robbery," I said. "Hand me the bills as though you're making change."

The clerk handed across forty or fifty dollars, which I pocketed along with the cigarettes. "Now the rest of it," I said. Automatically you say that, because there's almost always a plant. The clerk reached under the counter and came up with a cigar box. I took the box, said, "Thanks," and walked out, unhurriedly. If the clerk had had a gun he could have shot me dead when I turned my back. But right then clerks with guns were the least of my worries.

I drove off. I pulled into the first service station I saw, pocketed the money I took from the cigar box and washed up in the men's room. Then I combed my hair. The mirror on the wall told me I looked half human. But I didn't feel half human. I didn't feel any part human. My eyes didn't want to focus. My head continued to expand—and contract.

I had to hurry. I had to get to Tim's. I booted the Chevvy out into traffic. When I saw a liquor store I double-parked and bought a pint of whisky and took two or three big slugs as soon as I got back to the car. I was hoping the whisky would help. It didn't. I started seeing double, and flung the bottle.

I thought about Judy as I pushed the Chevvy along Verdugo Road. Sure, all I had to do was go get her and take off, make a run for it. Of course that would be involving her, risking her life, and running out on friends. But who would worry about such minor points of ethics in this kind of crisis? It would be a cinch to rationalize making a run for it with Judy. A little devil told me that Judy would want to be with me no matter what the risk and that in this variety of jackpot a guy should look out for his own skin first.

But I held the nose of the Chevvy pointed toward Tim's and kept the accelerator pedal rammed against the floorboard. And damn the rationalizing and all the little devils in the world! Groggy as I was, I still wasn't ready to run. I still wasn't ready to expose Judy to police bullets or to the women's quarters of a jail.

The street was dark, quiet. I drove slowly by the parked car. It didn't look like a police car. I kicked in the clutch and revved the motor. "All right, you bastards," I shouted, "I know you're there!" Still nothing. No movement. No sign of bulls. At an intersecting street I U-turned and drove back, kicking off the headlights. I glided to a stop at the curb in front of Tim's, clutched my gun, waited. Five seconds. Ten seconds. Fifteen seconds. Nothing. I alighted, walked as swiftly as I could along the driveway to the rear of the front house, then cut between it and the little place in the rear.

I knocked. No response. I tried the doorknob; it turned. I shoved open the door, peered into the darkness. "Tim?" Nothing. No answer. "Bill!" Silence. I felt for and found the light switch. I squinted against the sudden blaze of light. The place was a shambles.

And no Tim, no Bill. I guessed the truth, but not all of it.

The bulls had been here. They had gone to the front house. Tim's mother had called him. The bulls asked Tim about me. I wasn't there, Tim said. The bulls wanted to see for themselves. So they came around to this little place here in the rear, walked in unannounced and found Bill in bed. Taken by surprise, Bill sat up and glared at them.

"We want to question you," Detective Fred Bovier of the Glendale police told Bill. "Better get up and get dressed."

For reply, Bill whipped a snub-nosed heavy-caliber revolver out from under the covers and thrust it against Bovier's abdomen, squeezing the trigger. At the same instant the detective grabbed for the gun, his hand closing behind the hammer. For a few seconds there was an intense struggle. Then Detective William Weaver drew his own gun and slammed Bill on the head with the gun butt until Bill relaxed his grip on the snub-nosed revolver and had it jerked from his hand.

Bill and Tim were handcuffed. The cops were on fire at Tim for not warning them about Bill. They ransacked the place and found another gun—one of the two taken from the radio-car bulls almost a month earlier. Then they knew what really hot suspects they had. The pieces were beginning to fall together. Bill and Tim were rushed to the Glendale jail. They were told: "This guy you call Tuffy is dying and you two are lucky you're not dead. We caught another one with Tuffy and we got a lead on two more of your gang. But Chessman got away. What we want to know is, where can we find him?"

Bill swore he didn't have any idea, but Tim, separately questioned, threatened, growled at, said, defiantly, "He'll come back to get me and Bill if he can."

The police rushed reinforcements to Tim's place. Cops with sub-machine guns were strategically located. A battery of recreation lights from the back yard of an apartment house next door was turned to face the front house at Tim's, then extinguished.

Ironically, the trap the police set had been baited by their quarry himself; all they had to do was wait to spring it. They waited, ever so patiently. . . .

I snapped off the light and, gun in hand, stood in the doorway, straining to hear some tell-tale sound, to catch some suspicious movement. I remained frozen there for a full two minutes. The cops outwaited me. I pocketed my gun, not wanting to be waving it at any chance passers-by, stepped out the doorway and began walking along the driveway to the street.

Then it happened. A blinding blaze of light. A glimpse of armed men crouching in the surrounding darkness, waiting to pounce. A voice ringing out, sharp and clear and assured:

"All right, *Mr.* Chessman, put up your hands!"

23

Deus Ex Machina—with a Twist

The bulls had us racked up or on the run and the newspapers had a field day. Headlines shouted: L.A. "BOY BANDIT" GANG ROUNDED UP. LOS ANGELES DEVELOPS ITS OWN DEAD END KIDS. POLICE GUNS WRITE FINIS TO YOUTHFUL CRIME SPREE. *Gunfights wreck boy bandit gang; 2 shot, 3 jailed, 2 others at large.* "Youth shot by police is near death." "Girl, 16, Companion Seized in Young Bandit Roundup." *Alleged boy bandits joke as high bail set on 39 counts.*

The stories beneath those headlines were the usual breathless, excited stuff ground out for such occasions:

"Five tough young eggs . . . carnival of crime . . . swaggered into municipal court to be arraigned on 39 felony counts . . . charged with various counts of robbery, assault and attempted murder . . . Chessman . . . assertedly the leader of the gang . . . held for lack of $60,000 bail . . . amazing way in which they had organized to stage a reign of crime . . . widespread activities of a junior crime club . . ."

Plus all the details, real and imagined. And with great emphasis, always, on how police had "smashed" this boy bandit gang, this "juvenile crime empire." Nor was there a lack of pictures to accompany the big, black headlines and the adjective-laden stories. Pictures of the "suspects," "the young desperadoes," "the tough young eggs." Pictures of their captors, the cops. Pictures of the "arsenal," the many guns taken from the gang. Pictures of the demolished, bullet-riddled Ford.

And then came the inevitable editorializing, the inevitable articles on Los Angeles' "young crime wave." *

"Who," one of the inevitable editorials demanded, "is responsible for the abnormal situation which makes mere children the small counterparts of Dillingers and Buchalters?"

The answer: "Nobody—and everybody."

Getting back to us and our plight: Tuffy didn't die. An emergency operation was performed on him and he was then placed in a high-custody room in the jail ward section of the General Hospital. His shattered hand repaired, Little Andy was locked in an adjoining room. Tim and I were first questioned at one outlying police station before being taken downtown to the Hall of Justice for more questioning. Those inquisitorial periods got pretty rugged. Most cops aren't at all pleased with young gangsters who slug, beat, fight, shoot it out with, disarm and appropriate the squad cars of their brother officers. Be assured this isn't something I inferred from vague rumblings; it's something I was told, monosyllabically, emphatically and with an impressive show of aroused indignation. Cops are usually objective and impersonal when dealing with crimes against the citizenry, but crimes against cops—well, that decidedly is another matter. That's a personal affront, a challenge, heresy of the worst sort.

Tim was the first one to be questioned privately. They took him to a small back room where eight oversized dicks, a police stenographer and a chief of detectives impatiently awaited him. They growled at him

* If the implications weren't so tragic, this excited, periodic rediscovery of the juvenile delinquency problem by the press would be amusing. The problem is always good for a splash, but never a penetrating sustained drive. The same huge metropolitan daily which ran the above series of articles in March of 1941 was doing the same thing during April, 1953, this last time in knock-down, drag-out competition with another Los Angeles daily. And every time these articles appear they almost invariably ascribe a new cause or new causes for juvenile delinquency, which reflects a certain admirable originality on the part of staff writers but hardly a devotion to the facts. Since the problem of juvenile delinquency is presently a greater problem than ever, one must question whether such articles ever do any good.

a couple of times, crowded around him, and he began to talk. He told what he knew.

Bill was next. He volunteered nothing, cautiously admitted no more than appeared certain the bulls already knew.

I was last. And I was their boy. The chief of detectives, a tall, thin, sharp-faced gentleman, was a picture of grinning, breezy self-confidence. "Well, Chessman, I guess you want to tell us all about it." And the eight big bulls nodded their respective heads, as though that indeed must be my wish. The steno had his pencil poisèd expectantly over his notebook. Ten pair of eyes were on me.

"Tell you all about what?" I countered blandly, outwardly all grinning, polite contempt, for cops and their inquisitions and their smugness—and for what I knew came next. Inwardly, however, I was tense, wary, very angry.

I was told: All about everything, from the beginning. About—and then the chief glibly rattled off what he knew or guessed concerning our criminal doings, which was much too much. But still, significantly, there was also much the omniscient chief didn't know—and, thank God, he hadn't mentioned Judy or Tuffy's wife!

So I said, flatly, "I prefer not to say anything until I've had a chance to talk with an attorney."

"Why not?" demanded the chief.

"Because I think I need legal advice very badly in the face of such serious accusations."

"Here's eight good men," the chief said, indicating the dicks with a sweep of his hand. "What's wrong with getting advice from them?"

"Nothing," I said. "Nothing at all. Except that they're cops."

The chief jumped to his feet. "What's wrong with cops?" he roared angrily.

"I don't think I should answer *any* questions until I talk to an attorney and get his advice."

The chief said, "Do you mean to sit there and deny that you were one of the three men who . . ."

I broke in. "I'm not denying and I'm not admitting anything until I'm allowed to get some legal advice from an attorney."

The chief glared at me. "I can see we aren't going to get anywhere by *talking* to this guy," he said ominously. Then he walked out, slamming the door behind him.

"The chief's right," said a dick. "This punk don't wanta be reasonable. He don't wanta talk."

"He thinks he's tough," said another, who grinned at me as he approached the chair where I was sitting. "He's a cop-hater. Ain't you, kid?"

"Why, no," I said. "I love cops. Just the sight of a uniform gives me a thrill."

"Shut up!"

"Don't be a wise guy!"

I loved cops, the cops loved me. Right then my feelings weren't too selective. I didn't try very hard to keep in mind that big, burly cops who question you in back rooms are in the minority. At the moment I was perfectly content to hate all cops with a fine impartiality. Right then I needed the hate.

An hour or so after this last inquisitorial session got under way, we were booked into the county jail on suspicion of virtually every crime known to man. As soon as this booking was completed, we were taken to the jail's "little green room" and the questioning got under way again. Another contingent of detectives was there to see what they could see, as it were. This group, however, was more amiable, more agreeable. The fine edge of official indignation had worn off. After all, we were in custody and they seemingly had enough evidence and charges to bury us, figuratively if not literally. Thus, law enforcement had triumphed, hadn't it?

"Here, Chess, have a cigarette."

"Sure."

"Light."

"Thanks."

"You know, you boys did give us a headache for quite a while."

"Yeah, come to think of it, I guess we did. Well, now it's your turn to give us one." I grinned wryly. "Or maybe I should say it's your turn to give me a worse one than I already got."

"Relax. With me this is just a job. We got a lot of unsolved robberies and other crimes on the books and we believe your bunch is responsible for quite a few of them. What we'd like to find out is, which ones did you commit and which ones didn't you commit."

"And the more we tell you the more charges we get filed against us."

"Not necessarily. You see, Chess, you know and I know that we got enough on all of you already to put you out of circulation for a long, long time if that was all we were interested in. But it isn't. We're interested in solving crimes, in finding out what you did and what you didn't do. Besides, we realize that all of you are just kids and we can make it a lot easier for your bunch if you all cooperate."

I nodded I'd heard. Then I asked, "How's Tuffy?"

"He's going to be O.K.," the cop assured me.

"And Little Andy?"

"He's doing all right too."

Off-handedly, the cop added, "And we don't intend to bother your girl friends."

I stiffened.

"Relax, Chess, relax," the cop said. "We know they really aren't in this thing with you."

"You seem to know a lot," I said.

"That's right, Chess. We always got people ready to tell us something. You know that."

Yes, I knew that. I knew the cop was unquestionably right. There were always people ready to tell the cops something, for one reason or another. Because they were professional finks. Because they were good, civic-minded citizens. Because they were trying to sell somebody else out to save themselves. Because the cops scared or third-degreed something out of them.

So far I had admitted no more than my right name. The tougher, the more rugged the back-room sessions, the less communicative I became. According to my code it was unthinkably wrong to betray friends and confederates; hence, stubbornly defiant, I had refused to "talk." I did, however, want to see that all of us got off as lightly as possible. And being defiant or acting smart certainly couldn't help any of us, not when the police were willing to treat us reasonably. Moreover, I was willing to take the weight on my shoulders, which was where most of it rightfully belonged.

So Chessman smiled and became as seemingly affable as his inquisitors.

Yes, I said, I was sure, so long as it did not involve turning against one another, that we would all be willing to cooperate. Yes, cooperating was the most sensible thing to do. We were then told that newspaper reporters and photographers wanted a crack at us, and as evidence of our willingness to do the right thing we posed for pictures with the cops. It was the way the newspapermen wanted it. The reporters asked a million questions. As politely as possible, we avoided giving more than vague and general answers. We said we preferred not to make a more detailed reply until the police had brought us all together and permitted us to talk it over between ourselves. The detectives agreed not to question us further until this was done.

The next morning Tim, Bill and I were driven under guard to the prison ward of the General Hospital and allowed to talk with Tuffy and Little Andy in private. Once greetings were exchanged, I got right down to business. "Look, you people, we have a problem; how to avoid growing old in one of The Man's prisons. I think we can solve that problem by keeping the gendarmes from wanting our scalps. So now we quote cooperate unquote. Without going overboard, we help the cops clear their books and they don't try to bury us too deep. Let me do most of the talking. Agreed?"

It was. At our signal, the detectives filed into the room. Tuffy, still far from ambulatory, was propped up in bed and we grouped around him. Deputy Sheriff John Toohey read off a long list of crimes which the police believed we may have committed. He read slowly and occasionally we would interrupt to ask a question about the manner in which the crime had been committed or what may have been said at the time of commission.

Then we would say, "You can chalk that one up to us."

Or, "No, that's one we didn't pull."

By the time the end of the list was reached, we had tentatively admitted to the commission of approximately thirty robberies and eight car thefts. We politely hedged when some of the gun fights with the cops were mentioned.

Then I said, "Now that we've kept our part of the bargain where does that leave us? Little Andy here, for example, isn't really involved at all, except maybe technically. And neither is Tim. What are you going to do with them?"

"If your story holds together after we've checked it and after we've run all of you through a show-up, then they've got nothing to worry about," I was assured. "We're not out to send any innocent men to prison. We don't do business that way."

And the cops proved to be as good as their word. Little Andy was allowed to plead guilty to one count of second degree burglary, a crime unrelated to anything "the gang" had done. No new charges were filed against Tim. He was sent to San Quentin for violation of probation only. (The cops carefully kept from us the fact Tim had talked, telling what he knew. Tim swore he had told nothing.) The Rabbit, soon apprehended after being fingered by Tim, was released for lack of evidence and later rearrested and sent to prison on a charge with which we had no connection. Similarly, a shoplifting partner whom Tim had also named was committed to prison for a crime in which we had not figured. Several of the others involved with us were never even arrested. These were mostly friends and confederates about whom Tim, fortunately, had no knowledge. Most importantly, the girls were never bothered, never questioned. The press never learned of their existence.

Immediately after our talk with the cops in the jail ward, there followed another lively session with the impatiently waiting reporters and photographers. More posed pictures. More stock, loaded questions. As spokesman for the group, I couldn't resist the opportunity to give the gentlemen of the Fourth Estate their money's worth, since I had already had a chance to glance over some of their sensationalized accounts of our activities and capture. For all their worldly wisdom, their glib sophistication, not a one of them seemed to realize that, with a coldly calculated objectivity, I was pulling their leg. I was—and this is an old, old device—focusing attention on myself and an ever-smaller number of our group, thus turning attention away from those who could be helped, cleared first. Slowly but surely, one by one, we would, so far as possible, take the weight off ourselves, and meanwhile the newspapers would happily and enthusiastically be thumping the remainder. We were more than willing to have the story of us and our activities molded to fit the stereotyped pattern—the familiar Procrustean bed. After a couple of sessions with the press, we became, in public print, such stock, standardized characters in such a stock, crime-doesn't-pay plot that we lost our individuality and hence our significance.

Typically, the newspapers reported that Chessman, "as spokesman for 'the gang,'" admitted commission of various crimes "boldly and without apparent remorse." And how incredibly easy it was to explain all! Let us look at the newspaper version of my explanation. Bill and I "were in Road Camp No. 7 in Las Flores Canyon. Auto stealing. You pick up ideas there. We did. And here we are."

Then Tim, described by the newspapers as "a dark-haired kid whom the [others] obviously sought to protect," is quoted as adding: "The rest of us were in Camp No. 1 in Soledad Canyon. Same rap. I've known Chessman all my life. We went to school together. So when we got out last autumn, we just naturally drifted together."

"But why rob?

" 'Lucrative,' said Chessman briefly."

Thus was narrated how "Police . . . smashed the last vestiges of a 'boy bandit' gang which owed its inception to whispered conferences at two County Jail road camps." (The newspapers made not so much as passing mention of the fact that Tim and I had previous long records as juvenile delinquents, that we had served time in the state's reform schools, and hence that the program then in effect for reforming the young delinquent was, at least so far as we were concerned, a conspicuous failure. What, then, of that much-praised "system which strikes at the undeveloped roots of potential criminal careers"?)

The newspaper accounts continued: "Two boys remain at large, authorities said, but their apprehension was expected soon.

"With this swift action by the law, the little band reached the end of an astounding trail of holdups, running gun duels with police, and automobile thieving. City and county law-enforcement agencies joined in compiling the docket, extending back several months, on the young 'mob' . . ."

But still no penetrating analysis of *why* the young mob, nor any objective reporting about it or its members. Like the iceberg, nine-tenths of who and what we were and what we had done remained beneath the surface, unseen, unreckoned. And there it stayed. We put on our masks; we played our assigned roles. Just a group of impulsive, talkative boys who had tried, rather ingeniously, to make a fast buck and failed. And our failure was rewarded. We were the beneficiaries of the *post hoc* fallacy that forever is advanced each time a gang, juvenile or adult, is "smashed." The faulty reasoning goes like this: "Hereafter potential criminals will have clear, stern warning they cannot possibly win if they turn to crime; therefore, on account of our smashing of this gang we have proved crime doesn't pay."

But this is specious, idle proof. This cops-and-robbers approach to crime is at best an expensive and dangerous consolation prize. Left unanswered, or only superficially and misleadingly answered, is the question: What makes youngsters willing and eager to buck the odds, to fight their society, recklessly to gamble their lives in the face of such "proof"? And what of the gangs and individual criminals never captured, of the crimes never solved? We know that only 13 per cent of the nation's criminals ever wind up in jail.

Thus, in this light, how does such unpenetrating and stereotyped cops-and-robbers, you-can't-win, no-matter-how-smart-they-are-they always-end-up-in-jail reporting help society and those agencies concerned with the administration of justice? The answer, of course, is that it doesn't help; rather it definitely and stupidly hinders.

Catching us and putting us in prison, in and by itself, solved absolutely nothing. It proved absolutely nothing. If we had been given twice or ten times as stiff a sentence this still would be indisputably true. It wouldn't have changed the fact that youngsters were then continuing and are now continuing to turn to crime in ever-increasing numbers. It wouldn't have explained why we had turned to crime. It wouldn't have deterred any of those youngsters following in our footsteps.

But the screaming headlines and the stories beneath those headlines led one to believe otherwise and hence made the work of law enforcement infinitely more difficult. The implication was that from the start we didn't have a chance, that the cops inevitably would catch up with us. The unrealistic inference to be drawn was that anyone, regardless of how clever he is, who picks up a pistol with robbery in mind inescapably will wind up behind bars, with the cops knowing every last crime he has committed. Accordingly, the public relaxes its vigilance. All is well. The police always catch the criminal. He is always convicted and put away. That is that.

Only it isn't.

To be sure, the 87 per cent of those committing crimes and escaping arrest are most happy with this situation, with these fictions by which society ignores or denies their predatory presence. But law enforcement isn't. It's handcuffed by the situation, the fictions. It's fully, keenly aware of its own limitations and of the fact that its job is to solve crimes as well as to catch criminals. It knows that convicting a criminal of some crime is important. But equally important is solving crimes. And a balance must be struck.

Conviction of just one robbery in most jurisdictions, particularly those with an indeterminate sentence law, permits society to imprison the offender as long as if he had been convicted of, say, twenty robberies. In California, for example, the punishment for first degree robbery is "not less than five years," and for second degree robbery "not less than one year," which means that the state's paroling and term-fixing agency can, in the exercise of its wide discretion, fix the term at natural life. Thus, while they may impress the public, multiple convictions rarely serve any useful purpose so far as maximum possible imprisonment is concerned. However, if run consecutively, they can greatly increase the minimum—and thus operate to defeat the very constructive purposes of the indeterminate sentence law. Both humane and economic considerations dictate that in the vast majority of cases society's goal must be to rehabilitate the offender and then return him to his community. Should law enforcement adopt a policy of endeavoring to "bury" every offender taken into custody, it would succeed only in jamming busy court calendars, in adding prohibitively to the bill the taxpayer must pay for the administration of justice, and in making it virtually impossible for the penologist to change the offender's attitude toward society and crime during the needlessly long (and, for the taxpayer, needlessly expensive) period of incarceration. Whether rightly or wrongly, the offender would be convinced that society's only interest in him is to take vengeance upon him.

The police know that most of those who commit the traditional offenses and who are caught haven't committed just one crime, one robbery or burglary or forgery or car theft, and they know they have a long list of unsolved crimes with only the vaguest description of the perpetrator in many instances. So they do the rational thing: they offer to file only a specified number of charges if the suspect will clear up for them all the crimes he has committed, and if he will aid them in recovering missing loot. If they didn't do this, the police would have an impossible task. Obviously most suspects would admit absolutely nothing if they knew that every admission would lead to the filing of another charge.

Tuffy, Bill and I were charged with an impressive number of robberies, as well as with one count of attempted murder, another of assault with a deadly weapon. Extremely high bail was set. The police worked feverishly to link Bill and me with a robbery-murder in Hollywood, but ultimately concluded we had had nothing to do with it. We hadn't. The newspapers played up our initial court appearances, had us swaggering into court. We pled not guilty. Two trial dates were set, one for each of two groups of charges. A nationally broad-cast "true" crime cases program dramatized the story of Los Angeles' boy bandit gang. The "High Power" tank where we were lodged had a radio and I was amazed by this "authentic" dramatization of our activities. At one point the script had me snarling savagely out of the side of my mouth, "All right, copper, where do you want it, in the head or the guts?"

Then came trial. Unfortunately, the case had been assigned to be tried before the same judge who had warned me that he would throw the book at me when he had put me on three years' probation, with the first six months to be served in the County Jail (road camp). My objections to being tried by this particular judge were overruled, a jury was called, and we were speedily convicted of four counts of first degree robbery. The district attorney's office then offered to let us plead guilty to one count of assault with a deadly weapon, with the understanding that if we did so—which we did—the remaining robbery charges, as well as the count of attempted murder, still scheduled for trial, would be dismissed. As soon as the guilty plea was entered and the dismissal order made, the judge sentenced us to three five to life terms and a one to ten term all to run consecutively, plus another five to life term to run concurrently. That added up to sixteen years to a possible four lifetimes in prison!

"Damn!" Tuffy softly exclaimed. "That's apt to keep us busy for a while!"

Bill grinned. "Let that be a lesson to you," he said, which was what, in effect, the judge had told us at the time of sentence.

We didn't cry, figuratively or literally, over the stiff jolts the judge had handed us. We didn't blame the other guy for what had happened. We had stood together and we had fallen together. Sure, we had failed, and to ourselves we admitted our failure. Well, now we would accept whatever the state had to hand out in the way of punishment. We wouldn't whine or cry or beg for mercy; we wouldn't try to excuse away what we had done. Instead we would look to the future and salvage as much as we could from it. We fully expected to find San Quentin a harsh, brutal, gray place. Well, we wouldn't let

The Joint, as it was called, beat us or defeat us. We'd do our time. We'd stick together and we'd get along. We weren't the swaggering, posing, tough-talking kind; neither were we the kind who could be shoved around, bulldozed or taken advantage of.

Tuffy and Tim were taken with a chain of prisoners on the long ride north to San Quentin a week before Bill and I were transported to the prison with a group of thirty-odd. The others followed in subsequent weeks. As soon as Bill and I exchanged our civilian clothing for prison garb, we had our heads shaved (a practice soon discontinued), were mugged, measured for Bertillon indexing, fingerprinted, and then assigned single cells in what was then the "Fish tank" section of the Old Prison. We spent slightly more than two weeks there, being interviewed by various institutional departments and were given thorough physical examinations. We were allowed the liberty of a small, fenced-in yard adjoining our cells, where we could walk, talk, sit in the sun and play checkers or chess, when we weren't being interviewed or examined. Tuffy, Tim, Bill and I spent most of our free time walking and talking about the future and what it might hold.

Ten days after my arrival at San Quentin, I celebrated my twentieth birthday and reflected, somewhat wryly, on that sixteen years to a possible four lifetimes birthday present I had given myself. Being healthy young animals, however, all of us regarded the prison years before us as an interesting challenge, not as a final, dreadful defeat.

When our initial detention period was up we were given "fish" (new man) job assignments, transferred to other cells in the big cell blocks and absorbed into the general population of this walled city of five thousand prisoners. We had begun serving our terms in earnest.

It seemed to me that at least half of the youngsters I had known at the reformation factory were doing time here, with one just executed and another on Death Row waiting to die, while a third was given a life sentence and a transfer to Folsom for beating another prisoner to death with a hammer less than a month before my arrival—all of which eloquently attested to the singular success of the reformation factory's "beneficial training program."

One of those who had matriculated to The Joint from the school was a smiling, adventurous lad. He had been sent here after the cops blew a hot car out from under him less than a block from my home. The first chance he got he ran up and greeted me. Then, half-seriously, half-jokingly, he asked, "What the heck took you so long to get here, Chess?"

What had been the delay? Why had it taken me nearly two years after leaving the reformation factory to get to Quentin? That hardly spoke well of my enterprise, did it?

My cell was on the fourth tier of the South block—the world's largest cell block, incidentally—a huge building containing one thousand cells, with two men assigned to each cell. (The block has since been divided into four more easily manageable sections.) When the bell for "music hour" rang that first night, my unsuspecting ears were assaulted by a din that, to the uninitiated, was nothing less than infernal. Musical instruments of every imaginable kind, as well as some unimaginable kinds, blared, honked, oompahed, beeped and boomed; simultaneously, scratchy, hand-wound phonographs equipped with extra loud needles screeched jive, jump, hillbilly and western tunes, with some opera being thrown in here and there just for the hell of it. When Pandemonium broke loose, I leaped to my feet, startled. What manner of mass madness was this? My cell partner rocked and rolled with laughter. He was finally able to stop laughing long enough to shout an explanation. I immediately set to work making a homemade pair of earplugs.

Thus began my indoctrination. While it was not the brutal, jungle-like place I had expected, San Quentin was still prison in every sense of the word, and I was often reminded of the fact during those first eventful days here. The high walls, the armed guards, the mass feeding, the shakedowns, the cell searches, the machinery of custody, the rules and regulations posted on the cell wall reminded me. And so did sudden and violent incidents which are a part of the warp and woof of any high-custody prison.

A man a few cells from me blew his top one midnight. He stood at the bars shouting hysterically, "Taxi! Taxi, you bastards!," until the night nurse and a squad of guards came and took him to the hospital.

Another time I was returning to my cell after the night meal when I heard a scream and some smart character with a twisted sense of humor shouted "Tim-ber-r!" Down hurtled a living, kicking, screaming body. It struck the cement floor with a thud. Two men darted out of line, to render aid I thought—but actually to snatch the shoes from the feet of the smashed and dying man. I watched these two human vultures make hurriedly off with their prize. The smart character cracked with awed approval, "Man, did you see *that!* They beat the fool for his kicks before the second bounce!" Whereupon, I am pleased to report, some indignant soul planted a number nine in the most appropriate part of the smart character's anatomy.

One day, in the Big Yard, a paretic Filipino ran amok with a butcher knife. In nothing flat, showing rare good judgment, prisoners and guards alike were fleeing for their lives in every direction. A dead-eyed guard calmly took aim with his carbine and shot the Filipino to death. . . .

Tuffy had gone to the Mess Hall and was working as a waiter. Tim and I had been assigned to the Jute Mill and I was then in the process of "learning a trade with a future in it"—namely, the running of a spinning machine. This was before the abolition of the con-boss system, and the con boss of my section was a ratty, self-important joker who had developed the habit of throwing his weight around. When he gave me some guff I belted him. The gun guard on the cat walk blew his whistle and came on the run, aiming and kicking a shell into the chamber of his rifle as he ran. I punched Mr. Yelling Self-Importance one more time and then held him up in front of me, as a shield. That way, to shoot me, the gun guard would have to shoot through one highly vocal and thoroughly alarmed con boss. The section's floor guard broke us apart. Then I got into it with the guard. That netted me a fast trip to the Captain's Office—The Porch.

The old lieutenant on duty heard what the guard had to say and then bellowed, "Thinks he's a fighter, huh? Well, let's send him on high and see if that doesn't cool him off."

"On high" meant the isolated punishment unit behind Condemned Row and on the top tier of the North block.

"Hell," I said, "give me a chance to get warmed up first."

"Are you arguing with me?" the old lieutenant roared.

I was positive I had discerned a twinkle in those old eyes. "Yes," I said, "I'm arguing with you—if it'll do any good."

It did. I didn't go on high. Instead I was given four Sunday lock-ups and lost my privilege card for thirty days, which was a relatively mild punishment for swabbing a con boss and having a run-in with a guard.

The Jute Mill, by the way, is no more. On April 18, 1951, it burned to the ground. . . .

Prison officials don't have too much to say about the very real problem of homosexuality in prison. What can they say? They are fully aware that prison breeds the problem; they do all they can to combat it, realizing all the while that the best they can do is to drive it underground, out of sight, and thereby hold it in a form of check. So far as possible, prison wolves or "jockers" are kept from preying on the young, frightened and physically or morally weak inmate. The known and aggressively active "queen" is segregated and, when possible, helped medically and psychiatrically. Morality is demanded and homosexuality made an offense. Reads California Department of Corrections Rule D1207: "Any inmate committing, soliciting or inciting others to commit any sexual or immoral act shall be subject to disciplinary action." Thus inversion in any of its forms is punished, often severely. Yet, nevertheless, the practice of homosexuality still flourishes, secretly. That it does so is inevitable.

The man doing time in prison has been locked away from women but he has retained his instincts, his hungers, his needs and his manhood. Sexually, he has three choices: to remain celibate, to masturbate, or to find an available male substitute. Such a substitute is not hard to find. In time, a man may think: "Hell, why not?" And that "why not?" is a question that every man in prison must answer for himself.

It was a question all of us had to answer for ourselves. I mention the fact because it is one which those who write of prisons and prison life too often find convenient to ignore.

San Quentin had a new warden, a kindly, practical, far-seeing man named Clinton Truman Duffy, and this bespectacled, thoughtful penologist was destined to write penal history in California.* It was he who would remarkably change the physical and spiritual face of this historic and what was then tough and trouble-ridden prison. Originally given a temporary appointment for a mere thirty days while a successor to a former warden was being selected, Clinton Duffy, his father a prison employee before him, proved to be the very man the appointing board and the governor were looking high and low for. He stayed on as Warden of San Quentin for more than eleven challenging years; then he accepted a gubernatorial appointment to the California Adult Authority, the state's busy five-man board charged, among other duties, with the responsibility of deciding how long each adult male offender will serve in prison and how much time he will spend on parole. It is no exaggeration to say that today's new San Quentin was born that July day in 1940 when Clinton Duffy, to his own immense surprise, heard himself named warden. Thus it happened that the dawning of a new summer day found San Quentin a prison of resurgent hope.

Our warder was no longer despair. We who were doing time were treated like human beings, not caged wild animals; like men, not faceless numbers. The outside world was brought closer to us and we were given every incentive to strive to become a useful part of that world. We were offered trade training, education, recreation, a library of good books, the right to keep or win back self-respect, the chance to take a close look at ourselves and past lives and decide where we wanted to go from here. It was possible, in short, for our prison experience to lead to a better, a brighter future.

* Clinton Duffy has himself engrossingly told the story of his years as warden of one of the world's largest prisons: *The San Quentin Story* by Clinton T. Duffy, as told to Dean Jennings (New York: Doubleday & Company, Inc., 1950). His book eloquently demonstrates what a clear-headed faith in people and humaneness can accomplish with even hardened felons.

We did very well at San Quentin. We worked hard, won good jobs, studied and took part in the sports program. We remained loyal to one another and it was a sad blow to us when we learned how Tim had secretly informed on us. We had a talk with him.

"We just found out how you put the finger on us, Tim. Now, other guys would beat your brains out. We're not going to. We don't intend to tell anybody else what you did. But we don't want you to rap to us again. From here on, you're on your own. You're not one of us any more."

I had gone to work, by choice, in the educational building, and when the Supervisor of Education's inmate secretary and chief clerk was paroled, I was given his job. With Warden Duffy's approval, another man and I built up the audio-visual department of the institution's growing educational plant, made it into a highly useful arm of prison education. This was in the days before the prison budget permitted the hiring of accredited teachers; and in addition to my many other duties, I voluntarily taught as many classes as I could find the time for—typing, shorthand, English, business English and bookkeeping, among others.

By far my greatest satisfaction was teaching an earnest group of illiterates to read and write. I scrapped the childish readers and wrote (mimeographed) my own beginning texts, and I still can hear one grizzled old convict say in awed triumph: "Hey, Chess, I read it! By God, I read it!" "It" was a simple sentence, falteringly read, but it was also a major triumph and it opened up a marvelous new world for this old con. I was also the youngest member of the San Quentin debating team, and we established a fine record against such formidable opponents as Leland Stanford University, the University of California, San Francisco State Teachers College, and others of equally high caliber.

Warden Duffy was no foolish coddler of felons; he ran his prison and he maintained discipline, but he didn't make discipline an end in itself, or custody a god to be blindly served. And he didn't hold himself up as the All-Wise One in matters penological. But he did have a constructive, pioneering program, a program that made sense, based upon his belief in the man doing time. He believed that those men who genuinely wanted another chance should have that chance. He believed the public should accept a man who had done his time and was trying for a new and honest start. He believed the public should be acquainted with his prison, that it should know what was being done here. So he invited many civic groups to tour San Quentin as his guests. He often brought them to the educational building to let them see for themselves what was being done and then, seated in the school's combination auditorium and classroom, he and other officials would explain their program and how it worked. Quite often he would ask me to speak, and I did so gladly.

"All of you have read about wild youngsters like me in the headlines of your newspapers," I would tell them. "You read where we were committed to long prison terms. But did any of you ever stop and wonder what happened to us after San Quentin's front gate clanged shut? Well, let me tell you. I think you will find what I have to say a revelation."

Then I would tell these groups about San Quentin. And make no mistake: I was no performing seal. I meant what I said and I didn't pretty up what I had to say. I believed absolutely that what Warden Duffy and his staff were doing was a fine good thing, a sound sensible thing. As one who had known the meaning of other kinds of treatment, I wanted to do all I could to see that what was being done at San Quentin succeeded, whether *I* did or not.

There were, frankly, those who believed that Chessman, for all his industry, his enthusiasms, his studiousness and his friendliness, was, deep down, the same old Chessman still, full of angles and violence and cunning. This perhaps may have been attributable, in part, to the fact that I had retained the good will and trust of the men in the yard, the cons, even the hating, defiant, intractable ones whom I helped when I could. I knew, too, that the prison's chief psychiatrist had tagged me a "constitutional psychopathic personality" and predicted that my chances for living within the law after release were slim.

In another respect, I knew I was one of the luckier ones, for Judy, who still believed in me, still loved me, was waiting for me faithfully.

She was then living with my mother and father, which proved a great comfort and help to my parents. The idea had been hers. "With Caryl gone, I think you'll need me," she had told them. Judy wrote almost daily and visited me regularly. She, my parents and all my friends were standing solidly behind me. I was by no means the forgotten man.

The Duke had never paid me. With my arrest, I had expected him to default, and was preparing to take desperate steps to collect through tough friends when I was informed the neurosurgeon had decided, after conducting further tests and studies, that my mother could not stand the shock of an operation and that an operation would be futile even if she could. There was, it appeared, nothing medical science—or stolen money—could do to help her, so I called off my tough friends, telling them that I would settle accounts with Duke when I got out.

When the Japanese bombed Pearl Harbor I again desperately wanted to go to war. It became a torment to find myself locked away from freedom when I had come so close to occupying the cockpit of a fighter plane and fighting for it. Now it appeared that I was doomed to spend most of the war in prison. And that hurt. Not until May, 1943, did California pass a "special service parole" law and even then, because of my many consecutive sentences, I was ineligible for induction for several additional months.

In July, 1941, California had opened a unique minimum security institution in the southern part of the state, and I was convinced for many reasons that my chances for induction would be greatly enhanced if I was at this Chino Prison. Further, in the interim, while shooting for induction, I wanted to be near my parents and Judy. When I began making inquiries about the possibility of a transfer to Chino, I was told to wait until I appeared before the Board of Prison Terms and Paroles, the old board which has since been replaced by the Adult Authority. Perhaps then I *might* be considered. The board saw me at the end of a year.

"Of course you realize, Caryl, that we cannot possibly fix your term or grant a future parole date this early?"

Yes, I realized that.

"However, we have some splendid reports on your work and attitude and urge you to maintain this fine record you've been making for yourself."

The board postponed further consideration of my case one calendar year. During that year I worked and studied harder than ever.

"San Quentin on the Air" was being broadcast from coast to coast by the Mutual network's more than three hundred radio stations; an immediate success, the program's national reception had been nothing short of amazing. Happily, I was privileged to be one of those who helped write the weekly scripts.

All the while I kept plugging for Chino. I didn't suspect it at the time, but Fate cunningly cold-decked me a few short weeks after my initial appearance before the old Board of Prison Terms and Paroles. Ironically, the day this happened, I was positive the world had been handed to me on a silver platter. So feverish and unbounded was my enthusiasm, I triumphantly scribbled these words on a piece of notebook paper:

"*Deus ex machina*—with a twist."

24

Operation Adolf

I had been at San Quentin about a year when I met an intellectual, darkly handsome young man with an unpronounceable Slavonian surname, a keen interest in literature and a remarkable talent and inclination for burglary. A couple of confirmed bibliophiles, we promptly struck up an acquaintanceship which ripened into friendship.

In the course of time, Renny told me how he had gone to Hollywood from the Midwest, how he'd spent several months prowling bookshops by day and the homes of the affluent at night. I gathered he had developed a proficiency for locating and getting into concealed wall safes and other places for the keeping of money and valuables. On one of these nocturnal excursions he had struck it rich, finding several hundred dollars in cash and a thick sheaf of documents in the safe of a palatial home in an exclusive residential district near Beverly Hills. Renny had pocketed the cash and had intended, as was his practice, to leave the documents behind when he had chanced to glance at them—and had his breath taken away.

"All right, all right," I said impatiently, my curiosity whetted. "Don't keep me in suspense. What the heck were those documents?"

"Chess," Renny said, "you won't believe me if I tell you."

"Try me and find out," I urged.

He did. When he finished, my look of amazement prompted him to say, "I told you you wouldn't believe me."

But I did believe him, yet I couldn't help being staggered by what

226

I had heard. I knew without doubt that the whole course of my life had been altered. That much was certain. Life suddenly held promise of being rare and good. Here was an undreamed-of chance to redeem the errant Caryl Chessman—or a truly inspired and speedy way for the said Caryl Chessman to join his ancestors. But then, emotionally, I was jerked to a momentary halt. Had Renny saved those documents? Were they where *I* could get them?

They were. "But what would you do with them?" Renny wanted to know. "Blackmail?"

I laughed the question away. "No, Renny, not blackmail; something much bigger than that. Something as big and as ironic and as marvelous as life itself."

Understandably, Renny failed to perceive the least justification for what amounted to poetic ecstasy, and he was puzzled. "You wouldn't turn them over to the F.B.I.?"

Promptly and emphatically I replied: "Hell, no!"

"Then what?" he asked.

My grin was knowing. "Now, friend Renny, it's my turn to say you won't believe me if I tell you. But I have an idea; if you'll pardon the adjectives, an impossible, irresistible, fantastic idea. And, with any kind of luck at all, it's just preposterous enough to work. If it does I am, thank you, a self-made man with a million dollars to spend."

"And, thank you, if it doesn't?"

"I'd probably get my neck stretched for treason."

Renny, burglar and bibliophile, winced. Even the thought of mild physical violence he found distasteful.

My unbridled enthusiasm, however, mocked at danger. The neck-stretching possibility simply added zest, spice to my plans. Wanting one such or not, Uncle Sam now had a brand new and singularly unorthodox ally who intended to direct a boiling, restless, tireless energy toward giving the *Herrenvolk* a lively time of it.

I hastened to make it clear to Renny that I had absolutely no intention of committing treason but would be obliged to convince certain fascistic personages that such was my intention, and if Uncle Sam found out, I might have a tough time explaining.

Renny's puzzlement had reached the point of acute agitation. Would I kindly stop talking in adjectival circles and explain?

"And if I do, you'll never say anything, no matter what happens, without my personal O.K.?"

"Not a word," he promised.

"All right. Here's the idea."

The idea was to take those papers Renny had acquired and return them to their rightful owner, a surprisingly important Hollywoodian who apparently was actively engaged in a sly plot to use the movie industry for propaganda purposes on behalf of Der Fuhrer & Company. By returning those papers I would, I hoped, win that fascistic gentleman's confidence. I would be on the lam; I would be darkly angry at this country for making me what I then would be, a hunted outlaw; I would be out for revenge; I would have a suggestion on how I could get it and, at the same time, gloriously aid The Cause; I would get myself shipped to Germany; I would proceed cheerfully to sell Brother Adolf's strutting stooges a curious bill of goods; I would be aiming toward wangling myself into the presence and confidence of the Third Reich's Chancellor; my object then, with the *Schutzstaffel* lulled, would be to ventilate said Chancellor's head with holes or put the snatch on him.

Renny's reaction to my idea, now that he understood it, was immediate and unreservedly enthusiastic. That the odds against successful execution of any plot to ventilate der Fuhrer's cranium or snatch him were probably a million to one troubled us not in the least. For here was that magic chance-of-a-century to fire a shot that not only would be heard around the world but that would reverberate far down the corridors of time. Thoughtfully, moreover, a million-dollar reward had been offered by certain solvent citizens to any enterprising party who succeeded in writing finis to the astonishing dictatorial career of Herr Hitler.

And certainly Herr Hitler was fair game. It was he and his gangster crew who insisted that man is a beast of prey. These worthies screamed the virtues of hatred, especially racial hatred. And Renny was a Jew whose grandparents had come from Eastern Europe; Renny was a burglar with some explosive hidden papers and a jubilant monster for a friend.

From such oddments could history be written.

But not without painstaking preparation.

So we tore the problem apart, examined all the kinks and angles. We turned to a bright, blond lad for some needed technical assistance. We studied propaganda techniques and the characteristics of German fighter craft. With a gimlet eye I pored through *Mein Kampf*. I began evolving the fantastic bill of goods I intended to sell the Third Reich's Mighty Ones. Artfully disguised, I reduced this plausible hokum to book form. Meanwhile we kept marshalling facts, figures, incidental intelligence. We got all the dope we could on truth serums, so-called. I quietly contacted Gabriella, who'd figured in my past, and a friend I'll call Jay.

We did all this without attracting attention or arousing suspicion. I stepped up my campaign to get transferred to Chino. I walked a tightrope. Whether I was rationalizing or not, I didn't regard what I intended doing as involving the betrayal of those who felt I was a changed and sobered young man who had earned a transfer to California's unique minimum security institution. Here was a chance to stand alone and pit myself against the forces of history, to rise up from the bowels of prison and reach out for the moon and stars. Only the tiniest, grayest, narrowest mind could have branded my proposed and preposterous gamble betrayal. That it failed so conspicuously attests only to the fact that, by and large, man has lost his capacity to dream boldly. And because that is so, I weep for him unashamedly.

On May 27, 1943, my twenty-second birthday, I was transferred by ordinary passenger bus with a group of thirty-three other prisoners to Chino.

The ride from San Quentin (in Marin County, near San Francisco) to the California Institution for Men at Chino (in San Bernardino County, approximately forty miles from Los Angeles) was a long one and consumed nearly twelve hours; yet, for me, every mile and every minute of that ride was fascinating. The last two years of my life had been spent in a walled and womanless place called prison, and now I was rediscovering the face of the world beyond—the face of a world at war. That face excited me, stirred me deeply. I was, if possible, on beholding it, more eager than ever to try my hand at stalking a Fuhrer.

At dusk we arrived at our destination, a unique and wall-less institution today deservedly famous. We were told that the fence around the grounds was not there to keep the inmate population in, but to keep the public out. And the atmosphere, as we found the moment we stepped from the bus, was friendly; the stresses and tensions often found in and inevitably a by-product of the high-custody prison were absent. Truly, here was a new kind of institution.

Just as Warden Clinton T. Duffy had been blazing a penal trail at San Quentin, so too had Superintendent Kenyon J. Scudder at Chino.

At Chino the man serving time encounters trained personnel genuinely interested in helping him be successful when released. He isn't surrounded by high walls, bristling gun towers. Custodial regimentation doesn't smother his individuality. Everything isn't all figured out for him down to the last tiny detail. It isn't the coercive presence of a gun bull, but his own sense of responsibility that restrains him from running off—to brief and dearly bought freedom. So he learns to face up to other problems and responsibilities confronting him And valuable trade training is available. Moreover, he's allowed to visit with his family and friends under ideal conditions.

To the prisoner, and hence to society, all of this means much. In point of blunt fact it often means the difference between success (the harmonious and productive readjustment of the ex-inmate to and in his community) or failure (the return of the ex-inmate to crime). . . .

I did exceptionally well at Chino. Assigned to the Farm Construction Crew, I became an inspired digger of fence post holes and repairer of barbed wire fences. I loaded and unloaded trucks with unfeigned enthusiasm. Work, manual labor, was what I wanted; the tougher the better. My object was to toughen the physical machine, to ready it for maximum efficiency under the most rugged conditions.

And not only did I work with a happy vengeance, but in my spare time I played with an equal vengeance. I swam in the Chino pool, lifted weights, boxed.

To keep as mentally sharp as possible, a couple of other prisoners and I formed the Chino debating team. For opponents, Mr. Scudder lined up teams from nearby universities and colleges. We more than held our own against them.

I volunteered for duty as an airplane spotter. A previously unused guard tower had been put to use as a post for reporting to the Interceptor Command in Los Angeles the presence and description of all airplanes sighted in the area. On a purely voluntary basis, pairs of men worked together in four-hour shifts (around the clock). I worked two and sometimes three nights a week on the twelve midnight to four in the morning shift. The tower we used was situated in a pasture, away from the other buildings.

Judy visited me almost every Sunday. And my parents found it possible to make the trip from Los Angeles once or twice a month. (I was granted special permission to visit with my mother at the car.) These three people, who meant so much to me, were happier than I had seen them in a long, long time. I was near them again and their hopes were high.

And all the while I was secretly making arrangements, contacts with the outside world. A friend of mine made me a key that would open the lock on Chino's unguarded back gate. While on duty spotting airplanes, I had two visitors, Jay and Gabriella. On three occasions we held whispered midnight conferences. To the man on duty with me, I passed these visits off as clandestine meetings with a girl friend. My policy was never to let my left hand know what my right hand was doing.

Dick, a handsome smoothie in his thirties, fitted neatly into my plans. By happy coincidence, he was scheduled for parole in the near future and without plans, funds or friends in that part of the state. I had a talk with him. I wanted to help him and, in return, I wanted him to do me a few small favors. The first one was to pair off with me spotting airplanes. He readily agreed and we had no difficulty arranging to go to the tower together a couple of nights a week on the midnight to four in the morning shift. That solved my final problem.

I received word from the outside. All was ready.

The day was Sunday. Judy visited. I dared not tell her what the immediate future held. The time passed too quickly, and as I held her and kissed her goodbye I knew, angrily, that if I failed I would forfeit all right to her. I vowed I wouldn't fail. "Judy Baby," I told her fiercely, "I love you!" I added, "No matter what happens, remember that—and try to believe in me."

Judy's violet eyes searched a pair of glittering brown ones. "But what can happen, Daddy?" she asked.

I grinned. "Nothing, Judy. Nothing at all."

" 'Bye," she said softly.

" 'Bye," I repeated, and my grin softened to a smile. My Judy was a fine, beautiful woman. God, how I loved her! And I was such a romantic fool, such a wild dreamer, I wanted to slay a dragon to prove it.

A group of us were lying around on the grass in front of the entrance to the mess hall waiting for it to open. Talk got around to Chino and what a fine place it truly was. One of the guys said, "Anybody who'd run off from this place would have to be crazy."

I agreed, repeating the words, "Anybody who'd run off from this place would have to be crazy." And eight hours later I had run off.

The details of flight and a tight time schedule had been worked out with patient care. I don't mean to imply that the escape itself presented any problem, since virtually all I had to do was walk off unchallenged. But unplanned, haphazard or spur-of-the-moment escapes have a way of getting one promptly back into jail. Actually, the escapee's real problem doesn't begin until the escape itself is an accomplished fact.

No one had been given any reason to suspect I intended to abscond. The remaining few hours were passed in a routine way. I spent the early part of the evening chatting with friends in the dormitory, ribbing and talking about everything and nothing. My boss, who was also the football coach, paid the dorm a visit and signed me (and others) for the coming football season. Then I wrote letters to Judy and my mother, telling them both how much I looked forward to seeing them next Sunday. After that, with nothing left to do but wait, I read. At eleven P.M. I stretched out on my cot, intending to relax for a few minutes before I checked out for airplane spotting duty. I closed my eyes. The next thing I knew, the supervisor in charge of the dorm was shaking me gently.

"Hey, wake up!"

I sat up with a jerk, looked at my watch. Five minutes past midnight! I'd overslept twenty minutes. I jumped up and hurriedly put on a light jacket. "Must've dozed off," I said.

The supervisor nodded. "When you failed to check out at a quarter to I figured that was what had happened. Thought I'd better check."

"Thanks. Thanks a lot."

Dick, whose quarters were in another building, was waiting for me at the desk. His look was quizzical.

I grinned and said, "Fell asleep."

We hurried to the administration building, got the sandwiches and the thermos of coffee prepared for each pair of spotters, and were then driven to the tower by a supervisor who patrolled the grounds. As soon as this supervisor drove off with the two men we relieved, I quickly set the scene.

Entrance into the tower was made by climbing up steel ladder rungs set in the concrete and then by passing through a trap door in the floor. I took off one shoe and made a long heel mark next to these rungs just below the trap door. I then ripped off the heel of this shoe and dropped it. Next, I climbed back down to the ground, cut myself with a knife, let blood drip around the base of the tower. After bandaging the cut, I took out a cheap pocket watch I was known to carry habitually and banged it against the cement base of the tower. Just then an airliner flew overhead and I scrambled back up into the tower and reported it, making sure the local operator in the institution's control room recognized my voice. I asked for and was given a time check. Then I hung up. Dick was looking out into a dark night.

"Well, Dick, I'm all ready and I'm late. I've got to get moving on the double. But first, are you sure you have everything straight?"

He nodded. "Everything," he assured me.

"All right, then I'm on my way into the wild blue yonder. Take it easy. I'll be seeing you in a couple of weeks."

"Check," Dick said. "And good luck." We shook hands.

I disappeared through the trap door, swiftly descended to the ground and stepped out to the center of the road leading to the institution's back gate. I hadn't gone fifty feet before I was beset by some hellish variety of night bird. This feathered monstrosity squawked at the top of its lungs at the sight of me and hurtled in to the attack. I responded by cursing it roundly and throwing an assortment of rocks and clods. At this affront, its outrage seemingly knew no bounds and I found myself confronted by and the target of an insane, squawking, diving, darting ball of winged fury. This being my first—and I fervently prayed my last—encounter with a psychotic night bird, I didn't know what to do except to get the hell out of there just as fast as I could. So that is what I did, remaining under attack all the while.

I continued on the double to the back gate, passed myself through with the aid of that key a friend had made for me, crossed the road and followed an irrigation ditch across a field toward a row of towering eucalyptus trees. Just as I reached the first tree, my tormentor was joined by a friend; salutations were squawkingly exchanged and both made one last pass at me before flying away, still squawking. I breathed a sigh of relief at their passing from the scene. Believe me, it is not a happy experience to be put to rout by an insane night bird at the outset of a prison escape. In fact, my relations with night birds as a class have been strained ever since.

Reaching the ravine, I dropped into it and uncovered a waterproof box which had been buried there for me in case anything prevented my meeting Jay and Gabriella, who were to be waiting for me a short distance away. I removed the automatic pistol and the money, and placed the thick sheaf of papers I had brought with me from the prison in the box and reburied it, hurriedly. Then I followed the eucalyptus trees to where a dirt road began. Jay and Gabriella were parked there in an almost new, powerful sedan. Seconds later, we were speeding on our way.

Back at the prison, Dick gave me an hour's head start before phoning in. "We've had an accident out here," he reported. "Nothing serious, I don't think. Chessman slipped and fell out of the tower. He banged himself up quite a little, cut his head and acted dazed at first. He's walking back in to the hospital and should be there in about four or five minutes."

They waited—five, ten, fifteen minutes. Still Chessman failed to put in an appearance. They checked. They searched. No doubt about it: Chessman had disappeared. Superintendent Kenyon Scudder was notified and gave the order. Law enforcement was notified. Teletypes began to clack. An escape bulletin was issued. *Use caution in apprehending,* it advised. *Subject may be armed and is considered dangerous.*

Subject was armed with a dream—*and* a gun.

We reached our destination, a dwelling place in a city I shall not identify. And then everything began going wrong; the dream became a violent nightmare. Jay went off to transact some business; he didn't return. He had a wild time of it and ended up doing time in one of the nation's toughest prisons. Gabriella left for another purpose; she didn't return—in time. Several big men with drawn guns came to this dwelling place.

I had just dried off after showering. I looked out a second-floor bedroom window and saw them below. I had only time to pull on a pair of pants, slip on a shirt and kick into a pair of shoes before I snatched the automatic pistol and ran out a back way, past them, and dove headlong from the stairway, squeezing the trigger of the gun, hearing its staccato bark. I missed by inches being impaled on a stake fence. A stake gouged the fleshy part of my right hand and I lost the gun. But I won respite. The big men had been too disconcerted by my impromptu firing swan dive to shoot. I picked myself up and ran, ducking out of sight.

The big men came pounding after me. Pursued, shot at, I ran, hid, ran, until I thought my lungs would burst. I gasped, cursed—and ran some more. Just as I was leaping a low fence, two shots rang out; I was knocked sprawling and threw myself under some shrubbery. Two big men ran past me. They kept going. I regained my feet, promptly collapsed, got back up, fell back down. I'd been shot. I still didn't know where and I didn't have time to find out. I had to get out of there—fast. I got up and, by putting most of my weight on my left leg, managed to stay up. I followed a fence, using it for partial support. Next, I did the same with the side of a house. By then I could walk again unsupported. Or at least I could stumble and stagger. So I dodged big men with guns and stumbled and staggered for ten or fifteen blocks, making my way toward the business section of the city. Finally I stood in the shadows of a home behind a gas station.

A big rig, motor running, was parked at the side of the station and its driver was gabbing with the attendant. When a passenger car drove in and stopped at the pumps, both men walked around to the front of the station. That was my cue. I made for the sleeper behind the cab, crawled in and closed the little door after me. A minute or so later I was on my way. I didn't give a damn where.

I had a nasty flesh wound on the outside of my right leg about eight inches below the belt line. I had also been shot, of all places, in the right, little toe. I dabbed at both wounds with a handkerchief and then felt around in the sleeper and found a leather jacket and a pair of field boots. The jacket was warm, and the boots, though a size or more too large, were better than my own shoes, the right one having been shot nearly off my foot. The shot toe kept bleeding. Three times I had to take off the boot to pour the blood out of it. My foot had swollen so badly I had difficulty getting the boot off the third time.

I grew woozy from loss of blood and either fainted or slept. The next thing I knew someone had jerked the sleeper door open and was tugging at me.

"Hey!"

I looked up. There stood the truck driver, a short, blocky young man with the face of a perplexed pug.

"Hello," I said, pulling my thoughts together. "Good morning. Or is it morning?"

It was morning. The truck driver told me it was. Then he asked, "When did you get aboard?"

I told him. "By the way, where are we?" I added.

We were just inside the Los Angeles County line. That meant I was virtually back where I started!

The truck driver said, "I was highballing into L.A. but the damned engine conked out on me and there ain't a garage nowhere along here. I'm in a helluva fix."

"Then that makes two of us," I told him. I tried to climb out of the sleeper and couldn't. "Give me a hand, will you, Mac?"

He helped me out. I had to grab at the cab to stay upright. While I held on, the truck driver looked me over. He saw I was wearing his jacket and boots. He saw my pants were blood-soaked.

"Mac," I said, "I know you must be wondering what my story is and . . ."

He interrupted. "The cops after you?"

I admitted they were.

Two and two suddenly made four. "Say, you must be the guy they were looking for back . . ."

It was my turn to interrupt him. "That's right, I must be. And so now you got a chance to make a big hero out of yourself by snatching me. I'm afraid I'm not in very good shape to resist."

"Shot?"

"Shot."

"Bad?"

"Not too bad."

A man in a Chevvy came along and stopped when he saw us. He rolled down a window and asked, "In trouble?"

The truck driver nodded and said, "Yeah, truck broke down on me."

"I passed the highway patrol up the road a ways. Want me to go back and tell them?"

"Sure, if you will."

We watched the Chevvy U-turn. Then the truck driver said, "Look, buddy, I'm paid to drive a truck, not capture guys that are on the lam. Can you walk?"

"If I can't, I sure as hell can crawl."

"Well, you better get moving then."

"How about the jacket and boots?"

"You can have 'em."

"I'd pay you for them if I wasn't busted."

The truck driver took out his wallet, removed a five-dollar bill and handed it to me.

"Thanks," I said. "You're a right guy."

He shrugged. "Like I said, I'm paid to push this rig."

I stumbled off through an orange orchard, carrying my shot-up shoes. Walking was a punishing proposition. Well away from the main highway, I paused to bury the shoes. Then I stumbled on. The mountains were near but I doubted if I could reach them. Suddenly my thirst became fierce. I came to a small grape vineyard and ate some dusty, hot, half-ripe grapes. I walked some more. Thirst once again became consuming. My right leg was on fire. My thoughts didn't want to connect. Adolf was a long, long way off; the horse trough ahead wasn't. I staggered to it and buried my head. I drank the cool water in great gulps. With difficulty I removed my right boot and pants and washed the wounds; they weren't pretty. They needed more than a washing in a horse trough. The realization sunk in that staying alive had suddenly become a very real and immediate problem. Regardless of the risk of capture, I had to get to Los Angeles without delay. Bleached bones couldn't dream.

So back I hobbled to the highway and stuck out my thumb. An old farmer driving a flat-bed truck came along and picked me up. He had a dead horse on the back which, he informed me, he was taking to a tallow factory. Spotting the blood on my pants he asked, "Butcher?" I nodded. From that point on we got along famously. He let me off in the industrial section of Los Angeles, on Alameda Street. It was mid-morning. I made it to a nearby eating place, customerless at that hour, and told the waitress, "A double order of ham and eggs for a hungry man, My Pretty."

· 25 ·

The Pull of the Orbit

The waitress looked at me as though she thought I was out of my mind and wanted to know where I'd been. Why? I asked. "Well, for gosh sakes, Mister, this is meatless Tuesday. There's a war on."

I grinned. "You're telling me? I've been in it. And now I'm starved. So I'll make you a deal. If you let me have my ham and eggs today, I promise I won't eat any meat tomorrow. How about it?"

"Well," said the waitress, pouting thoughtfully, "I guess that would be all right."

I cleaned my plate, drank three cups of steaming black coffee, and felt much better. Then I selected a package of cigarettes from the off brands available and handed the waitress the five-dollar bill. She started making change.

"All I want back is a dime. The rest is yours."

She protested, "But you got two dollars and forty cents change coming."

"The customer is always right," I reminded her. "Now give me my dime and let me get back to the wars."

She did, saying, "You sure don't look like no soldier to me."

"I don't feel like one either," I replied, and hobbled out. I took the streetcar to an outlying district and then walked—staggered—a block and a half to a house where I was positive I would find a friend and sanctuary. But the friend was gone—to a war job in another state. Ironically, he had left only the day before. And his absence left me on a delightful spot: flat broke, shot up, sick, badly wanted, and on the streets without transportation. Where could I go? The police would be watching, checking all known friends.

I hobbled along, racking my brains for an original idea. The day was hot, blazing hot. My head pounded, spun. I staggered on—to nowhere. Thinking became too great an effort. I knew I had a problem, but I couldn't recall what it was. A matter of shooting ducks. Or Fuhrers. I came to a park. And benches and a drinking fountain. I drank until I felt bloated, then sprawled onto a bench in the shade. Two chubby, golden-haired little girls playing nearby in a sandbox ran over and studied me solemnly.

"You're a funny man," one of them told me.

I agreed—I was a funny man. After a while the funny man's head cleared; he sat in the shade all afternoon and watched children laugh and play. Then he stood up and hobbled off, grimacing with pain. He had to go slowly. It was dark by the time he had covered the two miles to the home of an elderly lady who had taught his Sunday-school class years before. He found her at home. She invited him in, fed him. She knew he belonged in prison; he was AWOL, he admitted. He spoke vaguely, but derisively, of funny men who set out to slay dragons, of bold plans gone astray. He borrowed a couple of dollars. As soon as he left, she called the police. The funny man got away. . . .

A long night finally passed. I had breakfast at a drive-in. A girl I had known in my childhood, and whom I'll call Gina, was my last hope; she lived close by. I had to make it there. Somehow I did, hobbling up to the door of the small, vine-hidden bungalow and knocking. Sleep in her eyes, a housecoat wrapped casually around her, Gina opened the door. She blinked. "You!"

"Me," I agreed. I stepped inside, closed the door and grinned in the manner of the small boy who has paid a visit to the jam jar with calamitous results.

Gina's startled eyes swept over me. "Good Lord," she exclaimed, "you look like the wrath of God!"

My grin broadened. "In a way, I guess that's just what I am."

"I read about your departure in the papers and I had a hunch you might pay me a visit."

"I only hope the gendarmes don't have the same hunch. They haven't been around, have they?"

"No, but I saw Judy and your mother and dad yesterday."

"That's one of the reasons I came to see you. I want you to tell them that I'm all right and not to worry. Will you do that?"

"Of course, I will. But you don't look all right."

"Don't tell Judy or my folks that. Besides, I'll be all right after I take a bath and shave and plug up a couple of holes."

"Why did you run away?"

"I had amnesia," I said with a straight face. "I fell out of an observation tower and struck my head. The first thing I remember after that is when I found myself running through an orange orchard."

"Then, when you came to your senses, why didn't you turn around and run right back?"

"Because prison officials have suspicious minds and I don't think they'd believe a story like that."

"Frankly, I don't believe it either."

"I didn't think you would."

"Well, what are you going to do now?"

"Gina, my sweet, I am now going to do something bold and dramatic."

Gina managed a frown. "If you ask me, I think you should do something sensible and prosaic."

I protested, "But that wouldn't be any fun."

"Having your kind of fun will get you killed."

"It could," I admitted.

I bathed, shaved with a razor which Gina resurrected from some quarter, and "plugged" up the holes. Both wounds were infected; they had an ugly look and obviously needed medical attention in the worst possible way. The iodine I applied with great liberality burned, like fires of Hell. Grimacing, I hopped about the bathroom and cursed softly but with rare eloquence, convinced the iodine was eating its way through my leg and foot. After an eternity the burning subsided. Then I dressed and combed my hair. I found Gina in the kitchen.

"Well," she said, "you look like a new man." She had made up her face and her smile was dazzling.

"And you, Gina, look like a very beautiful woman."

This goddess of my childhood flushed with pleasure. I sat opposite from her and had coffee and a cigarette while she ate a late breakfast. The warm mid-morning sun came streaming in through the east windows of the kitchen. I found myself relaxing more and more, feeling comfortable and even domestic (and these assuredly were sensations, however transient, which should have been wholly alien to the grinning, driven psychopathic hunter obsessed with acting out a fantastic dream).

Lightly we talked—of what once had been when the world and Caryl Chessman were young—of all that had occurred since. Now, once again, our paths had crossed, and still the spirit of Gina was a tonic. She still loved life for its own sake, with a passionate fervor, and, her beauty had not faded. An authentic Bohemian, Gina was also a circumspect one. And so, when talk returned to the present and me, she was greatly concerned. I had risked too much and the danger was surely too great.

"Gina," I assured her, "there's never any need for worry about me. I live a charmed life."

"Oh, I know, Caryl. I know that you are more than able to look out for yourself. But I was thinking of your mother and father and Judy. For their sakes, don't you believe you should consider giving yourself up?"

The constant, terrible pull of the orbit; there it was. And there was the verbal thrust I needed. "Gina," I said, with exaggerated harshness, "I didn't come to you for advice. I came for help." I stood up. I lit another cigarette.

Gina looked stricken and I relented. Our eyes met.

"I'm sorry, Gina," I said quietly. "Please forgive me. You see, I just can't give myself up and I guess that makes me a hopeless case. But that is still no reason for us to quarrel, now is it?"

"No," she agreed. "You're right."

"And I'm forgiven?"

"Of course."

"Good."

I had a favor I wanted to ask. "I expect some important papers to come into my possession within two or three days. It may become inadvisable for me to hold on to them personally. I may find it expedient to mail them to you or have them delivered to you. So if you receive a package with a return address on . . . let's say Wabash Street, you're to keep it for me and, for God's sake, don't look inside or let anyone else know about the package. I'll pick it up later. O.K.?"

It was. I borrowed ten dollars. A sick dizziness engulfed me. I floundered and Gina helped me to a chair. She got me something to drink. Then I stood up unsteadily and insisted I felt fine. That was the blackest lie I have ever told. But I had to get moving and keep moving, relentlessly, or quit. Vaguely I remember bidding Gina adieu and hobbling off.

I caught the bus for Hollywood. Next stop make-believe land. Or was I already there?

It strikes you as an odd thing when you stop and think about it. All the police in creation can be doing their utmost to find a certain guy without having any luck at all and then you can find him in practically nothing flat.

It was that way with an escaped convict and professional burglar whom I will call Al Collins. An aging Raffles, Collins was then about as badly wanted as it was possible to get. His looting of two hundred odd fashionable homes in the Beverly Hills and Bel Air sections of southern California had won him the sobriquet of the Phantom Burglar and ultimate capture and sentencing to San Quentin. A few weeks earlier he had escaped from a prison road camp and I had a hunch he had returned to his old stamping grounds. A couple

of phone calls and bar visits confirmed that he indeed had. I was instructed to be at a certain bar at a specified time that evening if I
wanted to get in touch with him.

When he saw me, Al let out a whoop. He acted as though he had
found a long-lost brother. In a way he had, for I was one of the
brethren, if a decidedly shot-up and down-at-the-heels one. This troubled him not at all. "We'll have you all straightened out in no time,"
he said, and then he practically ran me into the bar and had me gulping a drink and acknowledging introductions.

"Look, Joy Boy," I protested, "I'm in no condition for this sort of
thing. I need sleep and a doctor."

But this genial, burglarious friend laughingly insisted that I first
needed a drink, and then another. He joked all the while with the
bartender and two or three sleek, unattached females. It was hard to
believe that such an inoffensively extroverted guy could be a Phantom
Burglar—and one of the most wanted criminals in this part of the
country.

Just as he had said he would, Al got me "straightened out in no
time." That night (or morning) he got me a hotel room, registering
me as Jonathan Edward Carlson, and gave me a loaded revolver. In
the forenoon he took me to a doctor who did not ask questions and
then to a clothier. After lunch we returned to his apartment and fed
his landlady a likely story. She rented me a tiny, sunny apartment
on the ground floor that was perfect for my purposes. Al saw to it
that the apartment was furnished as I wanted it. And within twenty-
four hours I had a draft card and other identification.

I was Jonathan Edward Carlson.

Within forty-eight hours I was able to get around without too
much difficulty. The doctor had checked the infection and my
wounds were on the mend. On the shot foot I wore a light slipper,
which made walking less painful. The second night after meeting

him, I went on the prowl with Al. We acquired some cash, more guns, an almost new Packard convertible and several thousand dollars' worth of jewelry, which Al promptly turned over to his fence. A day later the fence had a proposition for us. Why waste time prowling for ice in such a haphazard fashion? he asked preliminarily. Why not knock over those who dealt in it? He had something special and something big in mind. We listened attentively. The proposition was almost too attractive. Al was enthusiastic. We would clean up here and then beat it for the East.

"Look, Al," I told him, "I didn't take off from Chino just to steal and have a good time. I got other plans, and don't ask me to explain."

He didn't, although his bony face then wore an expression of utter bafflement. "Hell," he said, "you must be crazy."

That, as I remarked, was not an original idea.

My "other plans" were rapidly shaping up. Unquestionably, Al had saved my life and, without knowing it, had put me back in the Fuhrer-hunting business. I then possessed everything required to make the next move—the right sort of front, money, guns, transportation and a connection to buy all the black-market gas I wanted, using loose gas stamps Al had acquired by the gross. So it was time to set some wheels within wheels in motion.

I visited the library where Renny had instructed me I would find those documents which had sent me leaping eagerly for the moon, and, unobserved, I snatched them from their novel hiding place, concealing them under my shirt and coat.

Perched behind her desk, checking some books against a list, the middle-aged librarian looked up as I was leaving, smiled pleasantly, failed to note my sudden increase in girth, and asked, "Did you find what you wanted?"

"Indeed I did, ma'm," I assured her.

I drove to Griffith Park, parked, and was jubilant when I examined the papers. They were exactly what Renny had said they would be. Well, now it was up to me. Here was my chance of a lifetime and I mustn't flub it. By God, I wouldn't! I'd turn defeat into victory yet! I swung the Packard back onto Los Feliz, crossed Riverside Drive and pulled into a drive-in. I ordered, and while waiting to be served, used a public telephone. When a cultured voice answered, I asked to speak to—let's call him—Mr. Christopher. The voice wanted to know who was speaking and I said to tell Mr. Christopher that Detective S. Holmes was phoning and wanted to speak to him about a burglary that had occurred at his home two years back. I was asked to hold the line.

Then, "Hello, Christopher speaking. Now what is this nonsense about a burglary? And who is this?"

"A friend," I said, "who wants to do you a favor. I happened to run across some papers today that I believe came from your home when it was burglarized a couple of years ago."

"Who told you my home was burglarized?"

"The burglar."

Christopher's voice became wary. "And you say you're a detective?"

"That's what I said but it was somewhat less than the truth."

"Meaning you're not?"

"I definitely am not."

"Then who are you?"

"I told you, a friend."

"How do I know that?"

"For the best reason there is: because I have the papers and because I haven't turned them over to the police or the F.B.I. and don't intend to. Because I want to give them back."

"And you will expect, I presume, an . . . ah . . . reward, shall we say."

I let my voice bristle with indignation. "Look, Christopher, let's get one thing straight. This isn't a shakedown. I don't want a goddamed dime for your papers. I want your help."

"In what way?"

"In getting out of the country temporarily, for one thing. It just so happens that I recently escaped from prison and the thought of going back doesn't appeal to me."

"How can I be sure this isn't some trick?"

"Look, I don't want to argue. I'll tell you my name and I'll call you back in twenty-four hours. In the meantime, you can check and find

out if I'm on the level or not. My name's Chessman—C-h-e-s-s-m-a-n—
Caryl Chessman. Goodbye."

I returned to the Packard and ate. And thought. Holding those
papers was like holding history itself in my hand. They were a
strange, terrible kind of Power, and that Power, recklessly handled,
as it had to be, could easily blow me to an anonymous Hell, less easily
into History's book. Certainly the pedestrian approach was out of the
question. With the stakes so incredibly high, only a bold gambler
stood any chance of winning. Well, that was fair enough. I was in the
mood to outbluff the Devil himself.

As I aimed the nose of the Packard back out onto Los Feliz, I had
a hunch: Gabriella was safe and had returned to her swank Hollywood apartment. Fifteen minutes later I was knocking on the door of
that apartment. When Gabriella herself answered, I barged in uninvited, elated at finding her and immensely entertained by her open-
mouthed reaction to the sudden appearance of what, in her obviously
tipsy condition, she apparently was convinced was a ghost's ghost. A
brainy, imaginative female for all her allure, Gabriella had often
laughingly insisted that I must surely be reincarnate that long-dead
happy rascal and melancholy poet she knew I admired so much, François Villon.

Now she fixed me with a stern look of distaste and said flatly,
"François, you're not real—go away!"

"The hell I'm not real!" I replied, and to prove it bussed this attractive doubter with unfeigned enthusiasm.

Whereupon, my reality established, we had a thoroughly noisy
reunion. The fussy but well-heeled male friend Gabriella had been
entertaining left in a decided huff. We laughed him on his way. Then
we compared notes. Her escape from the big men with guns had been
as miraculous as mine. Our fellow conspirator, Jay, had not been so
fortunate. He direly needed help in the way of money and a lawyer
and shortly, at considerable risk, I saw to it that he got both. Having
brought each other up to date, Gabriella and I plotted the future
with a considerable assist from her bottle of Scotch.

Gabriella dressed and we took a ride. Brazenly, I returned to within sight of Chino and retrieved the papers I had hidden there. Then I paid a visit to the private residence of a very wise and kindly old man connected with the California prison system. With Gabriella standing guard, this old gentleman and myself had a long and earnest talk. Next, Gabriella and I reconnoitered Christopher's walled and guarded hill home. After midnight I returned Gabriella to her apartment, picked up Al and we went out on the prowl, having something of a hectic time of it for the remainder of the night. Sneaking through the enclosed back yard of a fashionable San Marino home, two huge dogs came dashing at us, snarling.

"Stand still!" Al whispered, sharply.

"Stand still, hell!" I replied, and leaped for a tree near a high fence. With a growl of brute rage, one of the dogs sprang after me. In the nick of time I scrambled out of range of that enraged engine of destruction. Then I whipped out my pistol, quite expecting to see my foolish confederate being torn to bits. Instead, I witnessed the unbelievable. Al not only wasn't touched but he sent the two dogs slinking off in shame for having perpetrated such an outrage in the first place. To this day, I still have no idea how he managed such a feat. I watched him stroll calmly to a gate and pass through into the next yard, whistling softly, unconcernedly. I hastily climbed out on a limb to the fence and then dropped to the ground on the other side, rejoining this overbold tamer of man-eating canines. He was enjoying my discomfiture immensely.

"O.K., O.K., Smart Guy," I said. "But after this don't ever again tell me that Chessman is the crazy one in this crowd. The only reason those damned dogs didn't tear you to pieces is that they figured you were too damned skinny to make a good meal."

I stood guard duty while Al, silent as a cat, hot prowled a mansion. We had parked the Packard some distance away and the loot was too much to carry, so we hid the loot in some bushes and rode off to the Packard on a couple of bicycles we had found in the mansion's three-car garage. The next thing we knew we were being hotly pursued by a night watchman with the voice of Stentor, also on a bicycle. This crazy chase lasted for several blocks. I am still convinced the only reason we finally managed to give our stentorian pursuer the slip is that he shouted himself out of breath. We made it to the Packard, abandoned the bicycles, returned and claimed the loot and then almost literally ran into two cops in a radio car. Another wild chase followed. I breathed a long sigh of relief when at last I ditched this most recent pursuit. We got back to Hollywood at dawn and caught a few hours' sleep.

I accompanied Al when he took some more hot jewelry to his fence. The fence still was urging us to knock over a volume dealer in precious stones with a place of business in Beverly Hills. The fence had a tip from an inside source that the dealer was to receive a large shipment of stones in the near future. If we took the dealer then, the fence said, he could guarantee us, cash on delivery, ten per cent of the total value of the stones we would get. By the most conservative estimate, our percentage would add up to a small fortune.

"All right," I said suddenly, "we knock the guy over. That's settled. Now let's have the details so I can look over the place and get ready to take it when we get the signal from you."

After a thorough briefing by the fence, we laid careful plans for the robbery and then waited for word the shipment had arrived. The prospect of possessing such a large sum of money for a few minutes' work was most satisfying. It would finance flight if my plan with Christopher fell through. I would have a financial lifeboat.

That afternoon I phoned Christopher. He had checked and now urgently wanted to see me. I saw him, at his home. He turned out to be a shrewd, granite-faced character with a cephalic index of not more than sixty. I smiled indulgently at his questions. No, I hadn't brought his papers with me; what I had brought with me were some papers of my own. I had taken the precaution of leaving *his* papers in a sealed envelope with a friend, and I had instructed that friend exactly how to proceed if I failed to call for those papers that evening. I also had had the foresight to place a note in the envelope which the police would find both interesting and informative should it fall into their hands. Now, with those preliminaries out of the way, was he ready to talk business?

Christopher hedged; he talked around his subject; he played it coy. The papers weren't what they seemed to be. Why didn't I just return them, accept a substantial reward, forget the whole thing? Then, ever so slyly, he suggested that it might be the safest and healthiest course.

"Christopher," I told him, "it's now your turn to listen to me, and I advise you to listen real carefully." Then I laid it on the line. . . .

Not many hours later we landed in Mexico City. Minutes after that I had been introduced to and was closeted with a nervous, pompous little man high in the un-angelic hierarchy of the Third Reich. It was apparent that this small peacock regarded his United States citizenship as an accident of birth at best. His vanity and a flair for the bizarre helped me hook him.

"You can be useful to us, Chessman. Most useful."

We flew back to Hollywood. Gabriella and I celebrated the occasion. I happened to glance at a calendar. Less than two weeks before, I had been just another obscure guy doing time. Now, shortly, I would be taking a long and perilous trip across the ocean and my situation would be incredibly unique. A psychopathic compulsion to dream an impossible dream, a tutored, insolent audacity, a perfect willingness to escape the orbit, to say to hell with the orbit—these, with a large assist from Dame Fortune, had put me into a position to play a weird but useful practical joke on history. While the free nations of the earth locked in titanic struggle with Adolf, Benito, Tojo and Company, I brazenly plotted to pull off my own crazy coup, nonchalantly, perhaps, at bottom, just for the hell of it. Perhaps . . . because I wanted to prove that it could be done.

And then it happened, suddenly. A familiar old devil called disaster strode upon the scene. In a matter of hours I was decisively cut down to size. Then, I became just another guy on the lam. Through an inadvertence on Gabriella's part, Christopher and crowd discovered my deception and the party got rough for a while. Al, my genial, burglarious benefactor, was captured in a bar one midnight while I was home in bed. I slept on while the cops came and cleaned out his apartment. Fortunately, they didn't then rouse the landlady. I discovered Al's absence the next morning, packed and got out of there in nothing flat. I literally hadn't been gone five minutes when the cops returned in force. While being questioned by the police, Al let it slip that I planned to spring a mutual friend from Chino and when I returned to that institution for that purpose, a couple of nights later, I found the place crawling with armed men. It was a miracle that I managed to escape detection and capture.

I was in a bad way and the situation, if possible, continued to get worse. I was hurt in a fight. I was virtually broke. Al's fence had disappeared. The stolen Packard had been recovered. I had two guns but ammunition for only one of them, and it was defective; I was lucky if the gun fired one time out of ten. The cops were hot on my trail and would remain there. Christopher and his goons were also after me; in trying to get me, they gave Gabriella a fierce roughing up before I got her away from them by massaging a few heads with a tire iron.

Checking, I found the Duke was still around, a more potent underworld figure than ever. Someone told me he was cleaning up in the black market. I phoned him and tried to bluff him out of the money he owed me. But he was "in" too solid to bluff and he hated my guts. "You smart sonofabitch," he growled, "the only thing you'll get from me is a hole in the head." So, to get by, I stole a car and pulled several hit-and-run robberies—and ran into more trouble. I grew disgusted, bitter, angry. Inexorably, I had been sucked back into the orbit. And if I didn't flee, I knew it would only be a matter of days or hours until I was caught or killed. I didn't care.

26

Stone Walls Do a Prison Make

I should have run. I should have laughed, packed, got Judy and lammed out of southern California. That way I doubtless would have lasted for a while: weeks, months, maybe even years. I should have run and robbed and raised hell until finally the gendarmes caught up with me. Meanwhile Judy and I could be having a second honeymoon, a stolen one. We could live for the moment, selfishly, for ourselves, defying a threatening world and knowing that each day might be the last. Certainly I was equipped and conditioned for the role of mad dog and in my frame of mind that role, with my beloved Judy at my side, offered an appeal I found hard to resist.

But still I didn't run, even knowing the alternative was death or prison. Death had lost all ability to menace me. Death was nothing more than a welcome release from this meaningless mockery called Life. But prison was another matter: so far as I was then concerned, stone walls did a prison make. I knew that once I found myself inside them I would begin to dream again, to plan again. That was the torment. Even now, galled by defeat, frustrated with the death of a dream, overflowing with anger and bitterness and hate, a small voice was trying to convince me that all was not lost, that prison could offer more than torment and empty dreams.

Well, I would let Life and Death draw straws to see who got me. I would stand pat. I would give the cops a crack at me and, at the same time, I would declare war on Christopher and his crowd and the Duke and his bunch of smart operators. I phoned the Duke a second time and told him I had decided to give him a chance to give me that hole in the head, adding that I was so fascinated with such a gift that I intended to try to make him a present of the same thing. "I think it's time you saw the light, Duke, and the only way I know how to accomplish that feat is to ventilate that thick skull of yours with some .38 slugs." Next I called Christopher and gave him a hot tip where he could find Chessman. Who was speaking? "This is Chessman's worst enemy," I replied, not untruthfully, I thought. "He's been running his mouth off about you. You better get him—and quick!"

The police had my apartment staked out. I spotted them seated in an unmarked police car and gave a kid on a bicycle a couple of dollars to deliver a note I scribbled on a scrap of paper. "Stop wasting the taxpayers' hard-earned money by sitting there on your fat asses waiting for me to blunder onto the scene." As I hoped it would, the note riled the two cops. They came looking for me. That gave me a chance to pay Dick a visit. Did he know where he could get hold of some .38 slugs? He did. Fine. I said, I'd be back after them. He wanted me to fix a definite time. "So that I'll be sure to be here," he explained. And he wanted to know, too, if there wasn't something else he could do for me. Anything at all. A real pal.

I studied the .38 in my hand, juggling it, and then looked from it to this "friend." Yes, I knew about the orbit and its pull. "I'll be on my way now," I said, crossing to the door. "But I'll be back. You can depend on that. And you can be sure, too, that I always repay favors." Then I limped out into the night.

I managed a visit with my mother and frankly told her what I had tried to do and how and why I had failed.

I concluded wryly, "So now, Mom, it appears that Uncle Sam and his allies will be obliged to win this war without my help."

And what would happen to me?

"Have faith, Mom, that whatever happens will be for the best.

Sure, it was evasion, but it hardly would have been a nice thing to have told my mother of the violent possibilities as to the fate of her only son. . . .

I had more trouble. I went looking for it. Then, by prearrangement, I met Judy. She picked me up late one evening.

"Dick's," I said. "But first be sure we're not being followed."

On the way, quietly, wistfully, without censure, she said: "Caryl, I wish you had stayed at Chino. You told me yourself, before you escaped, that you expected to be out in a year or two. And I was so happy, so eager for the future. Now I'm afraid of it. I'm afraid you'll either be hunted or locked up for the rest of your life, or that something even worse will happen. I can't help feeling it's useless to make any plans for a good future."

"I'm sorry, Judy Baby. I'm sorry I gambled and lost."

Judy reminded me, without bitterness, "You've gambled twice and lost twice. I'm afraid that will happen again and again. I don't think you'll ever be able to stop. And because I love you so much, Caryl, I want to help you, yet I know I'm helpless. I don't think anyone can help you. I think there is something inside you that keeps driving you."

"Some day, Judy, perhaps all this will be different," I ventured.

"Yes," Judy replied longingly, "perhaps some day all this will be different."

She parked in front of an apartment house on a side street. Dick occupied the first apartment on the left on the first floor. The front door of that apartment led directly to the street.

I told Judy, "Get out and go to the door as though you're alone. Dick has had a hint I am coming, so the place may be staked out. I want to find out. If the cops are around, remember—you weren't with me!"

A light over the door went on and Dick answered Judy's knock. They stood talking. I slid out of the truck and eased the door shut. The street was dark, quiet. Now for the test: I stepped out of the shadows and walked unhurriedly toward Dick and Judy. Just then, with perfect timing, the police car drove by. A flashlight or spotlight beam caught me. The driver of the police car jammed on the brakes and almost stood his machine on end.

I looked for a fleeting instant at Judy. I was seeing her, out of custody, for the last time. She stood silhouetted in the doorway, rigid with anxiety.

I jerked out my gun and sprinted for the darkness between two buildings. The police car was backing up, its motor whining urgently, and one of the cops had leaped from it to pursue me. The gun in my hand clicked twice—I intended to break a couple of caps as a warning—but each time failed to fire. I managed to give the first cop the slip and could easily have gotten away. But I chose to stay, to hide. Within minutes the district was swarming with police. The net kept tightening. But I still refused to leave; the legions of Hell couldn't make me go. I slipped into a house through an unlocked back door, locked it behind me, and encountered an old man and two teen-aged boys in the living room, listening to the radio.

"Sit still, please! And act as natural as possible."

They sat in plain view of a bay window and the searching police. I stood in a hallway where I could keep them covered and still not be seen from the outside. Minutes passed and the sounds of search died. I slipped out of the house and was cautiously making my way through the blackness of the front yard when I tangled with a child's fire engine, rang its bell, and crashed in a heap to the ground, twisting an ankle. The chase was on again. Somehow I made it to a church and crawled under, hiding behind a large gas meter. I smelled the gas—a leak in one of the pipes—but failed to associate it with my increasing fuzzy-headedness. The gas knocked me out and probably would have killed me if a breeze hadn't sprung up.

I revived. My head had grown to at least ten times its normal size. I laughed, "You got the big head now for sure." I climbed out from under the church and got unsteadily to my feet. I was all mixed up and I desperately wanted a cigarette but was afraid to light one for fear of blowing up. That was how groggy I was. When I tried to concentrate on where I lived, little men with jack-hammers went to work in my head. That head threatened to explode before I finally remembered the direction and location of my apartment. It was only two blocks away—the longest two blocks I have ever traveled.

The first time I had visited Dick I had been wearing a slipper (because of my shot foot). This fact had been reported to the police, who had concluded I must be living nearby. Accordingly, they made a house-to-house canvass of the area, showing my picture and asking if I lived there. They also showed my picture to the proprietors of all grocery stores, drive-ins, drugstores and restaurants within a radius of two miles from Dick's. When I learned of this door-to-door business, I decided to leave, to move. But I waited one day too long.

I was taken into custody on a Saturday morning. Gabriella came over early that morning to help me move. I went for the stolen car I had hidden (I thought) nearby. Walking along Glendale Avenue, I saw a familiar detective up ahead. He knew I was behind him, but he also knew I had the drop on him, so he just kept walking to his police car. "I realized the futility of attempting to flush the subject alone," he stated later in his report. He put in an urgent call on his two-way radio for reinforcements. Meanwhile, I ducked into a store and then back to the apartment, positive no policeman had tailed me. None had, but still I'd been tailed—by the young son of the store owner who had been present earlier when the police showed his father my picture. I had seen the boy but had, unwisely, never suspected he was following me. He ran back and told the police where I had gone.

I stood at the second-floor window of my apartment and watched the police close off the area and begin to move in. Hurriedly, Gabriella and I tore up and flushed Christopher's papers down a toilet in a bathroom across the hall. I left the bathroom door open, Gabriella concealed behind it. Then I sat down to wait, smoking a cigarette. Guns drawn, two detectives crept up the stairs and inched along the hallway to my door. They knocked.

"Come in, gentlemen," I called out. "I've been waiting for you."

Their prize in hand, he was rushed to the police station. *Cherchez la femme* didn't occur to the police until too late. When they dashed back to the apartment, Gabriella was gone. "All right, Chessman," they demanded, "who was that woman?"

"That woman, officers," I replied cheerfully, "must be a figment of your own overstimulated imaginations."

That was the first lie I told; it was, however, by no means the last. From then on, determined to cover my trail and to keep anyone from learning anything about my dealings with Christopher (for fear that he might revenge himself on Judy or my parents), I took the initiative and told whopper after whopper while being grilled by relays of detectives and questioned by Chino officials and the F.B.I.

I had told Al Collins that if he were caught first I didn't care how much he told the police about me if it would help him. Shortly after my arrest I learned that he had implicated me in more than a dozen burglaries, which made no difference, since detectives from practically every local jurisdiction were prepared to file robbery, burglary, kidnaping for robbery and other charges. I flatly denied commission of all crimes and actually had committed not more than one-quarter of those the police accused me of committing. Later, I secured the services of an extremely competent criminal attorney, who neatly eliminated the possibility of my being tried for my life, held to a minimum the number of serious felony charges filed, and arranged for me to plead guilty to a single count of armed robbery, with the escape and all other pending charges dismissed. The judge who sentenced me ran this new count of robbery concurrently with all those unfixed, indeterminate terms I was already serving.

As soon as the police permitted, Judy visited me at the Glendale station. She was glad, not that I was back in jail, but that my hectic misadventure was over and that I was still alive. But even with my safety assured, she remained troubled. I was Judy's husband; she loved me greatly, yet more and more I was a stranger to her, a man she didn't understand. Still her heart wouldn't let her admit she had been wrong to marry me.

After our visit, the police had a talk with Judy. They told her she was a good girl and that her husband was no good, a confirmed criminal. She should divorce me before I ruined her life. Their words made Judy cry, quietly. And later, one of the more cynical ones made a play for her, going to our home and questioning her thus: "That husband of yours got an $18,000 rare perfume collection from one of his burglaries. We think he gave all or part of it to you, and you know they put young ladies in jail for receiving stolen property. Now, of course, I could see that that didn't happen to you if . . ."

Actually, she never had received any perfume from me. Nevertheless, however innocent she might be, I saw how vulnerable she was as the wife of a notorious hoodlum and escaped convict who was headed back to prison to serve a lot of years. So, when she visited me again, I insisted she divorce me, be legally freed from me. She could wait or not wait at her option; that way, if the right young man came along, she could make a new life for herself; that way, she would not carry the stigma of being Mrs. Caryl Chessman. That way was the only way, I insisted, but Judy wouldn't listen.

I was transferred to the Los Angeles County Jail and confined to the "High Power" tank while the wheels of justice made the necessary turns. There I met a renegade ex-convict who, while in prison, had made a name for himself as a writer. However, his larcenous inclinations had led him back to jail as a result of involvement in the burglary of half a million dollars' worth of gilt-edged securities. The federals had charged him with transporting these stolen securities, in violation of federal law, from one state to another, and a jury had convicted him. He was positive, however, he would win on a technicality in the appellate court, which he ultimately did, and was then trying to raise the money—$2500—for an appeal bond. He made me a proposition: if I would go his bond, he could set it up so that a smart attorney could spring me from prison on a writ of habeas corpus. While his plan was not exactly legal, it was foolproof if handled correctly and if certain devious preliminaries were attended to. Since I had nothing to lose but the $2500, I arranged to make bond. All I could do then was wait and see if he would hold up his end of the bargain. I doubted it.

I was returned to San Quentin in January, 1944. During this period, all escapees, on arrival at the prison, were sent to the "shelf"—the isolated punishment unit behind Death Row—for twenty-nine days and often then shipped directly to Folsom, the state's grim maximum security prison. However, largely through the good offices of Tuffy and other friends, I avoided the shelf, which was an early and significant victory in my campaign to regain freedom as soon as humanly possible. A few days later I won another and somewhat ironical victory—assignment to the local Selective Service office, which was under the supervision of Mr. George Oakley, a very well-liked free man. The chief inmate clerk in the office was scheduled for parole release within a week and I was given his job. There was an abundance of work to be done and I welcomed the opportunity to keep busy while I awaited word of my friend's labors in my behalf.

I soon received that word, and it was disgustingly negative. My pal, as he had been confident he would, had won his case on appeal but then, inexcusably finding himself in serious financial difficulties, had turned to the pistol. Presently, for robbing several federally insured loan companies, he was a widely sought fugitive from justice. He had done nothing for me. That was that. Although his banditry grossed him more than $60,000, he never repaid the $2500.

Tuffy was transferred to Chino the day following my return to San Quentin. As a matter of policy, local officials had temporarily held up his transfer until my return, feeling that this would be in the best interests of all parties concerned. I had a long talk with this old comrade. He was sorry to see me back and facing all that additional time. Personally, he was determined to straighten out and make a go of it. "Dammit, Chess, I just don't like these places," he explained. "I don't like the idea of throwing my life away doing time." I heartily agreed. But it was a little late. However, even then I had made up my mind that I was serving my last jolt. If I ever gambled again, the stakes would be my life, not my freedom. Tuffy and I wished each other luck, shook hands, and said so long. We were headed in opposite directions, and both of us knew it. I was destined to be the spectacular failure of that much-publicized boy bandit gang of 1940-1941.

I had been back at San Quentin approximately a month when I received written notice that the institutional Classification Committee had classified me "Maximum, Folsom." This meant I was a maximum custody prisoner and Folsom bound. I told Mr. Oakley about the action of the committee and he went to bat for me on the ground that I was working hard at a key job, that I was staying out of trouble, that I deserved at least a chance to earn the right to remain at San Quentin. As a result, in subsequent weeks, those who made up the transfer lists kept skipping my name. Thus I managed to stay at San Quentin.

In the spring of 1944, Mr. Ward J. Estelle, institutional secretary to the two former prison boards, was looking for a skilled inmate stenographer and I was recommended to him.

In this job, too, I worked sometimes as many as twelve hours a day, voluntarily. I had no easy job because I didn't like easy jobs. I worked not only as Mr. Estelle's secretary but also as secretary to Mr. Fred R. Dickson. Mr. Dickson was then Associate Warden in charge of the prison's care and treatment program, and today is Business Manager at Chino. Additionally, Warden Duffy often used me on special occasions when he needed someone to take dictation or to record special events. And both boards seldom failed to have some project or assignment for me when they were meeting at the prison.

After a year I appeared before the Adult Authority and had my term fixed at forty years, with further parole consideration postponed another year. That afternoon the Authority reconsidered and reduced the forty years to twenty-eight.

Judy had moved north and was living near the prison. When she came to see me I told her bluntly about my twenty-eight years and again urged her to get a divorce. Before, she had put off a decision, saying there was no hurry. But twenty-eight years looked like an eternity and Judy had met a handsome young soldier whom she liked, perhaps loved, and who loved her. Still she refused to desert me, and so her divided love and loyalty left her in an impossible position.

"Judy, dammit, I want you to get that divorce," I lied, then becoming even more emphatic, more cruel. "I demand that you get it. I don't want a weepy, unfaithful wife to add to my troubles. Besides, a happy home isn't included in my plans for the future. I'm going to be busy looking out for myself, and I sure as hell don't want to have anybody around nagging at me about reforming."

My words stunned Judy. She looked stricken but she didn't cry.

"I'm sorry, Daddy," she said. "I didn't know you felt that way or that you would think that about me."

"Well, you know now," I told her.

"Yes, I know now."

Ashen-faced, Judy left, and I didn't think I would ever see her again. I tried to convince myself that I had acted in Judy's best interests. Surely one quick, clean thrust had been best.

I buried myself deeper in my work, and after work for a few minutes each day I would stand and look out across the sometimes turbulent waters of the bay, thinking thoughts that were not bright, not pleasant. I studied law from legal books and reports used in the office and was tutored by a former attorney serving a term for forgery. As a discipline, I wrote and rewrote—one bad book and one rather promising one. I severed almost all contact with the outside world, corresponded only with my mother and one friend. I was sardonically amused when the teletype began to chatter, demanding proof that Chessman was still at San Quentin. It turned out that the victims of a string of robberies in the Los Angeles area had been shown a picture of Chessman and had "positively" identified him as the perpetrator in each instance. This time I had a perfect alibi. My cell partner was a smiling, black-haired, coldly brilliant young man who was wanted for murder in Ohio. In the cell at night we often discussed life in terms of honesty versus criminality, examining every conceivable facet of our subject.

And in those discussions my twenty-eight-year jolt and Ohio's electric chair loomed large. . . .

In the spring of the year there was some unrest and a food strike at San Quentin. The rank and file involved, as well as the strike's leaders, asked me to act as spokesman for them, which I did—and found myself under a cloud with Department of Corrections officials.

August 6, 1945: for me, the date has a personal as well as a historical importance. A few minutes after a newscaster excitedly announced that the world's first atom bomb had been dropped on Hiroshima, a bomb was dropped on me. I was escorted into the warden's private office. Behind his large desk sat Warden Duffy, his face a stern mask, his blue eyes searching my face, accusingly—for what? On each side of the warden sat other high prison officials, their expressions equally stern.

I stood before the desk. "You sent for me, Warden?"

Warden Duffy nodded. "Caryl, I'm transferring you to Folsom immediately."

To say that I was surprised is to state my reaction mildly. I recall uttering one word that was laden with astonishment.

"What?"

Warden Duffy repeated that he was transferring me to Folsom immediately—for safekeeping. But why? I asked. The warden said he wasn't at liberty to tell me right then. I learned later that he was acting on a tip he couldn't very well afford to ignore. I was then under suspicion of falsifying prison records, dealing in large sums of contraband money, and planning an escape.

So, handcuffed, legcuffed and chained, I found myself occupying the back seat of a new Chevrolet speeding toward Folsom.

Folsom is an old, grim-looking prison that squats broodingly on the bank of the American River in Sacramento County, not many miles from the state's capitol. In the summer the sun beats down like some celestial blowtorch and the prison is . . . hot!

We arrived after the night lock-up and I was placed into a barren cell in the Back Alley—the segregated punishment unit. I managed with some sleight of hand to keep my cigarettes and a box of matches. When I stretched out on the mattress which, placed atop a cot-sized slab of cement, served as a bed, I learned that I had about a million hungry bedbugs for company. Figuring I didn't have enough blood to go around, and not wanting to show any favoritism, I paced the floor, smoked and thought for the rest of the night. And the more I thought, the more I was ready to give the cell back to the bedbugs. After all, they had been here first.

A great rattle of keys and slamming of doors heralded the arrival of morning. A guard and a trusty came along with a food cart. The guard unlocked and pulled open the almost solid steel door and the grinning trusty said, good-naturedly, without malice, "All right, here it is. Straight from the Ritz." He handed me a big tin cup full of potent black coffee and a pan containing what was officially called diet loaf and what the prisoners called a dog biscuit—an unappetizing but edible and dietetically adequate baked concoction containing vegetables, cereal, beans and occasionally some stew meat. I drank the hot, black coffee, poked with wonder at the dog biscuit, and inexplicably felt much better.

What was next on the schedule? Exercise, it developed. Half a dozen other men and myself were marched out to the main yard and allowed to walk back and forth near a guard tower. The day was a scorcher and the sun was blinding; still, the more I saw of it the more I was taking a liking to this hot, drab, grim gray prison.

Prisons, you see, have personalities, as distinct as those of the men doing time in them, and Folsom's was tough, contemptuous, challenging. Treatmentwise, a new administration had reformed the old Folsom—tamed it, you might say—and thus it was no longer a brutal, hopeless place, but its brooding, violent ghosts were still there to mock the change, and its function still was to hold California's most dangerous felons. As many prisoners told me in the next few days: "Chess, this is it. This is the end of the road." It was for a fact, and, strangely enough, I felt right at home. At the end of the road.

Judy came to see me one last time, in September, 1945. She had decided finally that she should not wait for me. In the spring of 1946 she filed for divorce; a year later she received her final decree.

Folsom was (and is) full of men serving long terms who, in the matter of their freedom, have turned rather savage and dream desperate dreams of escape. They continually scheme and plot and look and hope and curse their fate, the walls, their keepers, even each other on occasion. Among this group were many friends and men I had known for long years.

In January, 1947, I again appeared before the Adult Authority.

"Gentlemen," I quietly told its members, "my mother is dying of cancer and my father also is in very poor health. I'm needed at home and I've had my fill of prison. You can believe me when I say that I don't intend to do any more time."

The Authority granted me an eleven-year parole and set my release date for late January of the following year. My effective parole date was later advanced to December 8, 1947.

The intervening months passed swiftly. The day before my scheduled release I said goodbye to all my friends. I wanted to know if there was anything I could do for them after I got out.

As I was being checked out the next morning a wiseacre shouted: "If you promise to hurry back, Chess, I'll have the Captain save your cell for you."

"Don't bother," I said. "Chess won't be back."

27

"O Villain, Villain, Smiling, Damned Villain!"

The receiving and release sergeant drove me from the prison to the little town of Folsom. The instant we left behind us the walled, gray place that had been my home for so many months I experienced a sudden hungry awakening of mind, a quickening of keen sensory awareness, an angry triumph. I'd made it! I'd made it to the end of the road —and beyond!

That was all. I got up and left.

When I got to Los Angeles I hailed a taxi, giving the driver the address of my father's florist shop out on Los Feliz, between Riverside Drive and San Fernando Road, and telling him the kind of place it was.

I got a shock when I saw my father, who was sitting in the back of his shop reading a trade journal, his glasses resting on the tip of his nose. Hell, I thought, that's the way old men read. Then I was jarred into the realization that my father *was* an old man, older than his fifty-six years. His once handsome face was lined and drawn. My mother had written me that he had a serious heart condition. And his once highly profitable retail florist business had gone bust. He had given up one shop and was losing money on this second one. The debts were piling up. He was just about at the end of his rope.

I was his one hope. Somehow he had been sure all along that when I got home everything would work out for all of us. He looked up, saw me and was immensely pleased.

"Hi there, old timer," he said.

"Hi, Dad." We shook hands.

I got my second shock a few minutes later when, after we closed up the shop and drove home, I walked into my mother's bedroom. My mother was lying flat in bed; she was thin to the point of emaciation and her face was haggard. Still paralyzed, she was dying, slowly and terribly, of cancer.

She cried for joy at the sight of me. I bent down and kissed her and her thin arms encircled my neck. "We need you, Hon," my mother said in a whisper. "We desperately need your love and your strength."

And they had both, without reservation. But hate was hardly love's best servant. Loving my parents, I hated what had happened to them. And I hated myself because I was partially responsible. It was a bitter, bitter pill to swallow to know that, urgently wanting to be proud of me, they had to find pride in the fact that I had managed to get myself out of the state's toughest prison in almost record time.

My return home was a dark and hollow victory: looking again at my mother and father, seeing the brutal ravages of time and sickness and pain and worry written in their eyes, their faces, their bodies, I knew that I hadn't changed. I knew the hate was still bottled inside me, that it would soon find release. I knew that my strength was a betraying strength. For it would demand revenge. It would seek out an enemy, the most terrible enemy it could find to pit itself against. And in that moment of reunion I became aware of an ironical truth: the strongest, the most powerful man in the world is no more a free agent than the weakest and least powerful.

I smiled. After that I never stopped smiling. I hated and smiled. My mother was dying and my dreams were dead. I had no future. My mother had no future. My father had no future. We had perhaps a few tomorrows. But tomorrows weren't a future. War and violence and hating and savagery weren't a future. Before there can be a future there must be certainty that the war being fought has a purpose, that it will lead to a peaceful place beyond, to a place of meaning where one may live usefully, creatively, unmenaced, without hate and without discord. But such a place did not exist except in one's imagination.

It had no reality. Only the jungle had reality. And goddamn such a reality! I would personally destroy it yet!

I kissed my mother tenderly. I put a hand on my father's shoulder. For their sake I would pretend to be happy. I would pretend that all was going to be well for us now, that a miracle would take place, the God-given miracle of a future. I would promise my mother to keep at creative writing. I would sit nights away at her bedside and when the pain in her side were not too great we would talk about the books I would someday write.

I would encourage my father to sell his retail florist shop; we would lay promising plans for going into the wholesale florist business on a bold scale. We would be pals again, the three of us, my mother, my father and myself.

And as they talked so earnestly, I saw my mother's and my father's wasted faces. I saw the jungle, too.

I got a gun.

I recruited some guys to work with me who weren't known to be associated with me. And I was real clever, too clever, remembering the time at San Quentin when I had been "positively" identified. That gave me an idea how to drive the bulls slowly crazy.

I went to see a man in an adjoining county, a gambler with greedy ideas of empire who was looking for a striking force. We closed a deal. Bookmaking in the county was Big Business, fantastically Big Business, and this particular gambling gentleman wanted to cut himself a large piece of this bookmaking pie. I agreed to help—for a price. The plan wasn't novel; it *was* functional.

With confederates (whom I have never named) I began knocking over some of the larger places where illegal betting on the horses was being done.

I also began hijacking the collectors for the syndicate while they were making their rounds. At gun point I accepted their contribution to what I assured them was a good cause and lectured them, time permitting, on the error of their ways and the probable consequences attending it.

Needless to add, the syndicate had gorillas in its employ who were paid to eliminate grinning, wise-guy interlopers. And it had connections in pretty high places, and hence the means to get rid of them in other ways too. So I was warned to lay off—or else! I was told to get out of town and stay out. I told those who warned me to go to hell. I said I didn't know what they were talking about. And then the gorillas and I began to play games. It was great sport. The damned fools were trying to kill me when I was already dead. I was already dead and just didn't have sense enough to lie down. I liked to agitate and do battle with dragons too much. They were doing me a real favor, this smart syndicate bunch, when they began to mouth off and to send their gorillas to take care of me. They gave me a chance to declare war in the jungle. And I hated the jungle. I hated what it had done to me.

My mother kept sinking and twice almost died. I sat at her bedside as she hovered between life and death. In the same breath I prayed to and cursed God. The fires of hell burned in Mother's side and her face was contorted with pain, yet she managed to smile. She tried to speak and couldn't. Her suffering was terrible to see. I had a prescription of a powerful drug filled and gave my mother the fifty tablets. "Take these as you need them, Mom, and if the pain gets unendurable I'll understand if you . . ."

I was working out the details of a plan to rob a man who ran a big check-cashing business out in the Valley. That was one of his more legitimate enterprises. I enlisted the aid of a couple of bandit acquaintances and we equipped a special car to be used in pulling our victim over to the curb while he was on his way to his place of business after he left the bank. Then one of my confederates, who was overfond of marijuana, got loaded on the weed and got the bright idea of using our special car for another purpose. I read about the stupid manifestations of that idea in the newspapers, and gave my confederate a growl. He didn't take kindly to my criticism.

"All right, you smart bastard," I thought, "we'll take care of you after the Valley caper."

But the Valley robbery was frustrated. The morning it was to be pulled off, my marijuana-smoking, wise-guy confederate had our special car out. He had been gone all night and when he returned we got into a mean argument.

My friend had a gun. He pointed it at me.

"Don't you like what I did?" he challenged insultingly.

I didn't like it.

"Then do something about it. Do something about it in the next five seconds. Because then I'm going to blow your goddamn head off."

I did something about it.

PART THREE

DAMNANT QUOD NON INTELLIGUNT

· 28 ·

Three Times and Out?

VOTE DEATH FOR "CRIMINAL GENIUS"

That, in bold, black type, was the banner headline carried by the Los Angeles *Daily News* on Saturday, May 22, 1948. In part, the story beneath that headline read:

A jury of 11 women and one man last night invoked California's seldom-used "little Lindbergh law" to order that Caryl Chessman, San Quentin-educated criminal genius, be put to death for the kidnapings of two women.

Besides the two separate kidnapings for which the 12 talesmen exercised their right to fix the death penalty, a life imprisonment sentence was imposed for a still third kidnaping count.

After 30 hours of deliberation, the jury returned verdicts of guilty in an amazing string of 17 out of 18 felony crimes charged against the 26-year-old "red light" bandit.

The 26-year-old former convict, who conducted his own entire defense, heard the seemingly endless list of guilty verdicts . . . without flinching from the suave courtroom manner he had constantly maintained.

On the contrary, he smiled as the first obligatory death sentence was passed—the ninth count read by the court clerk following seven other guilty verdicts and one finding of not guilty.

Chessman explained afterward he "was afraid" he might have gotten life on all kidnaping convictions, while with the death penalties imposed he felt confident they would be reversed upon appeal.

Upon the rendering of a death penalty upon any plea, the state penal code calls for an automatic appeal without any action by the defendant or his counsel. . . .

Gray-haired veterans of criminal law had flocked to the trial to sit in amazement at Chessman's conduct of his own defense.

And with the same professional calm, the neatly-dressed defendant walked into the courtroom as word was received from the jury that it was ready to come in.

The clerk finally got to the jury's words: "We fix the punishment at death . . ."

I sat on my bunk in the High Power tank at the Los Angeles County Jail, scanning the above newspaper account of my conviction. Some "criminal genius"! I thought disgustedly. For the third time, I was headed back to San Quentin. And if the state had its way, it would be three times and out; when I left the prison next time, it would be in a box.

"He who defends himself has a fool for a client." That is what they say around jails and courthouses, and they have been saying it for a long, long time. And I had had a fool for a client.

Turn back the clock. For weeks a "red light" bandit had been terrorizing the inhabitants of Los Angeles County. A lone wolf, he drove a late model Ford equipped with a red spotlight (perhaps portable) and, some of his many terrified victims reported, a police radio. The Ford had the appearance of a police car. Capitalizing on this, the bandit's *modus operandi* was to prowl the lover's lanes, the deserted stretches of beach highway or the little-used roadways—near the fabled Malibu Colony, near Pasadena's Rose Bowl—and the less habited hilly areas—along Mulholland Drive, and the winding, unlighted roads lacing the Flintridge Hills.

When, while on these nocturnal prowls, he spotted a couple in a parked car he would approach, flash the red light and brake to a stop. And the prospective victims, believing it to be the police on a routine checkup, would wait unsuspectingly while the bandit got unhurriedly out of his car and walked to theirs.

"Got any identification?" he sometimes would demand, flashing a penlight directly into the faces of the couple.

"Sure," the man would reply, and produce his wallet.

"How about the lady? She got any, too?"

If the woman had a purse with her, she would reach for it to get out identification.

At that point, or sometimes immediately on reaching the car, without going through any of these preliminaries, the bandit would shove an ugly-looking .45 caliber automatic into the faces of his startled victims and growl, "This is a stick-up!" Sometimes, after demanding and taking the man's wallet and the woman's purse into his possession, he then would rifle both for money on the spot, afterward handing them back. Other times, he would retain the wallet or the purse, or both. Sometimes, on approaching the car, he would be masked; other times he would not be; sometimes he would approach the car unmasked and, only after giving his victims an excellent view of his face, would he then pull up a handkerchief mask. Sometimes, in an atonal monotone, he would repeat over and over, insanely: "If you don't do what I say they'll carry you away in a casket."

Sometimes he would carry off and criminally assault the woman. If she begged him to show mercy, he would listen without interrupting, his face expressionless.

Then he would ask in a lifeless monotone, "You through?"

If she said she was, he repeated his demands. If she burst into tears he sat unmoving and waited until she finished crying.

"You through now?" that terrible voice then would ask.

One young woman he kidnaped asked him why he did these things. He told her his wife had been unfaithful to him while he was serving in the armed forces during the last war. He said he was getting even.

He struck again and again. The reports of his bold, usually brutal forays kept mounting, and because he invariably threatened his victims with the swift loss of their lives if they reported his conduct to the police, law enforcement theorized that many of his crimes were not known to them, and they feared murder would soon be included on the fast-growing list of his offenses. They doubled and then redoubled their efforts to capture him. He could be no novice, they reasoned, so with victims they poured through police mug pictures, hoping for a lead. None was found.

Heavily armed police officers teamed up in pairs and, with one of each pair disguised as a woman, spent nights parked in the hills in ordinary looking autos, hoping to lure him into striking. He struck elsewhere. All points bulletins were sent out. Police officers in outlying areas were alerted. The search was intensified. Over and over the police radio barked out a description of the "red light" bandit and the car he was using:

> Male Caucasian, possibly Italian, swarthy complexion, 23-35 years, five feet six to five feet ten, 150-170 pounds, thin to medium build, dark brown wavy hair, close cut, dark brown eyes, crooked teeth, narrow nose with slight hump on bridge of nose, sharp chin, possible scar over right eyebrow. Armed with a .45 old-looking black automatic. . . . Uses small pen type flashlight. Believed to be driving early 1947 or late 1946 light gray or beige club coupe. . . . A red spotlight has been seen on left and right side of car . . . Possible radio which receives police calls with switch underneath dashboard, no antenna on car. Believe suspect when operating keeps license plate and spotlight in baggage compartment in rear of car and after leaving scene of crime replaces license on auto. Clothes worn by suspect vary . . . Interrogate any and all

occupants using above described vehicle . . . Use caution as suspect armed.

Friday night. January 23, 1948. 7:40 P.M.

Radio car officers May and Reardon, both young ex-servicemen, were cruising slowly south on Vermont Avenue at a point between Hollywood and Sunset Boulevards in Hollywood when they spotted a northbound Ford generally fitting the description of the red light bandit's car. Reardon, who was driving, promptly executed a U-turn, shifting into second gear, and sent his prowl car leaping in pursuit.

A hundred feet or more up the street, both officers observed the car they were after turn into a gas station at the corner of Hollywood and Vermont. Reardon speeded up, then braked, aiming the nose of his Ford into the service station, which the suspected vehicle was circling. The several hundred feet originally separating the two cars was cut to a car-length at the back of the station, near the grease rack. The Ford eased out into the southerly stream of traffic on Vermont. It speeded up. Reardon followed suit.

Luck can be bad, insufferably bad. That I can vouch for, for I happened to be the driver of the Ford May and Reardon were following, and I knew they were behind me. I had spotted them before they had spotted me. I thought about my eleven-year parole. Seated beside me, as I guided the Ford back onto Vermont Avenue, was another parolee, and I knew it was a violation of the terms of my parole to associate with ex-cons. I was operating a car—later proved to be stolen—without the permission of my parole officer, another violation of parole conditions. The back seat of the car, a club coupe, was filled with men's suits and other clothing—later established by police to have been taken in what was called a robbery-kidnaping of a clothier a few hours earlier. In short, if for no other reasons than those just given, whether or not I had stolen the Ford or had even known it was stolen, and whether I had or had not participated in the robbery-kidnaping, standing a pinch meant more long, dreary years in Folsom.

So I decided to make a run for it, convinced I could shake off my tail. All I had was a Hobson's choice. Convicts have a saying: "If I run, I get shot; if I stand still, I get stabbed." For some reason I didn't trouble to analyze, I preferred to get shot or, stated more nicely, shot at. Automatically I made the physical movements that would send the car I was driving hurtling through traffic at breakneck speeds. All this was done in a fraction of a second. But I didn't catch my pursuers entirely napping. The red light on the police car snapped on. That car's siren uttered a low-throated growl. Soon it would be screaming hysterically in my ear.

Both cars leaped ahead. The chase was on in deadly earnest.

Unexpectedly, while making a sliding U-turn—after careening through countless screaming-brake efforts to dodge bullets—Dave, my much overwrought passenger, leaped or bounced against me and I was compelled to slam on the brakes to avoid crashing a parked car.

At that moment the police car swerved around the corner and Reardon, who was driving with inspired skill, deliberately crashed into us, on the driver's side. Welcoming the opportunity, Dave hastily exited out the door of the Ford on the passenger side. I followed his example with equal alacrity. Simultaneously, May and Reardon leaped from their police car, and two more squad cars shot around the corner and ground to a bucking halt. I didn't hesitate after alighting; I immediately made a dash for a back yard.

May shouted "Halt!" and fired twice in rapid succession. I was at most twenty feet away from him when he fired and had just glanced back. May's marksmanship was bad. The first bullet zinged by me. The second grazed my forehead, gouging out flesh and hair at the hairline. It felt as though my head spun around two full turns while my body continued to travel in one direction. The impact of the bullet slammed me to the ground. The sensation was that I'd been shot through the head. I seemed to float to earth.

When I struck the ground I felt a sharp, wrenching pain and knew I wasn't dead—at least not yet. I scrambled back to my feet, tried with indifferent success to run, staggered blindly into an iron fence and was stopped, cold, in my tracks. I was seized, ultimately handcuffed.

The police told me I was the red light bandit; they told me they could prove it. And I told them that was what they would have to

do. At first I laughed at their accusations, but not for long. The game
we were playing soon became a deadly serious one.

At the trial two irreconcilably conflicting versions were given of
what was said and what transpired while I was held at the station.

I testified that I was beaten brutally, denied sleep, threatened with
further violence, not allowed to see an attorney or my father, grilled to
exhaustion and promised only two or three robbery charges would be
filed if I confessed to the red light crimes; that the police threatened
to send me to the gas chamber if I refused to confess, or kill me if I
failed to do so and then claim I had been attempting to escape; and
that, as a result, when these physical and psychological third-degree
methods became intolerable, I falsely and involuntarily agreed to anything the police said when the words were put in my mouth.

These disputed admissions and confessions were made orally only.

I still maintain my so-called "confessions" were false. I still maintain
I was severely, viciously beaten. I still maintain the "confessions" were
cynically obtained in the way I have claimed all along, with the use of
violence. I invite all detectives to submit to a lie-detector test with me.
If the test shows, with regard to this beating, that they are telling the
truth and I am not, I will abandon voluntarily all possibilities I have
of survival and withdraw any and all legal actions or proceedings that
may then be pending in the courts.

I extend this same invitation to other police officers who at the trial
denied extorting a false confession in the way I testified and still assert
they did. And I state my belief that the prosecutor contrived to get
those "confessions" admitted into evidence knowing they had been
secured in violation of the Constitution. I am prepared to take the
matter to court and back my claim.

One thing more: Ever since my arrest I have begged for a lie-detector test on the question of guilt or innocence but have never succeeded in being given one. So I make another stipulation. When I am
questioned about my treatment after being taken into custody, I want

also to be questioned about whether I am the red light bandit. If the test reveals that I am lying, when I flatly and unequivocally state I am not that bandit and that I did not commit the crimes for which I am waiting to die, then I shall abandon my legal fight for survival.

A Fool for a Client

After being held those three days for investigation at the Hollywood police station, I was transferred to the Los Angeles County Jail and, after being put through a show-up, was lodged in the High Power tank, old and familiar custodial quarters.

I immediately contacted one of southern California's better-known and most capable criminal attorneys, a small man with button-bright eyes. This was the same man who, with other members of his law firm, had represented me and got me off with a comparatively light prison sentence on that last occasion when I had been confronted with the very real prospect of being sent to the gas chamber.

He seated himself at the table across from me in the Attorney Room of the jail, looked at me quizzically and shook his head. "Looks like you really got yourself into one this time, Chess. Maybe, though, with a little work I can get you another deal. What will you settle for?"

"An acquittal," I told him.

His eyebrows shot up. "Quit kidding," he said.

"I'm *not* kidding," I replied. "And I'm *not* guilty. Maybe that's just a remarkable coincidence. But it also happens to be the fact."

My smallish counsellor's expression told me, before his words did, that he was frankly incredulous.

"That's what they all tell me, Chess. You know that. But let's face the facts. Let's look at the airtight case they have against you. I've already taken a look into it." He held up, outstretched, the five fingers of his left hand. Then, taking hold of them one at a time with his right thumb and index finger, he pointed out how the evidence damned me five times over.

"One, many of the red light victims identify you. Two, you are caught driving a stolen car which fits to a *T* the description of the one the bandit used. Three, a penlight, also fitting the description of one used by the bandit, is found in the glove compartment of this car. Four, the bandit used an old .45 automatic, and when you're arrested they find one near the car. Five, the police tell me you have already confessed. I should add, not to mention or count the fact—you are a notorious police character, a two-time loser, that you tried to make a run for it rather than submit to arrest which, the law says, shows a 'consciousness of guilt.'"

I told him, "I still say I'm not guilty this time."

I held up five fingers and, following his example, counted on them. "One, I was *mis*identified, not identified. It happens all the time and you know it, particularly when the police call the victim and say, 'We've got your bandit; he's an ex-con who's already confessed. Won't you please come down and identify him for us?' And before the victim comes down, he reads all about the guy's arrest in the papers.

"So, all right, let's take a look at the facts. I'm six feet tall and weigh over 190 pounds, and I look it. My build is what they call muscular. I wear a size 46 coat. All the police reports on the bandit definitely fix his height at between five six and five nine or ten and his weight between 140 and 170, with a thin to medium build. How about *that?* And some of the victims said the bandit was an Italian and had a slight accent and talked in a monotone. I'm not Italian. I don't have an accent, and anybody can talk in a monotone."

(You will doubtless question how, at that point, I knew all these facts. The answer is found in the trial record: while being held those three days for "investigation" the police showed me the police reports.)

"Two, three and four: I was caught in a hot car, they found a penlight in the glove compartment and a .45 near the car—all true. But there are thousands of Fords that look like the one I was caught in. You can buy a penlight in any drug or dime store. And all .45's look alike when you're staring into the business end of them. So, put all three together and say they add up to more than coincidence. Yet, when you get right down to it, all that means is that maybe this car, this penlight and this gun belonged to the red light bandit. That still doesn't, *ipso facto,* make me him.

"Five, the so-called confessions the police got from me were procured in such a way you would have confessed if they'd been asking you the questions—and telling you the answers. They just aren't true. And if I'd stopped and let them arrest me in the company of an ex-con in a car loaded with hot clothes, just to mention two facts, I'd have gone back to Folsom as a parole violator, maybe with some new charges, whether I was the red light bandit or not. So how does that show any consciousness of guilt?"

"All right," he said, striving to be patient. "Let's assume you've convinced *me.* Let's say *I* believe you. You're not the red light bandit. Somebody else is. But if that's the case, you must know who he is. So how do we go about proving his identity?"

"We don't," I said. "We prove my innocence."

"And how do we do that?"

"By alibi witnesses and physical evidence. I've been thinking back and I'm positive I can prove where I was when most, if not all, of the red light crimes were committed. By tearing down identification and taking apart the prosecution's other evidence, showing the obvious flaws in it. By proving their case is *too* good. By proving, if the prosecution tries to introduce them, that my alleged confessions were coerced and are phony. By letting me testify and tell the truth about the existence but not the identity of a third man in the car that night I was arrested and how I happened to be involved with him. By a lot of other ways that you know as well as I do."

"Look, Chess," my counsellor said, "you don't seem to understand. If you take the stand, the D.A. can and will impeach you with your prior felony convictions. No jury is likely to believe anything you say after that. And no jury will take your word over that of the police as to how the investigating officers secured a confession. As far as the alibi evidence is concerned, all that will do is create a conflict with prosecution evidence for the jury to resolve. Can't you see? You haven't got a snowball's chance in hell if you don't produce this third party, if he exists."

"He exists, all right," I said. "But look, I'm not saying *he is* the red light bandit. All I'm saying is that *I'm not.* All I'm saying is that there were three people in the Ford and one got away at the service station just before the chase began, and the one who got away fits the description of the red light bandit, and the car and everything in it belonged to him."

"That's your story?"

I nodded. "That's my story."

The small man with the button-bright eyes mulled over what I had told him. Then he said, "Chess, tell me something. Answer me truthfully. If our situations were reversed, would you believe me if I told you that story?"

"No," I admitted, after a moment's thought, "I don't think I would."

"Well, that's the answer then," he said. "I don't think you would either. It's not part of my job to decide whether you're telling me the truth or not. I'm personally inclined to believe you. The story's just wacky enough to be true and it's obvious there is just a whole lot more you could tell me that you're holding back. But take an old campaigner's word for it: no jury on earth will believe you once they hear about your criminal record and after those female victims get on the stand and point the finger at you and say you're the man. You'll be committing suicide if you go before a jury. Better take a deal if I can get one, and I think I can."

I shook my head. "No deal."

My counsellor looked sad. He said, "Well, Chess, it's your neck, but just the same I hate to see you stick it in the noose."

"In this state," I reminded him, "they gas you."

"That's right," he agreed. "And when they get through with the job you're awfully dead and you stay that way for a long, long time."

Those words brought our interview to an end. I was still determined, whatever the risk, to take my chances in front of a jury, yet I couldn't very well ask a man to defend me who genuinely believed that in doing so he would be sending me to my doom.

I promptly consulted another attorney, a tall, florid-faced, white-haired former member of the district attorney's staff, with a formidable reputation both for huge fees and an ability to work legal miracles in seemingly hopeless cases.

Puffing on a cigar, this attorney listened, absorbed, to my story. He had asked to hear it. When I finished recounting it, I asked, "How much to defend me and really do the job?"

He promptly quoted a fee of too many thousands of dollars. He also said he wanted a guarantee of several thousands more if he got me the acquittal I wanted.

I whistled. "Look, counsellor," I said, "I'm supposed to be the guy who goes around robbing helpless citizens, not you."

He laughed a deep belly laugh. "Son, I like to win," he told me jovially. "I like to win better than anything in the world. It's a religion —almost a mania—with me. I'd like to win for you, on your terms, but it would take money to do the job. It would mean turning investigators loose to dig up every shred of evidence there is in the case, both for us and against us. It would mean hiring a forensic chemist, using expert witnesses. It would mean spending more time than you can imagine digging around in law books, staying awake nights working out the angles and the kinks in the case, and spending days on end probing prospective jurors' minds to be certain we got the right ones." He paused to flick the ash from his cigar.

"You see, son, I'm no fixer. When I win it's only because I know more about the case, the evidence, the angles and all the rest than my esteemed opponent the prosecutor. Actually, the fee I quoted you was a bargain rate. I know it's probably twice as much money as you can afford to pay or can raise. Yet at the same time it's not a penny less than I could take the case for and still have a chance to win. Understand?"

I told him I did. I understood if an acquittal was legally for sale, I didn't have the purchase price. This fact was underscored when I contacted yet a third attorney, with the same results.

This meant if I still wanted to be represented by counsel at my trial I was left with these alternatives: either hire an attorney I could afford, or ask for an appointment by the court of the public defender. Ours being an adversary system of jurisprudence, a "protection of legal rights" would mean only a watchdogging to insure the presentation of available, favorable evidence, trial of the case according to established procedural standards, and full and fair instructions to the jury on applicable principles of law.

I needed more than a watchdog, however. I needed an inspired advocate—an Erskine, a Pruiett, a Darrow, a Fallon, a Rogers and a Leibowitz all in one—an unconquerable, dynamic legal gladiator eager and willing to punch gaping holes in the prosecution's case. I needed a dedicated champion willing to fight for me every inch of the way through the trial. That was what I needed, and I ended up with a fool for a client.

I decided to represent myself.

A courtroom and I were not strangers. I was then familiar, generally, with the rules of evidence and, although acquired informally (mostly from my studies at San Quentin), I possessed a working knowledge of criminal trial procedure. I could talk and argue convincingly, and I wasn't crowd shy. There was no danger I would suddenly find myself struck dumb when the trial got underway and I found myself on my own. Finally, I was in the mood to give the state a good battle for my life.

I thus believed I possessed sufficient skills, miscellaneous, legal and forensic, to justify my decision to have a fool for a client. That decision was made reluctantly but not halfheartedly. When I appeared for plea I informed the master calendar judge, who would take my plea (of not guilty) and assign the case to another judge for trial, of my decision. His Honor questioned me sharply in an effort to determine if I was sincere or simply claiming an intention to represent myself in order to stall the case along by allowing it to be set for trial and then, at the last minute, hiring an attorney who, necessarily, would have to get a continuance in order to prepare. I assured this judge I really did intend to try the case without an attorney. His

Honor wasn't so sure and warned me I must be ready to go to trial on the date set.

Being ready is, however, more than a state of mind, and it assumes a condition of fact. In my case that naïve assumption was not justified. Back at the jail, I ran head on into unexpected difficulties. My jailers pointedly informed me that their rules did not allow prisoners to possess legal books of any kind, or a typewriter or clerical supplies (beyond pencil and writing tablet paper), although legal books, typewriter and clerical supplies, as I pointed out, were essential to anyone undertaking to prepare a defense in his own behalf. The logic of what I said was met with a shrug, a grunt or a growl. Inquiry also resulted in my being told I would be restricted to two twenty-minute visits a week behind a thick mesh screen from friends or relatives (which included witnesses), notwithstanding the fact I was acting as my own attorney and direly needed to interview numerous witnesses.

Try as I might, I was not able to get these rules relaxed, and the result was that, for all practical purposes, I was foreclosed from personally preparing for trial. To my way of thinking, this was a strange situation indeed: both California's organic (constitutional) and statutory law expressly gave the individual defendant the right "to appear and defend in person," and yet apparently, in practical operation, when the right was asserted, it could be frustrated by forcing the defendant to go to trial wholly unprepared. The situation became even stranger when I attempted to write the trial court and complain. My letters were returned by the jail censor on the ground no prisoner could write a "personal" letter to a judge.

Not relishing the predicament I found myself in, I contacted a fourth attorney in whom I had confidence and made tentative arrangements with him to assist me in the preparation and presentation of the case. This attorney was to set investigative and other pretrial machinery in motion immediately upon receipt of a fee agreed upon, which was to be paid by my father, who planned to secure the money by making a loan on our house.

Then I suffered another setback. My father was seriously injured and hospitalized before he had completed negotiations for the loan, and my trial date on the first set of charges came around before he had sufficiently recovered from his injury to conclude these negotiations, even with the attorney's help. I was scheduled first to be tried on the clothier robbery and kidnaping charges jointly with Dave, the overwrought passenger, who had been named a co-defendant. On my application, my trial was severed from Dave's and continued for three days, when the red light crimes were to be tried. Although sought, no other relief was granted. On the date set for trial of the red light and other charges, I appeared before the trial judge (not the one originally scheduled to preside over the clothier robbery and kidnaping charges) and explained I was wholly unprepared to defend myself through no fault of my own. I asked permission to subpoena named jailers to prove I hadn't been allowed personally to prepare, and had my father and the attorney in court ready to testify. I motioned, consequently, for a brief continuance and for an order that either I personally be allowed to prepare or that the attorney of my choice be allowed to prepare the case for trial for me.

The motion was denied. The trial judge said it was my own fault I was unprepared, because I had turned down the services of a deputy public defender and had been warned to be ready for trial. He added that he saw no need for me to produce witnesses and that he couldn't "interfere" with the sheriff's "arrangements" that operated to prevent me from personally preparing. Then he ordered that all eighteen felony charges be consolidated for one trial.

The legal battle for my life was on and the struggle ahead looked rugged. I knew that, being wholly unprepared, I would be hopelessly outmaneuvered. Death sentence convictions would inevitably follow if I didn't get immediate help in contacting my witnesses and gathering physical evidence, things I couldn't possibly do in a jail cell. So I asked, and the trial judge agreed to appoint the deputy public defender assigned to his courtroom as my "legal adviser" until I could arrange for private assistance.

My legal adviser turned out to be an earnest young attorney named Al Matthews who had become a deputy public defender for the express purpose of gaining criminal trial practice experience in every kind of criminal case before my trial judge, the Honorable Charles W. Fricke, regarded in legal circles as one of the state's most learned trial jurists and in certain other circles as one of its toughest.

Al and I huddled that night in the Attorney Room at the county jail. He listened intently to my story, scribbling notes as I told it. I emphasized that I wanted to prove my claimed innocence, not another's guilt. I told him bluntly that I knew exactly what I was up against and that win, lose or draw, I would take the responsibility. I said all I wanted was a fair chance to defend on my terms. I remarked that I realized my story probably sounded incredible but asked that he accept what I said on faith alone and help me unearth witnesses and run down leads.

"In short," I said, "let's start with a hypothesis of innocence and try to develop it."

"Fair enough," he agreed.

And that's what we did. I felt much better when the trial got under way the next morning.

First was the problem of selecting a jury. The prosecutor, personally convinced I was guilty and a menace to society, wanted a jury that would vote the death penalty. He said so. He said considerably more. He told prospective jurors: "You might think he is just as insane as some people for the defense say" (although no one for the defense had said I was insane). He worried over the fact I "persisted" in representing myself, and added this would give me an opportunity "to grab some sympathy for [my]self in some way." He asked the prospective jurors if they would be able to cope with the "problem" of "defendant representing himself." He gratuitously argued the evidence would "be a veritable demonstration and not call for anything except the death penalty," even before the jurors had the faintest intimation of what the evidence would be or show. He said he didn't believe the "evidence" would show I had killed or murdered anyone *yet*. He demanded to know if the prospective jurors had any "quarrel" with the kidnaping law; he told them it took "courage" to return the death penalty and questioned their "courage" to do so.

In turn, I wanted a jury that would weigh all the evidence fairly

and impartially, and hardheadedly decide the question of guilt or innocence without being influenced by passion, prejudice and newspaper
or other hoopla. So each of us, the prosecutor and I, arduously questioned prospective jurors until, four days later, a jury was finally selected and sworn "to try the cause."

That meant the preliminary skirmishing was over.

I also had the uneasy feeling that it meant the battle, if not the war,
was lost before it had really begun. It seemed to me that the prosecutor, before offering a shred of evidence, had convinced the jury that
this was a death penalty case and that the trial to follow was simply a
necessary formality.

I heard my motion for a daily transcript of the trial proceedings,
invariably granted in capital cases, denied.

I listened as the prosecutor stood before the jury and delivered his
opening address. The theme he was to stress throughout the trial
was nicely summed up in a one-sentence paragraph of a news story
which appeared in the Los Angeles *Daily News:*

> In his [opening] statement to the jury Dist. Atty. J. Miller Leavy
> said Chessman was a "criminal genius, a one-sided personality
> with absolutely no social conscience."

An old hand at the game, the prosecutor forcefully and dramatically
presented his case in support of the charges, his "case in chief" as the
law calls it. Neatly he wove a convincing, damning net of direct and
circumstantial evidence around me. He called witness after witness to
the stand—several victims of the red light bandit who said, "That's
the man!" Forensic chemists who testified crisply, professionally with
regard to hairs and mathematical probability, and little nuts and pliers
and "adhering debris." Police officers who vividly detailed my capture.

I countered with a vigorous but necessarily improvised defense. Already, so far as I was concerned, the trial judge figuratively had handcuffed me when he had ruled I would have to remain at the counsel
table and would not be permitted to approach the witness stand to
cross-examine prosecution witnesses with regard to exhibits; nor

would I be allowed to take those exhibits to the jury box and pound home my point after I had ferreted out some piece of damaging information from a prosecuting witness.

We had so little time to find witnesses and dig out favorable physical evidence that my defense at times lacked the convincing coherence additional time for preparation would have given it. I was obliged to call several witnesses to the stand absolutely cold, without first interviewing them, and others after but a hurried interview. Still other key witnesses we never did locate. And there was the very real problem of trying to defend against eighteen serious felony charges simultaneously. All I could hope to do with such a rough-hewn defense was to create a reasonable doubt as to my guilt, which is all the law requires to warrant acquittal.

I took the stand in my own behalf and flatly denied being the red light bandit or committing his crimes. I weathered the storm of an intensive three-day cross-examination, steadfastly stuck to my claim of innocence. But the prosecutor was clever and in several ways made a fool of me. I had expected that to happen and considered it unavoidable, since what I was trying to do could be compared to a man in a stud poker game who declares he has an ace in the hole but refuses to show it. I testified that three men had been in the Ford the night of my arrest (and earlier a fourth) but refused to identify that third person, and this gave the prosecutor an excellent opportunity to ridicule my testimony. He also, over my objection, forced me to admit that two other men and I had been associated with an individual engaged in closing down the "books" (places where illegal wagering is done on horse races) of a competitor, and that I had taken $2300 from one bookmaker at the point of a gun, a "robbery" not charged.

In rebuttal, to impeach and discredit my claim of innocence and to smash the then looming structure of my defense, the prosecutor sought to introduce in evidence my pre-trial confessions, after having asked me if I had not admitted commission of a crime charged. I challenged his right to do so and branded those confessions in sworn testimony as false and extorted. The prosecutor replied by calling to the stand investigators who testified I had not been mistreated and had

confessed freely and voluntarily. As a result, the trial judge overruled my objections and permitted the police to testify and relate those
confessions to the jury.

That evidence, in turn, brought before the jury startling accounts of
my violent criminal past, since, on invitation of the prosecutor, one
of the investigating officers testified these previous crimes and criminal acts—robberies, shootings, gun battles with police, escapes from
custody—had been discussed while I was being grilled with regard to
the red light crimes. This officer also testified I had bragged that I
would continue my criminal career posthaste if I ever got free again
but would be smarter and not get caught next time. I strenuously denied making any such statement, bragging or having discussed my
criminal past with the police, and offered other surrebuttal evidence
in an effort to combat the shock-producing effect I saw the prosecutor's rebuttal evidence had had on the jury.

In all, when both sides had completed their presentation of evidence, a staggering total of more than eighty witnesses had testified
on 120-odd different occasions and eighty-four exhibits had been
placed before the jury. When transcribed, the testimonial evidence
alone filled 1500 pages of the reporter's transcript of the trial proceedings prepared for use on appeal.

Of the prosecutor's argument to the jury, the Los Angeles *Daily
News* (on May 18, 1948) reported:

> Life of criminal genius Caryl Chessman is a burden and a men-
> ace to everyone, including himself, and he would be better off if
> he were put in the gas chamber.
>
> This was the theme of Dep. Dist. Atty. J. Miller Leavy in his
> summation to a jury in Superior Judge Charles W. Fricke's
> court today.
>
> "This young man is completely worthless," said Leavy.
>
> "Since he was 16 he has abused every privilege of society."

Then the prosecutor called the jury's attention to the fact that I was
being tried for three kidnaping charges punishable by death—so return
three death penalties! he demanded.

The news story just mentioned went on to state the defendant "appeared unimpressed by the prosecutor's demand that he pay with his life for the alleged crimes," and that "It is expected that the jury will get the case tomorrow, after Chessman, a very eloquent speaker, has made his pitch to the jurors."

I spent that night chain smoking, pacing the cramped floor of my jail cell, reviewing the evidence from every conceivable angle and forming in my mind what I would—or could—say on the morrow when I confronted those twelve grim-faced talesmen and talked for my life.

How do you convince twelve such people who have heard you branded a fiend and worse by the prosecutor, who have seen and heard witness after witness point you out and say you are the bandit, who have heard police say you confessed, who have heard officers tell of the violent episodes in your past and your asserted determination to return to a life of crime as soon as you got free again—how do you convince twelve such people you simply are not guilty of the particular crimes for which you are on trial?

The answer is, you don't. When the time comes you stand before them and quietly, with cold logic, with warm emotion, you argue the evidence and your claimed innocence. You say all that can or should be said. You hammer at the fact that the red light crimes were committed by a bungling amateur with a sexually twisted mind, not by a coldly calculating professional criminal. You ask them: Would a two-time loser who intimately knew the ins and outs of crime approach a car unmasked and proceed to commit penny ante crimes punishable by death, knowing all the while his picture was on file in practically every police station in the county and that it probably would be one of the first to be shown to robbery victims? You pound at this theme and dissect the evidence for a day and a half. Then you sit down.

You listen as the prosecutor closes with another blast at you. He appeals to the jury to render "cow county" justice. You listen as the judge gives long, complicated instructions to the jury. You know what is coming thirty hours later when you are brought into court and the foreman of the jury tells the trial judge the jury has arrived at verdicts. On slips of paper these are passed to the court clerk. He reads the verdicts aloud. The jury has found you guilty on seventeen of the eighteen charges. On two it has fixed the punishment at death.

You know then that the long, tough battle for survival, rather than just ending, is just beginning. You know you are headed for the Death Row and that you will be lucky—damned lucky—to come off that Row alive. You remember then what a grizzled old convict once told you: *When it gets too tough for everybody else it gets just right for me!*

The reporters and photographers swarm around you. Flash bulbs explode in your face. Questions are hurled at you.

No, the death penalties didn't surprise you, but they did disappoint you. You had hoped for an acquittal. Yes, you still absolutely claimed to be innocent. Yes, with the death sentences, you believed your chances for reversal on appeal were good.

What happens if you lose the appeal?

The answer is simple. You practice holding your breath.

After that the reporters aren't quite so flip with their questions. They sense that inside you aren't amused.

And you're not. You've made up your mind you will put up the damnedest legal struggle any human being ever has before they get you in that ugly green room.

· *30* ·

"What Do You Think about It Now, Sucker?"

June 25, 1948—the date I was sentenced to death—fell on a Friday. It was hardly a typical Day of Judgment. No thunder boomed in black, turbulent, wind-swept, rain-lashed heavens. No somber background music, gradually increasing in tempo, rose to a crashing finale. On the contrary, it was a warm, languorous day of early summer, and through an open courtroom window I could glimpse a patch of sunny blue sky and haze-shrouded mountains off to the northwest. Familiar, commonplace city sounds and smells drifted up from the street eight floors below. And distantly, perhaps from a car radio, I heard, mingled with other sounds, that phenomenon unique to our modern society, the singing commercial.

Heavily guarded, I had been brought to court a few minutes early and, while waiting for the judge to arrive, Al Matthews and I spent the time smoking and talking about nothing in particular, our countenances far from funereal. When Judge Fricke, a slight, bespectacled little man then in his late sixties, with a surprisingly deep voice, entered and seated himself at the bench, we plunged our cigarettes into a handy sand-filled receptacle and ceased talking. In a bored voice the clerk formally declared court in session and I walked around and took my place at the counsel table. I leafed through my notes to be certain they were in order.

The case of *The People of the State of California versus Caryl Chessman* was called. The court announced itself ready to hear argument on the motion for new trial I had made. Heard, the motion was

295

denied. Was there any legal cause why sentence should not be pronounced? After hearing me, the judge said there was none, and that
made the traditional question an interesting bit of rhetoric.

Then, matter-of-factly, I heard myself sentenced to death. Twice
over—because the jury had fixed the punishment at death on two
counts—the following words were spoken in a rumbling monotone:

"The jury having returned a verdict . . . finding you guilty of
the crime of kidnaping for the purpose of robbery, and fixing the penalty at death, it is the judgment and sentence of this court that for
that offense that you, the said Caryl Chessman, be delivered by the
Sheriff of Los Angeles County, State of California, to the Warden of
the State Prison of the State of California, at San Quentin, to be by
him executed and put to death by administration of lethal gas in the
manner provided by the laws of the State of California. The Sheriff
is directed to deliver you, the said Caryl Chessman, to the said
Warden of the State Prison at San Quentin within ten days from this
date, to be held by the said Warden pending the decision of this case
on appeal. Upon the judgment herein becoming final, to carry into
effect the said judgment of this court, the time and date hereafter to
be fixed by order of this court within said State Prison, at which time
said Warden shall then and there put to death the said Caryl Chessman by the administration of lethal gas."

At the same time I listened to Judge Fricke sentence me to fifteen
terms of imprisonment, with an order that all sentences except those
imposing death or life imprisonment be served one after the other,
consecutively, and that service on the first one not begin until I was
discharged on all prior sentences (in the year 2009!).

(Two parenthetical comments are in order. First, California law
does not permit a judge to run life sentences consecutively. Second, I
am of the considered opinion that, if ordered to do so, "the said
Warden" would find it more than a little difficult to put a condemned
man to death more than once. The California Supreme Court con-
curs in this view. Recently it had occasion judicially to pronounce
that "there can be but one execution of [a] death sentence." This
being so manifestly so, why did the state go to the trouble, burden

and expense of trying me on eighteen charges instead of just one if the prosecutor really believed evidence of guilt was so overwhelming? Interestingly enough, if I had been tried and fairly convicted on but one capital count—assuming but at the same time denying that a fair and legal death penalty conviction was obtainable—I would have been long since dead!)

This formal business of imposing those many sentences took considerable time. Once completed, I directed the court's attention to the fact that the court reporter, Ernest R. Perry, had dropped dead of a heart attack two days before. Then I made an oral motion to have the judgments just imposed set aside and a new trial ordered. The motion was made under a section contained in the California Code of Civil Procedure which provides that the trial judge, in *civil* cases, can grant a new trial with the death of the reporter if, in his opinion, it would be impossible to produce an acceptable trial record for use on appeal.

As I anticipated he would, Judge Fricke denied the motion, first upon the ground that the section in question applied to civil cases only and second because the moment a sentence of death is passed, "jurisdiction of the cause" is transferred to and resides exclusively in the California Supreme Court. But my futile motion still accomplished its intended purpose.

Judge Fricke took judicial notice of the fact that the reporter was dead and that he consequently could do nothing further toward preparing the record for the appellate court. Judge Fricke added, however, that this did not necessarily mean a record could not be prepared by some other reporter from the deceased reporter's notes. Taking his cue, the prosecutor then said that he had been authorized to state for the record that his office would do everything possible to assist with the preparation of such a record and that he understood the reporter had dictated a portion of his notes before his death. As a result, Judge Fricke made an order directing that "to the limit of human beings in their use of human ingenuity . . . the entire record of this trial be prepared in as complete a manner as possible . . ."

The order terminated proceedings that day in the case of *The*

People of the State of California versus Caryl Chessman. Again hand-cuffed and carefully guarded, I was hustled back to the High Power tank at the county jail. Within ten days I would be transported to the Death Row at San Quentin. The question of the record would have to be fought out in the higher court.

So far, I had been fighting for my life on terms dictated by a formidable opponent. Right then I wasn't so certain I was willing to continue doing so. I wasn't fascinated with the idea of having to accept a record prepared by one reporter from another reporter's notes and with "assistance" from the prosecutor's office. My suspicious mind took a dim view of what the result might be.

I had thought I was getting a break when the court reporter died. I would certainly get one if they couldn't produce any record at all, for in that case it was almost a cinch I'd get a new trial. But what if something that read plausibly were produced, and that missing from it, or watered down in it, were the legal errors that might get me a new trial? What then?

As I saw it, either I could go to San Quentin like a good little boy and hope the State Supreme Court would require the local officials to produce an accurate record or reject what was offered and order a new trial; or, with the help of some people I knew, I could say to hell with all this judicial hocus pocus.

By that last I mean that I could make arrangements to have myself liberated on my way to San Quentin. I could, given any kind of break, get foolproof evidence that I was not the red light bandit, and then surrender with it. There was, of course, the possibility that I wouldn't be able to get the needed evidence. And if I were caught without it, I would go straight to the green room.

So I had a decision to make. Which would it be, a gamble with the courts or with a gun? I took out a half dollar and gave it a flip.

Heads I win; tails you lose.

The sheriff's office and not the flip of that coin decided the course I would pursue.

Acting on a tip or a hunch, my transfer to San Quentin was effected with elaborate care. On the seventh day following the imposition of sentence, without forewarning, the turnkey assigned to the High Power tank shouted, "Chessman, roll 'em up!"

I was on my way. The boys in the tank wished me good luck as I rolled up my bedding and pocketed a few personal letters. Carrying the bedding and property, I was let out of the tank.

"Stand right here a minute," I was told.

"Yes, *sir*," I said.

From an adjoining tank stepped Dave, my passenger on that ill-fated January night. Separately tried for robbing and technically kidnaping the proprietor of a Redondo Beach clothing store and one of his employees, Dave had been convicted and sentenced to two terms of five years to life for robbery, to life with possibility of parole for kidnaping the employee (by moving him a few feet within the store), and to life without possibility of parole for similarly kidnaping the proprietor and striking him on the head with a gun butt. I had flatly testified at Dave's trial that Dave had met me in Hollywood a few minutes before the chase, that he hadn't been with me earlier that evening and hence could not have been a participant in the robbery. Other witnesses, including an employer, testified to his whereabouts during the afternoon and evening and established an alibi that wasn't shaken. Still conviction had followed on the strength of his arrest with me and his "positive" identification by the two men who had been robbed. Stunned for a moment by the severity of his sentence and angered by his conviction, Dave had made up his mind to give the state a run for its money in the appellate courts and his case was to have widespread ramifications.

Dave and I exchanged greetings. Four officers were waiting for us and escorted us along the mammoth jail's labyrinthine corridors to the bathroom. Brought there before us were eight other men being readied for transfer to Quentin. These transfers, incidentally, are referred to as "loads" or "chains." Dave and I were bathed separately and our property and persons were carefully searched. Then we were thrown our civilian clothing, and we dressed. Throughout this readying process there was an atmosphere of hustle and bustle, for it is one of tradition's paramount demands that jailers shall always be in a hurry to check their charges in or out. And this is so notwithstanding the fact that during the period intervening between "in" and "out," long, dead months often drag by while the sometimes creaky machinery of justice grinds and grinds and grinds.

As soon as it was readied, the load was herded to an anteroom off the Attorney Room, and there held in guarded isolation for half an hour before the Attorney Room was cleared. Then, closely watched by lynx-eyed deputies, those of us on the scheduled transfer who had visitors were called out into the Attorney Room and seated across from those who had come to see us off. A solid wooden partition extended from the floor almost to shoulder height, separating visited and visitors.

My father had been notified by telephone a very few minutes before and was there to see me, looking dazed and haggard.

"Dad," I said reassuringly, with a smile, "don't worry. And don't let Mom worry. Everything is going to work out all right for me. I guarantee you I'll never die in the gas chamber. That's just not going to happen. And I wouldn't be surprised if I was back on the streets a lot sooner than anybody thought possible. I . . ."

My father broke in, his eyes pleading. "Son," he said quietly, "your mother hasn't much longer to live. So promise me one thing. Promise me you won't try to get out by violence. If you did, the shock would kill her. We know how you feel and how bitter you must be. But get ting out that way wouldn't solve anything for you. I've had several long talks with Al and he tells me you've got a darn good chance to win on the appeal, especially since the reporter died. So for your mother's and my sake, son, go on up to San Quentin and give the Supreme Court a chance to see you get justice. We'll both stand behind you all the way. And your friends still are behind you too. They all believe you got a raw deal this time. They refuse to believe you're guilty. So give the courts a chance, won't you?"

I hesitated. "Dad," I finally said, "the way you put it leaves me on something of a spot . . ."

"You mean you won't?" my father asked. He was a picture of defeat, and he seemed to lack the strength to withstand this final, crushing blow.

"Let's say, rather, that for reasons I can't explain the choice is no longer mine."

My father's tired, sad eyes focused intently upon my face for a long moment before he spoke. "Son, there is something I never intended to tell you but . . . now I must. You remember after you were arrested that I begged you to tell who this other man in the car was and you refused?"

"I remember," I replied.

"You didn't tell me why, son, but I think I know why you refused to identify him. You thought that man was your friend. You thought had he been in your situation he wouldn't squeal on you. You thought it would be wrong if you told on him. I believe you still think that. For some reason I don't understand, you'd risk going to the gas chamber for crimes you didn't commit rather than tell the authorities anything. You believe that would make you a squealer or informer.

"But here is something you didn't know. A few days after you were arrested your mother received a telephone call on the extension I have for her. It was from your friend. He told your mother to send you word to keep your mouth shut. He said if you didn't, he'd blow your mother and me sky high some night, but if you kept quiet he would look out for you in his own way. He warned your mother not to say anything to anyone about his threat to blow us up."

I didn't permit my face to betray the way I felt, but the hate raged within me.

"Dad," I said, speaking very quietly, "that call may have been made by some screwball trying to be funny. But if it was made by the 'friend' you've mentioned, don't worry. I can take care of him my own way."

"Time's up," the guard at the end of the table called out.

My father and the other visitors (some of the female ones sobbing) remained seated, as they had been instructed, while I and the others on the load stood up and said our last hurried goodbyes before marching from the room. I winked at my dad, again said, "Don't worry. And give Mom my love."

Four or five minutes after the load was back in the anteroom, plainclothes officers with chains and handcuffs—the transportation squad—entered, and one of the officers whom I knew, chewing on a cigar butt, said, "Line up in pairs."

Desiring to be handcuffed together, Dave and I held back while the handcuffs were being snapped on the other eight men. One man had a handcuff placed on his left wrist; the man on his left had his right wrist cuffed. A three-foot length of chain ran back to another set of cuffs and the two men directly behind the first pair were then cuffed. A second group of four was handcuffed similarly. The cigar-chewing cop then said, "All right, men, out this door here."

Dave asked, "Hey, how about us?"

The cop grinned and replied, "I got orders to leave you and Chessman here. I think they took you off the load."

I grinned back. "Very funny."

"Yeah," he said, "isn't it?"

Dave and I were left in the anteroom for an hour and a half. We smoked and paced the floor, waiting.

"Do you think they really left us off the list, Chess?" Dave asked me.

"Hell, no," I said. "They're just playing games."

"What do you mean?"

"I mean they're not taking any chances. They know we know the routine. They know I got friends." (I almost spit out that last word —*friends!*) "They know we know the weak link in their chain is at the train depot. They know we know they take the load down there on a regular schedule and feed them, always at the same time, always at the same table in the same restaurant. They know we know that restaurant's always crowded and that either in there or while taking us to the train there's a golden opportunity for some enterprising party to shove a shotgun in their fat bellies and say, 'Give!' And they know I'm not exactly rendered ecstatic with these death sentences."

"Oh," Dave said. He thought over what I'd told him for a couple of minutes while we continued to pace back and forth and smoke. Then he grinned. "I'm surprised at them," he said, "thinking things like that."

"Yeah," I agreed, "they must have been reading too many detective stories lately."

"Or seeing too many gangster pictures," Dave added.

We laughed. But neither one of us was amused.

John Law had outfoxed me and I didn't like it. Here all along I'd been so certain that the only way I could get out of the frying pan was to jump into the fire. I'd been convinced that the only conclusive way I could prove that I wasn't the red light bandit was to produce him —or, put more accurately, his mortal remains. And the danger there centered around the perfectly obvious fact that, finally analyzed, whether one is executed for kidnaping or for murder, one remains just as thoroughly dead. And who would believe me when I said I had killed in self-defense? So I had desperately needed my freedom that I might get the proof I had to have before it could be destroyed.

Four tough, burly members of the robbery-gangster squad, sometimes called the major crime detail, came for us. Dave and I were handcuffed together, whisked nonstop to the basement of the Hall of Justice and bundled into a waiting squad car. Two of the detectives piled into the front seat of the car. A third got into the back seat with us. The fourth went back to a second squad car parked behind us and occupied by additional members of the robbery-gangster squad.

Followed closely by the second carload of armed detectives, we were sped to the Glendale station, which was the first stop the train made after leaving Los Angeles on its run north. We arrived just ahead of the train; when it pulled into the depot passengers and the crowd were held back by a cordon of police while Dave and I were hustled aboard and seated inside the specially and functionally designed prison car, apart from the other eight prisoners. As soon as we were seated we were chained securely, to put it mildly, and two hefty members of the transportation squad were posted directly behind us.

Chains were placed tightly around both of my ankles, my waist, up around my neck and under one armpit and then run over to Dave, who was secured in an identical fashion. Next we were leg-cuffed together.

The cop who did all this surveyed his handiwork with a critical eye. "There," he said approvingly, "that ought to do it."

"It should," I conceded. . . .

The trip to Richmond takes twelve hours on the milk run, with the train clanking and rattling to a stop at every station. Through the gathering dusk, the long sleepless night, the early morning hours, I sat and smoked and watched and thought bitter thoughts. My eyes were glued to the lost world just outside the sealed window at my left shoulder.

Cities, hamlets, rural areas. Highways stretching out like ribbons. Cars whizzing by. Depots. People. Life, and the evidences of it: a little girl on a scooter, a blind man in a frayed coat selling newspapers, a young couple strolling hand in hand, eternity stretching out invitingly before them. The lustrous night sky. The grayness of dawn. The lonely deserted stretches.

I knew how probable it was that my eyes were seeing all this for the last time, and rebellion flared within me. I fiercely wanted to curse, to fight, to lash out at my captors. I wanted to be free that instant. The need for freedom was irrational, overwhelming. It consumed reason, and I struggled to stand, straining at my chains.

"Something on your mind, Chessman?" one of the oversized members of the transportation squad posted behind me inquired.

The question mocked me, reminded me that those whom the gods wish to destroy they first make mad. So I grinned and said easily, "Yeah, how about going to the can?"

An hour later the train pulled into the Richmond station—our destination. Local police in patrol cars, alerted for our arrival, ringed the area. There was a casual, admirable precision in the way we were taken from the train, marched to waiting taxis, bundled inside (two prisoners and two guards to a taxi), and, with escort from the local cops, driven to the Richmond Ferry.

Three miles across the waters of the San Pablo Bay, the grim, uninviting outline of San Quentin was starkly visible. On the way across we were fed in the ferry boat's dining room. I shut off thought and turned my attention wholly to what promised to be my last meal in the free world—a double order of ham and eggs, toast and coffee. Then, the meal over, we were taken on deck, still chained together. The briny smell of the bay was clean and good. As the ferry docked, I busied myself with absorbing last impressions of the world I was leaving behind, perhaps forever. The piling of the landing creaked as the ferry edged against it. The morning sun was warm. The distant Berkeley Hills were visible. And the battlements of San Quentin loomed large up ahead. Our journey—my journey—was almost over.

An old yellow bus with a driver from the prison was waiting for us. We were seated in it, near the back, with our guards up front. This vintage, jaundiced carrier ground through the gears, rumbled along the pier and then bounced along the half mile of winding road to the prison's front gate. There the transportation-squad members checked their guns before we completed the last two hundred yards of our ride. We jolted to a stop in the shadow of a huge arsenal tower.

After alighting, we were passed through a gate in single file and then we entered the walls. In a receiving room just within, we had our handcuffs and chains removed and were seated on wooden benches.

A transportation-squad member, before leaving, asked me, "Well, what do you think about it now?"

Probably he should have added "sucker."

"Nothing to it," I told him, showing him teeth, and he walked away shaking his head.

My reply set a pattern. He and his kind were on one side of the fence. I was on the other side. He made it simple for me, and I chose to leave it that way. For a while. He saw it as an uncomplicated case of social black and white. I did nothing to disturb his simplification, for it made my problem of survival easier. I was a villain. I was sentenced to death. That was my role, and I accepted it casually. When and if it came, I would accept death equally casually, but without any display of false bravado, without, as they say, looking back. It was best if they said, "That Chessman is a bad one," and let it go at that, leaving me "free" to do the expected—to fight for my life, subtly, savagely, defiantly.

The business of checking new arrivals in is old hat for San Quentin's custodial staff. Each year hundreds enter the prison; as many hundreds are paroled or discharged. Many of the latter return. I was one who had. While the others on this Los Angeles chain were bathed (in a shower stall), searched, their personal property checked and outfitted temporarily in overalls, I talked with a correctional sergeant. We skipped anything controversial.

Dave and the others were taken away. Just before he left Dave said, "Drive slow, Chess. I'll see you later." I was tempted to ask him whether he meant in this world or the next. But I only grinned and replied, "Yeah, Dave. Sure. We'll be back in Hollywood practically before we know we've been gone."

"That's right," Dave said, tongue in cheek, "they can't do this to us."

I was showered, searched. Two officers took me to the Identification Department. There I was fingerprinted and mugged. Then I was taken to the Distribution Department and outfitted in soft slippers—the distinguishing mark of the condemned man—and jeans, denim work shirt and light jacket, all new.

Next stop was the Row. We crossed the Big Yard. Men I knew called out to me. It was old home week. The prodigal had returned—to be fattened up, then gassed into the Great Beyond. A real success story: Horatio Alger had nothing on me. We entered the North block rotunda. Up we went in the elevator. The double doors were unlocked and opened for us. We stepped through, were met by the two floor officers. The armed guard stood in his cage, watching, appraising the new arrival.

I glanced down the long, fifteen-foot-wide corridor fronting the condemned cells. I heard the muted voices of the doomed. And I wasn't enthralled by my arrival at this gloomy unit. It looked so sterile, so senselessly sterile, and its sounds were not like any you would hear elsewhere in the world of the living.

"Stand over there by that pile of blankets and other supplies," the officer in charge instructed me. "And take off all your clothes."

I did, was again searched, then told to dress. As soon as I had my clothes on, the second Row officer, a tall, heavy-set person just turning to paunch, with pale blue eyes, addressed me in a quiet, impersonal voice.

"All those blankets and other supplies you carry to your cell," he told me, indicating the items piled near me. Then he said, "Chessman, I'm told you've done time at the prison before. Now, we have certain rules up here which have to be observed. You must understand that. I'll explain those rules to you when we put you into your cell. If you cooperate, you will make it easy on yourself. If you don't cooperate, you will just be making it tough for yourself. My advice is try to get along."

Something New in the Way of Villains

I merely nodded, acknowledging I had heard the officer's "advice." Then I reached down and picked up the blankets and cell supplies. The officer in charge unlocked and opened the first door of the double-doored, bird-cage-like enclosure which leads into the Row corridor. Two other guards and I stepped within; the door was locked behind us. Then the second door, double-locked and bolted, was opened and I followed the two guards along the corridor to Cell 2455. When the cell door was swung open for me, I stepped inside and set my load down on the mattress of the cot. I heard the safety bar drop, the click of the door lock. I knew what those sounds meant—Chessman was as far in prison as it is possible to get.

The paunchy officer with the pale blue eyes and the quiet, impersonal voice said, "The rules."

The inevitable rules. The we-have-everything-figured-out-for-you, don't-think-for-yourself rules. Here they were.

I would be fed twice a day, shortly after eight in the morning and in the mid-afternoon, on a cafeteria-style tray and from a food cart pushed along from cell to cell by an inmate waiter (not a condemned man) who would serve me what I wanted. The knife, fork and spoon issued me at mealtime would be picked up when I finished eating.

Every morning the officer would come by with razors. If I wanted to shave, I would tell the officer and he would issue me a razor and blade. (The razor is a locking, institutional type.) An inmate porter would accompany him with hot water. (Only cold water is piped into the cells.) I would shave promptly, then return the razor.

I would be allowed out in the corridor with the other condemned men for a two-hour exercise and recreational period each day (and the other twenty-two hours a day I would remain locked tight in my cell). During the two-hour period I could walk, talk, play checkers, chess or cards. But no horseplay or fighting. Breach of any rule could mean a suspension of this privilege of coming out into the corridor, perhaps confinement in a "quiet" cell at the far end of the Row or in the isolation unit on the other side of the building.

I would be allowed to bathe twice a week, Sunday and Wednesday mornings. On these mornings I would be issued clean clothes and would turn in my dirty clothes.

I had been issued a set of earphones with a rather long cord. These plugged in at the jack fastened to the back wall of the cell. Programs were selected at a master control booth in another part of the prison. The earphones would be on from seven in the morning until eleven at night (and presently one side of the double jack is left on all night for those who cannot sleep). If I monkeyed with my set I would see the earphones taken from the cell and otherwise would be disciplined.

A set of sheets and a pair of pajamas had been issued to me. Every Friday morning I would hang these on my cell bars to be picked up, sent to the laundry and returned that afternoon. (Later the Row was furnished prison-made bathrobes—called spook robes by the doomed —to be worn to the shower.)

I would be allowed to write and receive a reasonable number of letters from approved friends, relatives and attorneys, and to have supervised visits from them.

I could order up to fifteen dollars' worth of canteen ducats every month, provided I had money on the books, and could purchase tobacco, candy and other items with these ducats from the institutional canteen.

Library books and daily papers were furnished the men on the Row. The daily papers were passed along from cell to cell. Also the Catholic Chaplain visited the Row every Saturday afternoon and passed out several of the popular magazines. I could subscribe to a newspaper or magazines, if I wished, and have the subscription price deducted from my account.

I would be permitted to talk to the men in the other cells around me, but loud talking or noise of any other kind was prohibited. When the lights were blinked at 10:30 P.M. this meant silence until the next morning.

So long as the men on the Row remained on good behavior, they were shown a sixteen-millimeter film every Thursday at the far end of the corridor during the exercise period.

Did I have any questions? No, I did not.

The paunchy officer left. A minute or two later he returned and handed me a package of cigarettes. "From your friend up the line," he said.

The "friend up the line" the floor officer had reference to was a man I'd known for many years.

My cell, I saw, had been recently swept and mopped. I pitched in and gave it a good scrubbing, made my bed and arranged the few cell articles I had been issued on the shelf above the bed.

With no especial enthusiasm, I visually inspected all that was visible of my world.

On the ceiling directly in front of the cell was an electric light. (It burns twenty-four hours a day.) High up on the vertical bars separating the Row corridor from the gun walk behind it, and also directly in front of the cell, was an office-size electric clock. (Its mate fronts a cell on the upper end of the corridor.) I looked thoughtfully at its white face, black numerals and black hour and minute hands. I watched the red sweep second hand completely encircle the clock face before I turned away. The time was twenty minutes after eleven. In another ten minutes the exercise period would begin. During those ten minutes I paced slowly back and forth the length of the cell, smoking and thinking. Wondering.

What lay ahead?

What possibly could lay ahead?

It was Saturday morning, July 3, 1948, and little did I dream that before this ordeal would be over I would have spent more time on Death Row under death sentence than any other condemned man ever previously had.

Years and years were fated to pass in slow and violent procession. And you would read in your newspaper about a doomed man named Caryl Chessman and perhaps when you did you would wonder what sort of strange creature he could be.

Sometimes Chessman would wonder himself.

Sometimes what was happening to him didn't seem as though it could possibly be real.

But it was.

"This place really puts it on your mind," I was told by a doomed man the day of my arrival.

"In that case," I replied with a grin, "this place and I are going to be putting it on each other's minds."

And that is precisely what "we" did, for years on end. Yet it took many, many months before the real, the deeper meaning of those words became brutally clear to me. At the time I made no effort to understand them. Why should I? I was interested in survival, not psychological data.

When you dance you have to remember that the fiddler may demand payment. At first I watched men take that last walk by my cell without batting an eyelash. In the eyes of some—those who couldn't help identifying themselves with the fate of all the other doomed— that made me a cold fish. I was supposed to get all worked up emotionally every time they marched some condemned man off to his death. A few actually got indignant because I didn't weep and wail.

"Look," I said, "you characters look out for yourselves and I'll look out for Chessman. And let's understand each other: I haven't got the time or the inclination to feel sorry for Chessman, so I sure as hell haven't got the time or inclination to feel sorry for anybody else."

Row time would be dead time as far as I was concerned. The present didn't count except insofar as it afforded me the opportunity to slug it out with the state for a future. Meanwhile I wasn't asking any-thing except to be left alone. I didn't give a damn about creature comforts or whether or not anyone regarded Chessman as a good boy or a bad one. I didn't want anyone holding my hand or feeling sorry for me or worrying about me.

By deliberate choice, but not affectedly, I was a cold, angry, remote machine. Human warmth was a luxury I didn't feel I could afford, not then; in this unnatural environment it appeared to be a weakness that could prove fatal. Funny thing, death itself didn't bother me. But the possibility of failure did. If I let the state win, I would be failing. If I let this place beat me in any way, I would be failing.

I didn't intend to fail.

And I haven't. Still, you can't spend more than five years in such a place as Death Row and not change, radically. In time the place gets inside you; it eats its way in; it writhes around in your innards. And once it does, you'll never be the same again.

Do you doubt this? Do you think you could spend close to two thousand days, more than sixty months, well over five years, on the Row, fighting defiantly for survival, existing all the while in the very shadow of the gas chamber, and not change? That you could watch approximately half a hundred men take that last dreaded walk by your cell and believe that, in some insidious way, it doesn't eat at your mind? That you could observe many of the doomed driven either insane or to the borderline of insanity by the stark fear of impending death, and not feel the slugging impact upon your own personality? That you could see men hounded to suicide or attempted suicide by fear and depression and stay wholly impervious to the sick-ening tug of environment upon your own mental processes? That you could witness your fellow condemned suddenly, savagely attack their neighbors or yourself and personally remain aloofly indifferent to the gargoyle-faced goading of frustration? That you could observe the baffled minds and tortured emotions of others of this condemned fraternity laid naked and raw by the mocking imminence of death, and not experience an inner upheaval, an indwelling turbulence?

I had made up my mind the Row wouldn't change me, wouldn't

touch me. It finally did. But don't mistake "change" for "break." I didn't break. And I didn't suddenly "see the light." I am suspicious of those who say they have. Successive crises can strengthen and constructively change the personality of even society's Chessmans, but this change doesn't take place in a magic moment midst the blinding glare of revelation. Revelation, when born of one crisis piled upon the other, can merely light the way; it cannot effortlessly waft you to a brighter and happier land. There remains a long journey to be made, a trying journey, and it is you alone who must make it.

December 2, 1949, the Protestant Chaplain brought me a telegram. "Is there anything I can do?" the Chaplain asked.

"No," I said. "There is nothing anyone can do."

My mother was dead. She had died of cancer—and a broken heart. She had died, I learned later, expressing her faith in me.

I smoked. I paced the floor. I thought what once had been. I looked around at what was. My mother was dead. After endless years of pain and poverty, she was dead. And her son was on Death Row waiting to die. And her husband was an old and broken man.

My dad flew up to see me. He was sick and sad and he missed Hallie, the gentle Hallie who had suffered so much.

"Mom's found peace now," my dad said, and that was doubtless true.

But what a cruel price she had paid for peace.

My mother was dead.

Something in me was dead, too. I doubted, then, if that something would ever be reborn.

• *32* •

"The Check on Chessman"

I came to the Row with one driving, dominant goal—to conjure up a legal miracle and leave the Row alive. To fight my way off the Row. To cheat the executioner out of his day off and his hundred-dollar fee.

Guilt or innocence aside, to my mind there was something peculiarly ignominious in gulping hydrocyanic acid gas fumes when signaled to do so and while being gaped at by "at least twelve reputable citizens," as required by law. Those twelve reputable citizens would simply have to do their gaping at somebody else.

And I must add that the fact that the law permitted me to have five friends or relatives in attendance offered no inducement to me to pay a visit to the time machine. Having friends or relatives present seemed a little too ghoulish even for my toughened sensibilities.

To get right down to it, no matter how nicely, efficiently or scientifically the state proposed to dispatch me into the Great Beyond, my psyche still balked at the prospect of such a departure with all the willful, stubborn obstinacy of a Missouri mule.

Dying in the gas chamber simply didn't make sense; not so far as I was concerned. Why, I asked myself, should I die there? Why should I passively submit to the mandate of the state if, somehow, I could fight free? If I had a potential bag full of tricks, why should I hesitate to use them? What else should or could society expect? Society hadn't apologized to me when it declared my life forfeit. Why should I apologize to society for fighting for existence?

314

I boiled down my problem of survival to its simplest terms. I took a long, piercing look at exactly what confronted me. The people of the State of California, speaking through their judicial processes, had decreed I must die. They had charged me with the commission of crimes punishable with death. They had convicted me. They had pronounced what the courts are pleased to call "solemn judgments" of death against me. They had imprisoned me in a formidably barred and guarded cell. They would have the death chamber in readiness to snuff out my life as soon as their Supreme Court should affirm the validity of the convictions. They had veteran, hard-fighting attorneys to protect those judgments against legal attack. They had armed guards who watched me day and night with shoot-to-kill orders if I tried to escape.

In short, they had a "Check on Chessman," as *Fortnight,* the California News Magazine, later was to remark while reporting that "The State of California has been playing a game with Caryl Chessman, and his life is the stake in the match."

Certainly, then, analogizing my situation to a game of legal chess, with *my* life the stake in the match, the people of the state, in whose name I was scheduled to die, could not very well take umbrage if I elected to play the game to a decisive conclusion rather than concede loss in despair.

Shorn of its troublesome moral considerations, what was to be tested was my legal "right" to survive. The decisive question to be answered was not whether I was a good man or a bad one. It was, rather, whether I had been legally and fairly convicted of committing specific crimes denounced by the laws of the state. And I was unable to perceive any reason why I should not put to extreme test the validity of those convictions. On the other hand, I was able to conceive of several persuasive reasons why I should try to return those death sentences unused.

I would be obliged, I realized, to play this legal chess game according to the rules society, through its judicial and legislative arms, itself had formulated. The arbiters of the game would be society's own courts. Opposing me would be society's most skilled legal chess play-

ers, old pros who knew all the gambits. They would relentlessly press
for a quick victory; that was their job. Mine was to keep from being
blitzed into oblivion while I maneuvered myself into position to
counterattack.

Analogies aside, I was literally, physically trapped, and the very
nature of the trap wryly amused me. I had to admit there was an
unmistakable poetic irony in the way my condemnation had come
about. My life had been punctuated with violent episodes, incidents
where death had eagerly waited to snatch me if guts, guile or luck
had run out. But they had not, and I was still very much alive. The
Fates had slyly seen to that. Clotho, Lachesis and Atropos had not
wasted their precious talents proving the glaringly obvious fact that
any foolish mortal can get himself prematurely laid out on a slab in
the morgue with no difficulty at all. All one has to do is invent some
pretext for awakening the fearful self-destructive impulses which lie
dormant in all of us. Do that, and you are on your way.

I was fully aware I could claim no personal credit for having
lived long enough to get myself doomed by the state and brought to
the Death Row. And, once here, I didn't try to kid myself my condemnation suddenly had assumed any cosmic importance. It was just
one of those things, and a peculiarly casual one at that. In the patois
of the big house, "Ya buys yer ticket and ya takes yer chances."
I had bought my ticket. I had taken my chances. I had taken my
chances when, just before my trial had begun, I spurned an offer to
plead guilty and accept a sentence of life imprisonment with parole
eligibility at the end of seven years.

So here I was, caged, doomed. And this raised the question: What
could I do about it?

I could and would maintain that I was not the red light bandit,
and be rewarded with knowing, skeptical looks, if not downright
indignation that I should have the audacity to persist in a claim of
innocence. One interviewer blandly assumed my unquestionable
guilt and inquired, "Tell me, why did you do it?"

With a perfectly straight face, I countered, "Tell me, why did you
kick your poor old grandmother this morning?"

The question flustered my interviewer, who managed to stammer, "Why, why, I didn't."

"Well, neither did I."

Then I got raised eyebrows and the same old argument. Everybody seems to covet certainty; I simply had to be guilty. Why? Because the courts in this modern day and age function in such a way that it would be impossible for an innocent man to be doomed. Accordingly, there was an element of brash immorality in my claim of innocence. This was so because, since I *must* be guilty (because I had been convicted), I should be overwhelmed with remorse and should spend full time crying out loudly for forgiveness, between cries of "Unclean! Unclean!"

Innocence could hardly be regarded as an advantage when looked upon as an impertinence. As wryly observed by Mr. Justice Jesse W. Carter of the California Supreme Court in a recent dissenting opinion, "If lack of penitence is shown by clinging to one's honest assertion of innocence, then innocence is a crime rather than a virtue."

Just before sentencing me to death, Judge Charles W. Fricke had asked me the traditional question: "Is there any legal cause why sentence should not now be pronounced?"

And I had promptly replied, "The defendant is absolutely innocent of these charges."

"That," His Honor had said, "is not a legal cause. That is merely an assertion."

Legally speaking, Judge Fricke was correct. Even patently guilty, justly convicted felons can *say* they are innocent, and often do. Proving innocence is another matter. I had one chance and failed. A jury convicted me. To be sure, I claimed, illegally; and I have persisted in that claim. But right then, when I stood before the man who would pronounce judgment against me, I was, without qualification, *legally* guilty. From that point on, because the law declares they must, the numerous courts to which I have been have indulged every presumption in favor of the validity and correctness of the jury's verdict. From that point on, the burden has been on me to prove otherwise. Moreover, reviewing courts decide only questions of law; they do not decide questions of fact, and guilt or innocence is such a question.

If there is any evidence contained in the trial record from which the jury could rationally have "inferred" guilt, regardless of how much evidence the defendant may have introduced to show his innocence, the reviewing court to which an appeal is taken from a judgment of conviction of crime will and must allow the conviction to stand unless it appears that the conviction was obtained illegally or unfairly (in a well-defined constitutional sense).

And once a judgment of conviction has been upheld upon appeal and becomes final, it is only vulnerable to what is called collateral attack; that is, by a petition for a writ of *habeas corpus* or *coram nobis,* or a motion to vacate. Each of these actions has its own special function to correct a particular kind of legal wrong, but they have this in common: they lie (are available) only when the trial court had no "jurisdiction" to pronounce judgment. This can mean when it is conclusively shown the conviction was had in flagrant disregard of a defendant's fundamental constitutional rights and appellate review either was not available or proved inadequate to protect those rights.

So, when brought to Death Row, my job was plain: establish, if I could, an illegal or unfairly obtained conviction. Fail and die. At bottom it was that simple, and yet I knew that job would take an awful lot of doing.

The staggering immensity of the task is best suggested by citing a few facts and figures. Thus far, originally based upon 2400 pages of trial record, litigation of the case has involved the preparation and filing of seven appeal briefs, four petitions for writs of mandate, two petitions for writs of prohibition, nine petitions for writs of *habeas corpus,* four petitions for rehearing, four petitions for a certificate of probable cause to appeal, five petitions for stays of execution, four petitions for writs of *certiorari,* with either supporting briefs or memorandums of points and authorities usually accompanying the petitions; two motions to augment and correct record, three motions for hearings, and a complaint in equity; plus numerous other incidental papers necessarily prepared and filed. These documents listed contain more than 450,000 words in all.

I estimate that at least three thousand hours were consumed in actual preparation, while I have spent, conservatively, another ten thousand hours in study. (Attorney fees are computed ordinarily at $20 an hour. At this rate, even assuming only one-tenth of the study and research I had made would have been necessary for an attorney, it would have cost me a minimum of $60,000 and probably closer to $100,000 had I paid counsel to litigate the case for me.)

My legal study and research has involved the partial or complete reading of some two thousand legal books, journals, reports, texts and the like. Notes taken from these total another half a million carefully organized words. Because I was unable to find texts bearing precisely on what I needed and wanted, I drafted for my own use a two-hundred-page text on *habeas corpus* and a four-hundred-page text on federal practice and procedure as it relates to state court convictions.

Opposing me at one time or another, either singly or in groups of from two to six, have been eleven different lawyers for the state. In addition to those, there are several more lawyers working for the state who have had a hand in opposing me but who have not formally appeared as counsel in the courts.

On several occasions since coming to the Death Row, I have been removed from the prison and personally appeared in the courts to prosecute habeas corpus proceedings in my own behalf. And I have been obliged to write and receive more than two thousand letters of a legal character while conducting the litigation and digging out facts and evidence from every imaginable quarter.

All this simply in fighting to keep myself alive!

· *33* ·

This Thing Called Judicial Justice

I've fought long and hard against almost impossible odds for survival. Moreover, I'm the first condemned man ever to defend himself at his trial and then handle all subsequent litigation of the case without being represented by counsel. I soon shall have spent more time on Death Row than has any other doomed man in the history of California, and the struggle is still far from over.

Perhaps this background qualifies me to make some comments I believe are relevant.

Most people have a tendency to look upon litigation in the appellate courts as an abstruse and suspicious business at best. I was one of those casually inclined toward this view prior to being brought to Death Row. While I didn't share the notion of some that appellate court judgments emanate from Olympus, much of what went on in such courts seemed to me to be beyond the comprehension of an ordinary mortal like myself. I was willing to believe that because, throughout my pre-Row days, what took place in reviewing courts was a matter of complete indifference to me, just as it is to most others who are not directly touched by this phase of the "administration of justice." But after more than five years of continuous litigation and personal contact with all things juridical, I can assure the reader there is nothing at heart esoteric, mysterious or Olympian in all that goes on in the temples of justice.

To be sure, everyone—the judge, the justice, the prosecutor, the policeman, the defendant and appellant's attorney, the defendant himself, the man and the woman on the street—looks at the law through different eyes. An uncounted number of books, both technical and popular, have been written dealing with the subject which bears the imposing title of "criminal jurisprudence." Just as with politics, everyone has his own ideas and pet theories in this field. Legislators are forever tinkering with, changing and modifying criminal laws. Experts and non-experts alike are certain they have "the" answers to the perplexing problems that press for an answer here.

But rarely, if ever, does the public get the opinion of the criminal. Rarely, if ever, is that individual given voice. More often than not, the public assumes the criminal to be neither literate nor articulate. A great many people refuse to believe the criminal capable of thought or entitled to think. Such gratuitous assumptions confound the problem. After all, we must keep in mind the fact that it is the criminal who is causing us all the trouble. (Yet I really should not say "all" the trouble because we, in our zeal, to borrow apt words from an old Chinese proverb, have called in a tiger to get rid of a dog, and we must beware lest in striving to eradicate crime we destroy our heritage of liberty under the law.)

Not alone for novelty's sake, then, let us take a careful but human look at post-conviction criminal litigation through the eyes of a man whose life is the stake in the match—myself. Alarmists of one school have set up the hue and cry that there must be something awfully wrong with the law "when a Chessman can flaunt it." In one breath there is an indignant demand for my neck and for the doing of justice. The short answer to such windy alarums is that I haven't been flaunting the law and that justice is a relative concept. Just because, in one general sense, justice is defined as meaning "merited reward *or* punishment," it does not follow that the punishment ordered by the trial court in my case is merited, no more than it follows that my conviction was legally obtained.

I began my quest for this thing called judicial justice. At the time I didn't realize this search would turn out to be an endurance contest that would go on and on.

You will recall that the case of *People v. Chessman* had taken a disquietingly unique turn with the death of the elderly court reporter. Resultantly, I found myself wandering about in a hazardous, uncharted legal wilderness, without compass. State law required the state high court to review the entire record of the trial proceedings; it required those proceedings to be prepared by the court reporter who had attended the trial and to be certified by him as correct.

With the reporter quite beyond the reach of mortal law, that record lay hidden in the old-style Pitman notes of the dead reporter, and literal compliance with the law was thus impossible. However, the trial judge had ordered that, "in the proper administration of justice and to the limit of human beings in their use of human ingenuity," a record be prepared and had directed the prosecutor to find a reporter who could transcribe the dead reporter's notes. The first several expert shorthand writers contacted examined the dead reporter's phonographic symbols and declared they could not be transcribed with any reasonable degree of accuracy. The prosecutor finally found a reporter, Stanley Fraser, who said he believed he could prepare a satisfactory transcription. I heatedly disagreed and sought a writ of prohibition against preparation of such a record from the State Supreme Court, which was denied after attorneys representing the superior court filed written opposition, arguing that a record had to be prepared, and filing affidavits by the prosecutor and the court reporter to the effect that a "good" record could be prepared within a reasonable time. So preparation of the record, by this unique means, went on.

Meanwhile, and from the time of my arrival on the Row, I began and continued to tug at the coattails of prison officials and the courts until I finally overcame objections to my use of a typewriter on the Row. It took me a year almost to the day to convince then Warden Duffy and his staff that the typewriter would not constitute a threat to custody.

The typewriter was sent to the Row the day my next-door neighbor was executed. Friday, July 1, 1949. At the same time, one of the Row cells, 2437, just inside the bird cage, was designated for use in preparing legal documents by condemned men working on their own cases. (I was the only one.) With the approval of my keepers, I converted this cell into a functional legal office. After numerous changes and refinements, every inch of space has been utilized to best advantage, and the cell is beginning to bulge with books and other legal matter.

A pressing necessity on arrival, in addition to clerical facilities, was access to law books, codes and rules of the courts. As promptly as I was able, I secured the procedural rules of the various courts and studied these until they were as familiar to me as the back of my hand. Then I arranged to borrow needed legal books from the prison legal library and, if not available locally, from the state library at Sacramento.

While waiting for the record to be prepared, I began cramming legal knowledge into my head. "The law," I was counseled, "seeks no unfair advantage over a defendant, but is watchful to see that the proceedings under which his life or liberty is at stake shall be fairly and impartially conducted." That being the case, I was certain the law wouldn't object if I made sure the law didn't relax its concerned vigilance. The appealing defendant's attorney is expected to give the highest fidelity to his client; I reasoned that the "fool" who represents himself could hardly be expected to show less vigorously alert loyalty to *his* client.

Only a preposterous combination of circumstances had made me my own reluctant advocate, but that is the precise point where reluctance ended—when I decided to fight. Psychologists recognize that there is a peculiar kind of person who does his best when the competition is deadliest, and I think there is left no room for doubt that I belong to the breed.

Litigation is legal warfare, actually, not hyperbolically. For me, when I was brought to the Row, litigation was a means—seemingly the only means—to an end. That end was survival. And I knew too well what a long, tough, rugged struggle lay ahead if that end were to be reached. I wasn't thinking at the time that my contact with the law would ennoble me. I was doubtless as frankly suspicious of the judiciary as it was of me. The courts and I were reluctant bedfellows at best, and we kept a wary eye cocked in the other's direction.

When this legal war began, I was candidly interested in only one thing: results. Winning. I wasn't concerned with acquiring the legal graces. Those who may experience disquietude, fearing I intend to convey the notion that a convicted criminal can make a mockery of the law, should be at ease. My purpose is precisely the opposite. Yet I must approach the subject candidly, one step at a time. Remember that your judicial institutions are operated by human beings, not gods or godlings. Similarly, those who make your laws are mortal, with mortal limitations.

The law is a science, but we often forget that it is a human science. To believe in its infallibility is to believe in a myth, and to do it a grave disservice. Indeed, it should be remembered that the reason there are reviewing courts is that the law itself recognizes trial courts are capable of erring, of denying legal rights, and so appellate courts are present to prevent injustice. But they do not probe for injustice, they do not search it out; it must be brought to them and proved by the attorney representing the aggrieved litigant or by the litigant himself, and even then before the court can act it must be shown that the court has the "jurisdiction" to do so. Some law must declare that the particular judgment or order sought to be appealed is appealable, or that the original collateral proceeding sought to be instituted is an established and cognizable one. The controversy must be justiciable. And even between the different reviewing courts there is an inevitable difference of opinion as to what is legal and constitutional and what is not. As we all know, the highest court in the land is the Supreme Court of the United States. Mr. Justice Jackson, a brilliant member of that ultimate tribunal, tells us that "We are not final because we are infallible, but we are infallible only because we are final." His words are worth remembering.

The ironic thing is that today I think very highly of the law and its processes, but I must emphasize that this good opinion did not come from blindly embracing the numerous juvenile platitudes that obscure the administration of justice. I think fact, reality and rationality are far better servants of justice than those self-professed champions who do their championing with quaint and childish myths regarding the perfect and Olympian characteristics of the adjudicatory process, and who damn as blasphemers those who critically inspect this most cherished of myths. The myth-makers might do well to keep in mind that both our Federal and State Constitutions are a limitation and not a grant of power upon those acting in the name of the sovereign—the people—and that it is not the arms and agencies of government, but the individual himself, who retains certain inalienable rights. No man's life, liberty or property may be taken by the state "without due process of law," and unless the state has accorded the individual "equal protection of the law." Those words from the Fourteenth Amendment to the Federal Constitution have a living, dynamic meaning. While their contours are vague, their core is hard, visible and stable.

The law tells us that there is a remedy for every wrong. But the mere academic presence of a remedy for a wrong, and convincing a particular court in a particular case that one is entitled to a particular remedy under a particular set of facts are two entirely different matters. In other words, because the general must be applied to the specific, a court can only dispense "substantial" justice, and often only in direct ratio to the skill, enterprise and forensic strength of the prevailing litigant.

Put bluntly, you do not send an amateur against Joe Louis and expect to win; neither do you win in the courts unless you are competently, skillfully and energetically represented. I knew that when I was brought to the Row. I realized what a prodigious amount of study, planning and concentrated effort effective self-representation entailed.

So I began to study and I have never stopped. What is the law? Why is the law? Who is the law? I often have spent as many as eighteen hours a day, seven days a week, seeking the answers to those three questions. It didn't take me a day to learn how little I knew of the law. Odd—one can spend a lifetime in lawlessness and still know practically nothing of law or its disciplines.

I enrolled myself in legal kindergarten.

• *34* •

"Kill Him if You Can."

I have concluded the law can never be a machine that infallibly dispenses impartially perfect justice. There is no such thing.

The law declared that I was entitled to have the entire record of the trial proceedings reviewed by the California Supreme Court for the purpose of determining whether my convictions had been fairly and legally obtained. The law further expressly directed that the record of these proceedings was to be made up by the court reporter who had attended the trial. But that reporter was dead, with the result that literal compliance with the law was impossible. This posed a problem. An easy but hardly legal solution would have been to gas me to death without any appellate review. Wisely, the Constitutions of both California and the United States expressly require that all those similarly situated be accorded equal protection of the laws. And obviously a defendant shouldn't be penalized because of legal infirmities not of his making.

To keep the law from finding itself hoist with its own procedural petard, the trial judge had ordered preparation of that record by "human ingenuity." Months passed. Numerous extensions of time were allowed. Thousands of dollars were spent. Then this uniquely prepared record—called a "Reporter's Transcript"—was finally filed with the clerk of the trial court. Appellant's—my—copy was mailed to me. I read this transcript and regarded it as grossly incomplete and inaccurate.

Yet here I was, locked in a death cell.

In the directest possible language, I challenged both the validity and adequacy of the transcript in papers which I prepared and filed in the trial court. Not only did I propose numerous corrections, but I formally asked the trial judge to produce *me,* as he had said he would and as the prosecutor had sworn he would, and give *me* the opportunity, by calling hostile and unwilling witnesses, to prove my claims that the transcript was grossly incomplete and inaccurate and that it had been prepared by incompetent and illegal means.

The trial judge ignored my request. He had the prosecutor go over my list of proposed corrections with the reporter, and then allowed eighty-odd corrections, disallowed more than one hundred forty others and "approved" the transcript, which was then forwarded to the California Supreme Court, along with the personal statements of judge, prosecutor and reporter on how hard each had tried to produce a record.

Angrily, perhaps even bull-headedly, in mesne or intervening proceedings, as the law calls them, I tore into that record in the state's high court. I charged extrinsic fraud in its preparation. I claimed the notes of the dead reporter couldn't be read with reasonable accuracy. I branded as inadequate the transcript before the court. I contended that in its present form it foreclosed me from showing I had been unconstitutionally convicted. I filed exhibits to back up my contentions. I demanded hearings and an opportunity to prove every last one of those contentions. I asked the court to refuse to accept the record. I said it might as well hear an appeal based on a record prepared by a ouija board as the one before it in this case.

Attorneys for the state filed a lengthy brief discussing their view of the law and urging acceptance of the record. They said it was a good transcript; the court should accept it, without holding hearings.

In a closing brief, I pressed for hearings more vigorously than ever. If hearings weren't allowed, how could I prove anything? Obviously I couldn't. Well, should I lose my life simply because judges had the naked power to refuse to produce me in court?

The state's attorneys had also cast a quizzical look at the fact that I had represented myself and seemed to be complaining because I had

exercised a constitutional right to do so. At the same time they seemed
to be suggesting that this self-representation was somehow wrong.

Why? I wanted to know. I was able to present competent argument
in my own behalf. I knew the subject matter and the law relating to it.
I would conduct myself properly before the court. I could be produced
safely. The law itself allowed me to represent myself. Yet the court
wouldn't listen to me—simply because I was a condemned man—although it was willing to listen to any attorney at all who might be
representing me. To me that seemed an overnice preoccupation with
form at the expense of substance. In a formal application to be produced I said all this. And once more I was bluntly told to get an attorney or go without oral argument. Then an attorney was appointed
for me but immediately relieved when I refused to turn over full control of the litigation to her. In lieu of oral argument I filed written
argument. The matters were placed before the court "for consideration."

And the months once more began to roll around.

Eight months after all papers in the case had been filed, the court,
with two of its justices strongly dissenting, accepted the transcript as a
basis for hearing and deciding the appeal—refused to grant hearings—
but ordered that certain missing portions of the trial proceedings be
added to it before the appeal would be heard.

My petition for a rehearing was denied, as were a petition for a writ
of habeas corpus sought as an aid of appellate jurisdiction and a petition for writ of mandate. The United States Supreme Court declined
to review the state high court's decision and opinion accepting the
record.

It took the reporter seven months, and cost Los Angeles County
thousands of dollars, to prepare this additional record ordered by the
California Supreme Court, although it ran to only three hundred
pages.

Meanwhile, I stepped up the intensity of my legal campaign. Somehow, some way, I was determined to get at that record. In swift succession, probing for a chance to launch a frontal attack, I carried my

fight against that transcript to the lower United States courts, through its intermediate reviewing courts and finally back to the Supreme Court of the United States for a second time.

I went back to my law books and dug out ammunition; I read fine print until my eyes blurred and my brain reeled. I walked the floor of my cell into the wee hours of the morning, until my arches became outraged, while I critically sorted and classified and analyzed what I had read, and boldly planned the mounting of a legal offensive, a way to queen a pawn.

Hallowe'en, 1950. The newspaper headlines for that night and the next day screamed "RIOT ON SQ DEATH ROW!" and I found myself in a "quiet" cell on the isolation unit, charged with being a ringleader. As might be expected, my reaction to this turn of events was neither meek nor submissive, philosophical nor passive. I made it very plain I didn't like any part of this routine. I managed to get hold of a few sheets of paper and a pencil and wrote a petition for a writ of habeas corpus in longhand, addressing it to a judge of the Marin County Superior Court. As usual, the Bay Area dailies picked up the story. Here's what the San Francisco *Examiner* had to say on November 15, 1950.

WRIT ASKED BY RIOT LEADER

Caryl Chessman, ringleader of the recent riot on condemned row at San Quentin, yesterday filed a [petition for a] writ of habeas corpus in Marin County Superior Court in San Rafael.

Chessman, currently in solitary confinement at the prison, charged in his writ that he is being deprived of his legal rights to continue his fight for freedom . . .

When results were not forthcoming within a reasonable time, I wrote out another petition for habeas corpus, directing it to the District Court of Appeal in San Francisco. I later learned unofficially that phone lines began to crackle. The *Examiner* reported the result on November 29, 1950.

Superior Judge Edward I. Butler of Marin County yesterday
signed a writ of habeas corpus designed to release Caryl Chessman, ringleader of the October 31 death row riot at San Quentin
prison, from solitary confinement. Application of the writ, which
is returnable December 6, was prepared in pencil by Chessman
himself.

I was taken from the hole, as the prisoners call it, and returned to
my cell on Condemned Row. Heavily guarded, I appeared in court on
December 6, and the writ was ordered discharged on the ground that
I was out of solitary and no longer had cause to complain.

A few days later I got into a rather violent argument with two other
condemned men. Back I went to the isolation unit. But this time my
legal books and papers went with me. I'm the only condemned man
ever to do time in the hole with a cell-full of legal books and papers.

When the additional record was filed and my objections to its accuracy rejected by the trial judge, I was in the mood to slug it out with
the state's attorneys in California's high court. Right then, more than
ever, I didn't much give a damn whether I lived or died.

"He who defends himself has a fool for a client." Every day it was
becoming clearer why this was so. And every day it was becoming
clearer that I would lose the appeal when it was finally heard.

Why? Because Chessman was a "bad" man. The newspapers said so.
He hated the Row. He fought back at it and what it stood for. He
refused to fit into the pattern. He didn't give a damn what anybody
thought about him. He didn't bluff; he refused to scare. Once he got
into a slugging match with another condemned man. The armed
guard ordered him, once, twice, three times, to stop fighting. Then the
guard pointed his gun through the bars at him. "Stop! Stop or I'll
shoot!" Chessman didn't stop. "Go ahead and shoot and quit talking
about it!" he shouted at the guard.

Yes, Chessman was a "bad" man. He had the "wrong attitude." He
hated; he refused to conform. Hence he didn't "deserve" to survive,
did he? Death in the gas chamber was probably too good for him.

Well, kill him then. Kill him if you can.

A Victory None Would Comprehend

I began a final draft of *Appellant's Opening Brief.* When completed it was a two-volume, 495-page whopper. In conformance with court rules, I first summarized the facts of the case, outlining what the evidence showed, and then launched and sustained an attack on every single one of the seventeen judgments of convictions.

Attorneys for the state, six of them, filed a reply brief in which they stressed the legal sufficiency of the evidence to support the convictions, argued according to their lights that I had been "legally convicted," warned the court "The record also shows that the appellant led a life in the commission of violent crimes and was beyond the possibility of rehabilitation," and accordingly urged affirmance of the death and other sentences imposed.

Beyond the possibility of rehabilitation!

I filed a closing brief calculated to rip apart the state's argument and reasserted my demand for reversal of all convictions.

Once again the court refused to allow me to appear for oral argument and submitted the case for decision on the briefs previously filed. I had another long wait. Through the spring, the summer, the fall of 1951. It was like hugging a time-bomb, never knowing whether that bomb would blow me to Hell or back to Hollywood.

Dave, meanwhile, had been fighting his convictions of robbery and kidnaping for the purpose of robbery. He had been transferred to Folsom, and unless relief was forthcoming he would spend the remainder of his life there. Not a happy prospect for one who, notwithstanding his conviction, could very easily be innocent of any connection with the crime. Dave's attorney, Rosalind G. Bates of Los Angeles, had appealed unsuccessfully to the California District Court of Appeal, Second Appellate District, which had allowed all convictions to stand. Then the California Supreme Court had granted an application for it to review the case. Mrs. Bates contended that Dave's innocence had not been proved beyond a reasonable doubt and that mere robbery should not be held to be punishable as both robbery and kidnaping. The court said it was for the trial judge (who had tried the case without a jury) to find guilt or innocence and once he had done so a higher court could not interfere with that finding unless there was no evidence at all to support it. On the second claim urged, the court split four to three, the majority holding that, under the kidnaping for the purpose of robbery statute, robbery is kidnaping and hence punishable as such, while the minority emphatically contended such a construction did violence to the spirit and language of the statute and was absurd. The bare majority prevailed; the kidnapings were affirmed, but since the law doesn't permit double punishment for a single offense, the lesser offenses (the robberies) were reversed.

A storm of controversy immediately followed. Up shot the eyebrows of California's leading law schools. What's this? Robbery *is* kidnaping! Well, then, why have the robbery statutes been left on the books?

When it met, at the 1951 Regular Session, the California Legislature promptly did something about the court's holding. Section 209 of the California Penal Code, the "kidnaping" statute, was amended so as specifically to require a *kidnaping or carrying away for the purpose of robbery*. Robbery—that is, mere seizure or detention during a robbery or attempted robbery—no longer was punishable as a "kidnaping."

The Legislature at the same time granted parole eligibility to every person convicted under the section as it had read before amendment and who had been sentenced to life imprisonment without possibility of parole. In other words, every person but the one primarily responsi-

ble for the change in the law was granted blanket relief! That one—
and the only man sentenced to death under the law whose sentence
hadn't been executed—had been forgotten.

*I was, then, in the unique position of being twice sentenced to
death for acts (regardless of by whom committed) no longer triable
and punishable at all under the kidnaping statute.*

A rule of law entitles every defendant convicted of a criminal offense to the benefit of any favorable legislative change in the law
made subsequent to conviction and before the judgment becomes final.
When the case is appealed finality attaches once the appellate court decides the appeal. And since a decision on my appeal was overdue, I
would be obliged to act swiftly. But I had to be sure of my ground.

I immediately contacted one of the senatorial sponsors of the bill
and procured a formal and lengthy opinion from the legislative counsel regarding the effects and meaning of the change in the language
of the statute. Definitely there had to be a "kidnaping" or "carrying
away" with the specific intent to commit robbery before one could
now be punished under this "Kidnaping for the Purpose of Robbery"
law.

Armed with this and other information, I wrote the court, setting
forth my opinion that the death sentences—putting aside the question
of who had committed the acts forming the basis of the crimes—were
void because of this legislative amendment. Should the court be in
doubt about this, I asked the court to permit me to augment my letter
with a formal presentation. The court didn't request that presentation
and before I had completed researching the law dealing with this subject, I got into a serious hassle with prison officials and, for disciplinary reasons, was separated for a time from all my legal papers and
books.

When it finally handed down its decision, the court allowed the two
death penalty convictions to stand. Here are the reasons it gave for
doing so: the intent behind the movement—whether for the purpose
of committing robbery or sex crimes—was for the jury to decide and,
having resolved that question against me (but remember the law
hadn't yet been changed and thus the jury could not have resolved

the question against me!) the court couldn't say "as a matter of law" that the movement *had not* been for the purpose of robbery. (Couldn't or wouldn't?)

The court went on to assert: ". . . the offenses for which defendant received the death penalty here were not mere armed robberies. [The perpetrator] by threat of force transported his female victims—Mary for a considerable distance . . . , Regina from the car of Lea to the car of [the bandit]—pursuant to a plan which purposed [but when? at what point?] the commission of robberies and the infliction of bodily harm (the sex crimes). . . . It is the fact, not the distance, of forcible removal which constitutes kidnaping in this state."

But it is also the fact of *intent* which constitutes kidnaping *for the purpose of robbery* in this state. As far as I was concerned the court had said much and yet nothing—except that I should die. Its reasoning wilted in the strong light of analysis. To begin with, the court first had said it could not find facts (which it was not and is not constitutionally permitted to do) and then it had unhesitatingly done so. It had flatly declared the purpose of the movement *was* for robbery *and* sex crimes. But the evidence flatly contradicted this statement of "fact." The movement, at the time it had taken place, could not have been for the purpose of robbery. Moreover—and this the court had ignored altogether—the jury had been instructed that mere seizure or detention (in a nonphysical, purely legal sense, and without any movement whatever) was sufficient to warrant conviction, and that the "kidnaping" began with the initial detention and was a "continuing" offense. Thus, even though the jury may have firmly believed that the robbery intent may have been abandoned by the perpetrator before the victim was moved and even though the jury may also have firmly believed that the movement had been for a purpose other than robbery, it still was required to find guilt under such an instruction (assuming that it believed the defendant was the perpetrator of the offenses). Further, the prosecutor had vigorously argued for conviction upon the theory that the "kidnaping" in each case had begun with the initial technical "seizure" before the victim had been moved and admitted that the robbery motive in the case of Z, if it had existed at all originally, may well have been abandoned before the movement had taken place!

Under that law, that state of facts and that reasoning by the state's highest court, my life had been declared forfeit.

Could I get a federal court to intervene? That remained to be seen. I took considerable comfort in the fact that the Supreme Court of the United States recently had ruled that, to conform to federal due process of law, the defendant was entitled to have the validity of his conviction (including the question of the constitutionality of the statute under which conviction was had) appraised on consideration of the case as it was tried and as the issues were determined in the trial court. This meant that while the state high court (in my opinion) may have pulled a fast switch on me, I still had plenty of ammunition to keep blasting away at the legal target.

The long wait for a decision on my appeal was over.

Six days before Christmas, during our exercise period, one of the Row's wits was scanning the San Francisco *Chronicle* when he let out a yelp. He handed me the paper, pointed his finger and cracked, "They just gave ya a Christmas present."

I read, "Caryl Chessman, San Quentin's death row legal expert, yesterday lost his latest appeal to the State Supreme Court. In a 5-2 decision the court said the death sentence was just punishment . . ."

Some Christmas present!

An application for rehearing of the case was denied in January, 1952, and so was the petition for writ of habeas corpus filed many months earlier.

On February 6, 1952, I received a note:

Dear Sir:
   On this date I received Death Warrant in your case, issued January 25, 1952, by the Honorable Charles W. Fricke, Judge of the

Superior Court of the State of California, in and for the County
of Los Angeles, fixing date for Friday, March 28, 1952.

> Very truly yours,
> H. O. Teets
> Warden

If I intended to be still breathing after ten A.M on that last Friday
in March I had to hustle.

My next move was to take the case for the third time to the United
States Supreme Court. But time, always the condemned man's Nemesis, was needed. Time to get the record put together, indexed, certified, forwarded to the nation's highest court; time to research, prepare and file the necessary *Petition for Writ of Certiorari,* with a
supporting brief; time to permit attorneys for the state to file written
opposition at their option; time for the court to consider.

The next several weeks were hectic ones. First, I won a postpone-
ment of my appointment with the executioner when Mr. Justice Jesse
W. Carter of the California Supreme Court granted my application
for a stay of execution until the United States Supreme Court acted
upon my petition for review. Then, working under tremendous pressure, I managed to complete and file all necessary papers. I waited.
Soon the state's attorneys filed a brief urging the court to refuse to
review. In a reply brief I accused those representing the state of trying
to oversimplify the case right out of court. I again hammered at the
fact that I had never been given any opportunity to prove that the
record upon which affirmance of the death sentences had been based
was grossly incomplete and inaccurate.

For reasons known only to itself, the Supreme Court gave me the
brush-off; on March 31, 1952, it denied without comment my request
for it to review and, following review, to reverse the judgment of the
California Supreme Court affirming the death and other sentences and
rule I was entitled to a new trial or to a chance to prove my allega-
tions concerning the record and the means used to obtain my convictions, with a consequent voiding of those judgments of conviction if
I carried the burden of proof.

My stay of execution was terminated. The death sentences again could be enforced. The procedural wheels of justice once more began to grind. I had my earphones on listening to the ten o'clock news from San Francisco one April evening when I heard the newscaster state that Los Angeles' notorious red light bandit had been sentenced to die in San Quentin's gas chamber on June 27th next.

A neighbor called me. "Did you hear that, Chess?"

"Yeah, I heard it, John," I said, not enthusiastically. Then my ghoulish sense of humor rescued me, and I quipped our old tongue-in-cheek favorite: "You know, if I didn't really know better, I'd be tempted to believe these people actually mean to kill me."

"Naw!" John said.

You don't let anyone know how you feel. You grin, hideously perhaps, but still you grin. The newspapers say you "must" die on June 27. Well, why *must* you die? Who says you must? And why the 27th? Sure, you're ready to die; you've been ready for a long time. Only you're still obstinate. You still aren't ready to let them kill you. You aren't ready to let them win. Sometimes some small inner voice tries to tell you that you still have a future, and that is when you want to laugh uproariously. Because this is your future. The gas chamber is your future (at least symbolically). Death is your future. And the Death Row is all there is for you. And what a joy it must be to society, what a comfort, what a pride—this stupid, obscene place called Death Row.

And what a perfect thing is your Hate. It drives you forward; it sustains you; it gives you a terrible sanity, and the strength to fight fire with fire. It gives the raging, the consuming inferno, meaning, does Hate. *Ah, Hate,* you cry out to this fanatic friend. Between the two of us we will go a long, long way. We will go right to the center of the inferno and there we will stand, taunting those too timid to follow, but ever so gently, ever so subtly. There we will stand, and our greatest triumph will be that none will comprehend it. Our victory will be unqualified, yet none will even know that we have won. What more could we possibly ask? What more than flaming destruction in an inferno that society feeds, and indignantly denies that it does so? What more appropriate end to this solemn farce than the one you and I, friend Hate, have plotted?

All roads but one were blocked off. That one led back to and through the Federal District Court. It was a narrow, doubtful road.

Thirty-eight days in advance of my scheduled execution, I filed a petition for a writ of habeas corpus. The petition was denied. No hearings were held. Attorneys for the state were not required to answer. I had eighteen days to live.

Only one man and one piece of paper stood between me and the grave. That man was Judge Stephens of the United States Court of Appeals. The piece of paper was my application for stay of execution he was considering. If he ruled no stay, that would be it. That would be the end.

I had nine, then eight, then seven, then six, then five, then four days to live, and still no word. Death was near.

The Sergeant-in-Charge of the Row called me to the cage at the east end of the corridor. "I don't like to have to ask you this question," Sergeant Perry said. I knew he didn't, for he was a friendly man, and I knew what the question was—the Warden's Office wanted to know, in the event the information might be needed, what disposition I wanted made of my body. I told him.

I made arrangements with a friend on the Row to destroy all my personal and legal papers in the event I didn't get a stay. "What do you think your chances are?" the friend asked. For answer I made a coin-flipping motion with my right hand.

A panel of three San Quentin psychiatrists had examined me, had certified I was legally sane. I had been notified that the governor had reviewed my case and had found no grounds for extending executive clemency. (I had made no application for such clemency.)

This looked suspiciously like the end.

The editor of the Los Angeles *Mirror* sent Bernice Freeman, a long-time acquaintance and ace newspaperwoman and feature writer for the San Francisco *Chronicle,* to interview me. Hank Osborne, the *Mirror's* assistant editor, wanted a story of my life (and he got it in exchange for a promise, made through Mrs. Freeman, to send his paper to the men on the Row). He wanted to run a series of articles, starting the first one on the day I died. He wanted to sound a warning to youngsters following in my footsteps.

Mrs. Freeman and I talked in the office of Douglas C. Rigg, San Quentin's deceptively boyish-looking Associate Warden in charge of custody. Just outside the office and visible through a large window, a garden was in full bloom, a riotous profusion of color. Overhead sea gulls soared and the sky was intensely blue. Against this tranquil background Mrs. Freeman heard the story of Caryl Chessman—heard it narrated in a detached way that was almost clinical. Her expressive, handsome features mirrored its horror, its humor, its subtlety, its savagery.

When I finished, Mrs. Freeman said, "Tell me, Caryl, are you afraid?"

I considered her question for a moment and then I shook my head slowly from side to side. "No," I replied quietly, "I'm not afraid."

And that, I'm convinced, is the most terrible thing that can happen to any man, for it means you are afraid of nothing because you believe in nothing, have faith in nothing. It means you have found life worthless and death consequently meaningless. It means you have traded fear for guile and hate and an angry, furious contempt, that you have turned against yourself and all that is warm and human. It means you are completely alone, securely sealed off from the reach of other men or God. Your coveted aloneness lacks only the finality that Death will give it.

At last you have reached the very heart of the inferno. Your journey with Hate is over. And you think of Swinburne and his Garden of

Proserpine. Yes, you are "tired of tears and laughter, And men that laugh and weep . . ."

And still your eyes want to look back as much as the quiet, hidden part of you wants to look forward. You know what might have been and knowing this you have a vision of what yet might be—a fleeting, fragile thing this vision.

Its after-image stays with you, haunts you, and brings forth jeering laughter from Hate.

• *36* •

An Awakening

It didn't make sense, not then. In a lot of ways, it was sordid, stupid, futile. They would walk me into the gas chamber, strap me down, seal the door shut. They would generate the gas. I would go to sleep for keeps. Then—*oblivion*. (What else? And if I did happen to wake up in Hell, why, what matter?)

CHESSMAN DIES IN GAS CELL, headlines would shout. Beneath would be the story in typical newspaperese. Who I was. What I had been convicted of doing. My long and violent criminal record. The years I had spent on Death Row fighting my case. A couple of human interest angles. The time the "pill" was dropped. The time I was pronounced dead. Some editorializing on a crime-doesn't-pay note.

Honest citizens would read the story casually before turning the page, perhaps to the sports section or the comic strips. Young toughs would read it, figure I was a chump for getting caught and then go out on a robbery spree. I had done the same thing. Three friends of mine had been executed in the green room during that nine-year period following my release from reform school and before I came to the Row, myself twice sentenced to death.

Sure, I'd had ample warning. I wasn't blaming society or crying about what had happened. I wasn't turning soft or getting wild-eyed. In fact, I wasn't really giving a damn. I was simply sitting in the legal cell that Tuesday morning, smoking, thinking, and trying in my own way to make sense out of my past and the fact I had no future, so far as I knew, beyond Friday morning at ten.

341

I was so absorbed in thought I didn't hear or see Warden Harley Teets come through the gate and walk up to the front of the cell. When he spoke, and I looked up and saw him, it seemed to me he had suddenly materialized out of thin air. He offered me a legal size envelope he held in his right hand.

"I believe this is what you've been waiting for," he said, and the tone of his voice or the expression on his face told me nothing.

I believe this is what you've been waiting for. Yes, that was what I'd been waiting for—a paper that would tell me whether I would live or die. I nodded, took the envelope, removed the two sheets of legal size paper, and read the typewritten words appearing on them. Judge Albert Lee Stephens of the United States Court of Appeals for the Ninth Circuit had ordered my execution stayed until his court heard and decided my appeal.

"Well," I said somewhat thoughtfully, if not profoundly, "a stay." I had spoken more to myself than to the warden, whose keen, pale blue eyes were focused intently on my face. He merely nodded, waiting, watching for my reaction, and I was soon to learn why. His concern was with something he regarded as far more important than the dramatic potential of the moment.

It took a couple of seconds for the significance of the piece of paper I held to sink in.

Yes, I could have put on a tough, casual front, said, "Yeah, this is what I've been waiting for," lit a cigarette and let it go at that. Or I could have acted childishly excited and exuded a lot of phony humility. But I did neither. Instead I said, making the words a flat assertion, "Another chance." And that precisely was what the piece of paper I held meant.

Then, really thinking out loud, I added: "To tell you the truth, Warden, here's a chance I didn't think I was going to get. I figured this time was apt to be it. And believe me, I was ready."

The warden nodded his head. I'm sure he suspected *how* ready I had been. He must have, for he asked, "I wonder, Caryl, if you really wanted another chance?"

"What do you mean?" I countered.

Ever so quietly, without histrionics, the warden told me I knew very well what he meant (and I did). He asked me what I was trying to prove, if anything. He told me he knew what I was, but he wasn't certain why. That, he admitted, was what troubled him, even at times baffled him, and not because he was especially concerned with what happened to me, but because of the larger implications and the fact there were so many of my kind. He observed I had carried what could only be interpreted as defiance to its absolute extreme, however refined my technics for doing so. I had used every last ounce of brain power, cunning and cleverness I possessed in doing so. Why? How did that make sense? I hadn't been deterred by punishment or fear of punishment. Not even the threatened and imminent loss of my life had seemed to have had any effect on me. Why not?

Did I think he enjoyed putting men to death? If I did I had better have my head examined, and that might be a good idea anyway. Society and its institutions were admittedly not perfect. But neither was I. The difference was society was continually trying to improve. I wasn't. I was willing to stand off and sneer and exploit and sabotage. I was 100 per cent negative and always looking for some angle, for some way to "beat" the system or belittle it. The tragedy was that I'd been so successful.

Did it ever occur to me, sermonizing aside, that it also takes guts to be honest? That if I'd spent one-half the time on the outside trying to do something useful with my life that I'd spent here on the Row ostensibly merely trying to save it I would have been successful in a much more satisfying and constructive way? Didn't I realize that a man's brains and skills and talents can be put to both a personal and socially acceptable use?

I had spent a life in crime, in prisons, outside the law. I seemed, deep down, to hate society and all it stood for. Why? There had to be a reason. And if there was a reason why was I afraid to tell it? Because I knew it was too childish? I had spent years on the Row, and I said it (and "legal execution") was no answer. All right, then what was the answer?

Did I ever stop to think that my own actions and conduct helped convince the public of the very things I said were all wrong? That I was making his job difficult? That his job was to try to help men?

The warden paused. Then, in a still quiet and calm voice, he said: "If you have the guts, Caryl, now you can make some sense out of your life and do something with it to repay Judge Stephens for the chance he's given you."

"Oh, sure," I said, smiling faintly. "But what?"

"Figure it out for yourself," he told me. He turned and walked away.

I dropped the copy of the stay order onto the typing stand. I lit a cigarette.

Figure it out for yourself. Declaratory not exclamatory. Figure it out for yourself. Figure it out for yourself.

I won't dress it up. I'll tell it in hard, clear words.

Here were the after-midnight hours, and a brooding quiet shrouded the Row. I awoke suddenly, and found myself staring at the walls and bars of my cell. They seemed to encase me like an insensate womb of death.

"Hell," I thought, "that's not metaphor, Chessman; that's cold fact!" I grinned, cursed, threw myself out of bed, kicked into my slippers and put on my bathrobe. Then I fumbled a cigarette out of a pack and lit it, inhaling smoke deeply into my lungs. I don't believe I had ever felt more wide awake or more strangely calm in my whole life than I felt at that moment.

I glanced at the clock outside the cell. The time was a few minutes past one. Wednesday, June 25, 1952. My 1,453d night on Death Row. More than 35,000 hours. Almost one-eighth of my life.

A few hours earlier—fifteen to be exact—San Quentin's Warden Harley Teets had brought me a copy of the stay of execution of my death sentences. The stay order would continue in effect at least until the Court of Appeals heard and decided my appeal from the Federal District Court's denial of a petition for a writ of habeas corpus I had filed, seeking to have my convictions set aside.

The stay came as a jolting surprise in a way. And it meant, in my life, that Friday would be just another day, not the end of the world. It meant I could still win in the courts—and work, work, *work*, against two hundred to one odds. But I didn't mind the work and I wasn't troubled by the odds. What troubled me was the warden's question— where was the sense of Caryl Chessman? How did I account for myself?

I paced the floor and thought about the day's happenings. Gradually the pieces began to fall into place. Slowly I found it possible to see my condemnation in terms larger than my own predicament. It was indisputably true that places like Death Row made sense only because people like myself didn't.

No man, I am sure, likes to feel his life has been completely wasted. Conversely, I am equally sure that every man wants to believe his time spent here on earth has been of some importance both to himself and to others. When one man turns against his fellows, there is a reason. When that man rebels and defies and hates, there is a reason. When he reaches the point where he believes in nothing, there is a reason. Most if not all of his fellows suspect this, but often the reason is buried, hidden in a dark corner of his mind and when he turns openly against them what he does seems to them unfathomable. They become piqued and they seek to force him to mend his ways by punishing him. When this fails and he reacts with increased hostility and violence, they have legal machinery to destroy him. And when he is destroyed, they say they have avenged themselves against a social evil. In a way they have. But—

I knew these men who turned against their fellows. I was one of them. On my record, I was one of the worst of them, notwithstanding a good intelligence, an excellent education, many valuable occupational skills, perfect health. I had lived defiantly and recklessly, without regard for my own life or safety.

I had been brought to the Row and then had spent four rugged, ugly years here, aggressively fighting for my life, and yet paradoxically giving the impression I did not give a damn about it or anything.

From all surface indications, I appeared determined to go to Hell, but equally determined to get there in my own way, on my own terms and at my own good time.

I have told here the story of my life for the first time, and my purpose in telling it is not to try to justify or to excuse what I have done. Perhaps my actions cannot be justified. They perhaps cannot be excused. But surely they can be understood, and a large social significance derived from them.

The story, in my opinion, clearly and forcefully demonstrates this important fact: The ultimate development of an antisocial personality is invariably the end result of the impact of powerfully felt extrinsic forces upon the young mind, spirit or soul (call it what you will).

As well, I believe the story demonstrates, with equal force and clarity, the fact that even those who, as adults, violently menace society do not spring full grown from Hell. They are a result of a complex called environment. They were young once, and something happened to them. They gave and give society ample warning of what to expect. The danger signals are always flashed.

The young are eager and alive. They are idealists, yes, and romantics. They hunger emotionally. They need love. They need to feel wanted; they want to belong. But reality can treat them harshly, cruelly. Fear can enter their lives, a fear that is ugly and unreasonable. They can develop terrible feelings of guilt, of inadequacy, of being unloved, unwanted, rejected, alone. They can feel tyrannized. They can become confused. They can rebel, and their rebellion can assume many shapes. It can carry them many places. It can carry them into a jungle world and give them a cause—crime.

That is when they need help and guidance most, but they cannot be helped and guided unless they are understood. And they cannot be understood unless someone they respect takes the time and spends the effort to determine the actual reason for their rebellion. To be sure, they should and must be disciplined, yet at the same time they should and must be made to understand the need for self-discipline. What's more, the idea that someone exercising an authority over them, whether parent, teacher, preacher, judge, reform-school supervisor or whoever, can scold, lecture, frighten or force them into being "good," which usually means no more than blind, submissive obedience to authority's will, is simply a fallacy. But authority—and society —seems to be infatuated with the idea anyway.

Yes, in a sense, I became a criminal and an outlaw by choice, but that doesn't detract from the fact there was a reason. When a youngster, whether with justification or not, I reached the point where I believed it was better to be anything than afraid. I gladly traded fear for guile and hate. My psychopathy became a shield, and the more those in authority tried to hound or pound it out of me, never attempting to learn why it was there in the first place, the thicker I built its walls.

And that is what, in my opinion, must be understood—such a rebellious, secondary personality would never be formed or forged if there wasn't a strongly felt need for it. Certainly it is never the result of spiritual spontaneous combustion. Moreover, however falsely, such a personality offers not alone protection but integration as well, and the opportunity to grow, to know purpose, to be "free," to have and retain individuality, to be a quantity that must be given social recognition and reckoned with.

It seemed to me, just as it usually seems to my kind, that society was simply trying to strip or rip off my shield, that it was willing to do so ruthlessly, that it didn't care about me personally, or the amount of humiliation or degradation it might inflict in the process. I stubbornly balked at being manipulated, regulated, or being compelled to conform blindly through fear or threat or punishment, however severe. Indeed, I came to question the validity of a society that appeared more concerned with imposing its will than in inspiring respect. There seemed to me something grossly wrong with this.

"We'll make you be good!" I was told, and I told myself nobody should, would or could *make* me anything. And I proved it.

One time a mammoth policeman growled at me, "You think you're a tough guy, don't you, Chessman? Well, you punks are all alike— you're all yellow underneath. We'll break you before we're through or we'll bury you."

I grinned. "Yeah, and you bulls are all alike. You're all a bunch of dirty sonsabitches. So shoot your best stick."

And I proved, because I had to, that I wasn't yellow underneath and that, if anything, it was decency and not cowardice I was hiding. Because I had to, I gave "them" a chance to break or bury me. Irrationally perhaps, destruction seemed trivial, unimportant, but not being broken or turning yellow, all important.

"You'll be sorry! You'll be sorry!" people kept telling me. I thought, Yeah, well, you'll never know it if I am.

"You can't beat us. It just can't be done. Crime doesn't pay! Crime doesn't pay!" I was told over and over. Smugly. Challengingly. "Admit you're wrong. Admit you're wrong or you'll be sorry. You'll wind up in the gas chamber!"

Well, so what? What's the difference? That's what you righteous bastards seem to want, so maybe I'll accommodate you. And you can be damned sure of one thing: I'll never come crawling back on my belly crying for mercy.

"Then we'll punish you. We'll keep punishing you."

Well, punish and be damned! You'll never extort good citizenship.

"Fiend! Fiend!" shouted the prosecutor, as though he were divinely commissioned to wield Jehovah's flaming sword. I grinned and thought: Maybe the joke's on you too, Oswald. Maybe society keeps scaring itself with self-created social villains, monsters, demons, fiends and fiendlings. And wouldn't it be immensely funny if this time I just didn't happen to be guilty?

I remembered the words of Dr. Johnson: "It is not sufficiently considered that men require more often to be reminded than to be informed." Well, I'd keep them reminded what happens when you twist the tiger's tail. Let them figure out for themselves why there are tigers.

"It's too late to save your life, so get down on your knees and beg God for forgiveness for this wicked life you've led!" cried the young preacher who came to the jail unsolicited to see me after my conviction. I shook my head, smiled and declined to do so. I preferred to stand on my feet, even if it was in Hell.

And so I did stand on my own feet, and I continued to do so when brought to the Row. I stood and fought for survival.

Each morning I would awaken to find myself surrounded by bars and walls and the aura of death. A cold, driving anger would return as the ugly immediacy of my situation closed in on me. Among other things, I would find helplessness, despair and naked fear all around me, and I would remember the lesson I had learned early in life: *It is better to be anything than afraid!*

It was better, I told the fear-ridden, to be angry and defiant. Better to be cynical and contemptuous and sardonic. I knew, though, the price I personally had paid to rid myself of fear, and I knew there was something more inherently terrible than fear. That is reaching a point where you believe it is a sign of intolerable weakness to believe in anything or the worth of anything, or to admit the need for human warmth or friends. That is when your own fanatic strength can destroy you.

I had made it crystal clear that I considered Chessman quite capable of looking out for himself. My briefs to the court were technically correct in every detail; they were exhaustively researched and were coldly logical presentations, but they were also written in acid.

Bullheadedly, I had virtually placed the state in the position where it must destroy me. I'd been a fool. And too seldom is the anatomy of folly understood.

· *37* ·

The Return from Outer Darkness

*But was it possible to tell—coherently, convincingly and dramatically
—what I believed should and must be told?*
With a relentless fixity of purpose, I set to work to find out. Now
I have my answer. Consequently, there is little—and yet much—left
to be said.

A month before I was scheduled to die that June morning in 1952, a
panel of three San Quentin psychiatrists interviewed me in the sergeant's office at the east end of the corridor and just outside the bird-
cage-like enclosure leading into the Row proper. This interview was a
formality, since its purpose was to inquire into the question of whether
I was legally sane (and hence liable for execution), and all three psychiatrists knew me. They knew me, to put it simply, as a character who
did inexplicable and seemingly crazy things but who was not crazy in
the legal sense. They also knew I would never feign insanity in an
effort to avoid execution.

The interview was not stiff or formal. We exchanged amenities. I
was invited to be seated in a chair facing them. I lit a cigarette. They
spoke pleasantly, and did not treat me as though I were a noxious
sort of bug under a microscope.

My long record of juvenile and adult crime was mentioned and
then discussed. Yes, I had been in reform schools, jails and prisons
most of my life. Yes, I had committed many, many crimes and had
ample warning of what to expect if I kept on. Yes, I had kept on

350

nevertheless. No, I was not guilty of the crimes for which I had been sentenced to death. I was not the red light bandit, but I would not belabor the claim. I was simply mentioning it as part of a paradoxical picture. Yes, I would say I was not the red light bandit even if I were.

One of the doctors commented that simply punishing or even capitally punishing the young offender did not seem to be the answer. It was not. Punishment itself just made him worse, more rebellious. Legally executing him only proved someone had failed to reach him in time.

What did I think was the answer? The question was flattering, but I didn't think I could spout out the answer in a few words. I wasn't even sure I knew the answer if there was more to it than what they already knew. All I knew I had learned from experience, and that had been largely a rugged, seemingly one-dimensional experience. I ventured the thought that perhaps after one spends a while in a jungle world he gets so he cannot or does not want to believe there is anything better, or that it is attainable in any case. Maybe hate has a lot to do with it. Hate for everybody, himself and psychiatrists included. God included. Maybe an X factor, on the other hand, is the key to this form of psychopathy.

I told them I could "say" it much better on paper. I thought I would like to try. What did they think of the idea? They all thought it was a good idea.

In spare moments, I began to draft the story of my life. I tried to tell a story of how a psychopathic hate is born and what it can do; I ended by letting Hate tell the story. And I saw convincing proof Hate was not a very good storyteller. I found myself running out of days, so I tore up what I had written.

Was life nothing but a battle in the jungle? Would it go on senselessly until I was finally destroyed?

I paced the floor of my cage. Smoking. Thinking. The time was 2:50 A.M. Only now it wasn't late any more; at least it wasn't *too* late. Yet both society and I had paid a needlessly terrible price to get Caryl Chessman to this hour of his life.

The price I had paid was two death sentences and a figurative million years' time to serve under maximum supervision if the death sentences were ever set aside. I had paid by spending more than thirteen years of my life behind bars, in reform schools, jails and prisons, on the Death Row. I had paid by giving up friends, a beautiful young wife, a normal life—everything, in fact, but life itself. And now I had only a most tenuous lease on the sole possession I had left, with the odds a conservative two hundred to one that an appointment in the green room still awaited me.

On the other hand, my so-called "life of crime" had cost society a conservative half a million dollars when totaled. Since my last arrest alone, it had cost the state thousands upon thousands of dollars merely to try to take my life, to liquidate what it regarded as a bad investment.

I realized then, with a new awareness, what a staggering price this was, and how society and I both and equally were on the losing end. I realized, too, that society well could say: "We heartily agree. But what else could we have done with you? What else can we do with any man like you?"

And that was what sorely troubled Warden Harley Teets. It was what had prompted him to demand an accounting, if I could give it. I knew he didn't want a lot of excuses. He didn't want me to say, "I'm sorry. I've been a bad boy. Now I'll be a good boy." He wanted to know *why*. And so did the psychiatrists. I saw that same unvoiced question in the eyes of the members of California's Adult Authority when they visited the Row. These men, and many like them, hold positions of grave social responsibility. They must deal with the convicted felon when he is brought to prison. They must decide when he is ready and equipped for release. They want to help him because in doing so they are helping society, and their view is the right one: the most sensible way to help the man in prison is to give him the opportunity to help himself. But some of the institutionalized sneer at the idea they need help. These are the ones called aggressive psychopathic personalities. These are society's terrible problem children.

They hate and rob and kill and defy and curse and throw away their lives.

And that isn't what they want at all, but they get trapped.

I knew then, walking back and forth, back and forth, that this was an awful social tragedy. For criminal violence is definitely reactive, and in every man is the ability to be either good or bad. It is, moreover, an ability that may atrophy but is never lost. Why, then, did society persist in needlessly confounding itself? Perhaps because it was overstocked with Pollyannas, professional do-gooders, amateur optimists, social evangelists, vise-turners, polemicists of vengeance, horror hucksters and the like. But the problem remained one of finding reasons and not fault. Blame-fixing for its own sake was a profitless practice.

I was one of the trees in this dark and forbidding forest. I knew what it meant to live beyond the reach of other men or God. I had "proved" everything I had felt the need to prove: that I couldn't be scared or broken or driven to my knees, that I didn't give a damn. But here is where the tragedy lies: this felt need is compulsive and negative only. It is a need to prove one can do without—without love, without faith, without belief, without warmth, without friends, without freedom. This negative need to prove becomes progressively greater and greater; a ruthless tyrant, it comes to dominate; it grows brash and boldly demanding. If not checked, the ultimate (conscious or unconscious) need is to prove that one can do without even life itself.

Whether in its first or final stage, it is essentially a self-destructive, probably masochistic need and is therefore more often satisfied than eliminated or even temporarily held in check by punishment. For that reason the use of punishment as a correctional device is self-defeating. And that is why the idea of social vengeance and places like Death Row merely tend to create and to aggravate a problem that is at once immense, vexing beyond expression, appallingly ramified and often decried vociferously—yet so little and so seldom understood.

Unwittingly, the public creates and puts into deadly operation a

Darwinian law of survival for the criminal. The smartest, the clever-
est or the luckiest murderer is not caught at all. It is even possible
that a perfectly innocent citizen will be charged with his crime. Of
those apprehended, the shrewdest will escape execution, if not always,
at least most of the time. If sociological and related "laws" have any
validity, then, by killing off the hapless and less resourceful of the
murderers, we are perfecting the strain. And if the suggestion is
sophistic, the reason for capital punishment is equally so.

Many responsible citizens are familiar with the facts above set
out—if not all of the inferences to be drawn from those facts—and
yet hold to the belief capital punishment is a necessary evil because
it acts as a deterrent to those individuals who otherwise would commit crimes punishable by death. Those who cling to this notion take
a pretty dim view of their fellow man and necessarily commit themselves to the proposition that, at heart, he is a homicidal brute who
can only be held in check by fear and force. That notion is wrong,
actually and morally. Guilt or innocence aside, the story of my own
life is proof that the doctrine of total depravity is both wrong and
dangerous when applied to social relations and relationships, and that
fear of being put to death does not deter the criminally inclined from
committing capital crimes. If it did, a neat solution to crime would
be at hand: make all crimes punishable by death and then there
would be no more crime.

Several states do not have a capital punishment law, yet their per
capita murder rate is no higher than those states with such a law.
Each year California executes nearly as many men as any other state
in the Union, yet hundreds of homicides continue to be committed
within its borders each year.

Four dozen men have taken that last walk by my cell and I am
yet to have the first one tell me he gave thought to the possible consequences of his act. Contrary to popular belief, most homicides simply
aren't the result of cunning planning or long thought. Many of those
I watched being marched off to the execution chamber were young
men who were of the opinion that taking money from honest citizens
at the point of a gun was an easy way to make a living. They were

shocked numb when their banditry was resisted and they pulled the trigger of their gun in their anxiety to get away. They were real life Walter Mittys who hadn't meant to play for keeps. They learned too late that when you buck society you aren't playing a fun game.

In addition to the necessary evil argument offered to justify capital punishment, less responsible and more cynical citizens are satisfied to have legal executions because they offer a "cheap" solution to the problem of what to do with criminals. They point out that a criminal can be put to death for less than two hundred dollars, whereas maintaining him in one of its prisons costs California slightly over a thousand dollars a year.

There are several answers to this bargain rate idea of what to do with the criminal wrongdoer. I shall limit myself to two. First, there are fewer than thirty men on the Row at the present time, while there are more than twelve thousand men committed to and serving terms of imprisonment in California's prisons. Hence, it is difficult to see how any substantial savings can be realized unless the whole bunch of them are done away with. And before we can do away with all of them we first will have to do away with all statutory and constitutional safeguards and we must develop an unprecedented bloodlust, as well as an unprecedented police state where absolute power to destroy is held by the few. The trouble with all this is that the advocate of the bargain rate solution to the crime problem may then find that his master regards him as a criminal who should be expended in the interest of another sort of economy.

Don't get the idea Death Row is a nice place. It isn't. It's a rugged, tough, ugly place, and not because prison officials make it that way. They don't. Its stupid horror is inherent, built in.

Let me briefly tell you something more about it. First, select at random between twenty and thirty men between the ages of eighteen and seventy-two. Their physical size or shape is immaterial. Put them in a situation beyond their capacity to control, or neglect to plant some essential seed in their minds which fills them with an awful sense of inadequacy. Causally or casually condemn them. Give them only a tantalizingly slim chance of survival in the courts or with the governor. Confine them closely in a special, isolated section of the prison. For a time each day let them commingle. Periodically march them off and execute them, one by one, or two by two. Replace the ones executed.

Do that and you have created the Condemned Row—with all its tragic pathos, its gripping tensions, its smoldering resentments, its flaring violence, its courageous, its cringing, its constantly clashing personalities, its secret hopes, its fear. Do that and you have created a limbo-like place where men are held suspended between two worlds, this one, and the next. Do that and you have erected a monument to futility. A social abattoir. That is Death Row. It is nothing more.

The Row's surface casualness is as deceptive as quicksand. For days or weeks at a time all will be quiet and orderly. Then tension will generate, a corrosive tension capable of eating its way inside you, in many ways an unintelligible tension. Nitroglycerine is known to be unpredictable, to explode suddenly, without apparent agitation, into violence. It is this quality the explosive and the Row have in common —ordinarily both when handled sensibly remain in a quiescent state. Yet both, without apparent reason, without extrinsically discernible provocation, are capable of exploding with an abrupt and shocking violence.

The seeming reason for such cyclic, savage spiritual convulsions is not elusive. The slugging impact of a death sentence upon the psyche is often terrible and always tormenting, with the result that as often as the Death Row ennobles it degrades. Some men reach the point where they would literally sell or sell out their own mothers for another day of life, and the knowledge that this is so can make you want to vomit.

With rare exception, the newly arrived condemned man does not want to die, at least not consciously. At least not in the gas chamber. At least not today, or tomorrow. Yet he finds himself suddenly thrust into a nightmarish microcosm where the spectre of death is all around him. He learns the man celling next to him has but two weeks to live. His first Thursday afternoon here he watches three burly guards march one of his neighbors off to his death. He reads in

the newspapers that still another condemned man's death sentence
has been upheld on appeal.

He realizes then he is up against a deadly serious proposition. He
is jarred, abruptly, into full realization why he is here—to die!

Sure, the Row makes the doomed man think; it wakes him up—
when it's too late.

And it does even more: it incites in the mind of the young rebel, the
psychopath, a hate. A terrible hate that he turns against himself and his
kind. For Authority is constantly threatening him with the Row, holding it over his head. And he fights back at that threat with a vicious,
destructive anger. ·

He says, as I did: To hell with the Row, the gas chamber! He
"proves" society can't extort submissive conformity.

Admittedly, he's as hard to "cure" as he is easy to recognize. And
quite a few of his kind are clever chameleons who, once imprisoned,
give every indication of having responded to a correctional training
and treatment program only so they can win release and continue, on
an increasingly more violent scale, their personal war against society.

Failing to understand the nature of their destructive affliction, the
public is often so angered by the seeming senselessness of their violent
conduct that it clamors for revenge and thinks hotly in terms of fighting them. But you do not kill cancer by killing, angrily fighting or
severely punishing those found to be afflicted with this dread disease,
and so neither do you kill the causes of an even more dreadful social
malady by waging a war against those suffering from it.

Rather, you seek out, determine and if possible eliminate the causes
of the disease, not its victims. And at the same time your goal must
also be to evolve a way effectively to treat and help the afflicted.'

All this, of course, is a job for specialists. Effectively helping the
"criminal psychopath," as well as all other men committed to their
custody and care, is a job specialists in California's Department of Corrections (and other state and federal correctional agencies) have tack-
led. It's about as tough a job as can be undertaken, and one requiring
the full cooperation and understanding of the public.

As well as any other human being, I know the enormity of that job. I know what it means to be eaten spiritually away, to hate and doubt and fight and sneer.

Not too long ago I was told, "Chessman, nothing can cure you but a pound of cyanide."

I grinned. "Thank you, Sigmund Freud."

That is how indifferent and sardonic you can get.

But there are periods of self-doubt and times when you know yourself for what you really are—an angry, hating, fighting *failure*. Usually then you curse your doubt and blaspheme the imagery of the self you see. A voice from within tells you not to waste time mocking yourself but to continue on your merry way to Hell. However, circumstances can combine in such a way that you refuse to heed the voice any longer. You fiercely resolve you will find a way to liberate yourself from the Thing that subjugates you.

The Thing is psychopathic bondage.

It is now late winter of the year 1954. Many months have passed since my appointment with the executioner was last suspended and I began work on my book. Much—more than half—of that time has necessarily been spent in litigating the case, in fighting all the while for survival. For the "race for life," the deadly competition with the executioner has continued without letup. Still, every minute I could spare, beg, borrow or steal from the legal work I have employed to write this book.

Prohibitive odds once again insist, and now more clamorously than ever, that I soon will be put to death in San Quentin's gas chamber. But odds don't tell the story, and odds can lie.

On Thursday, May 28, 1953, one day following my thirty-second birthday, the United States Court of Appeals decided the appeal by upholding the District Court's summary denial of my petition for a writ of habeas corpus.

This was bitterly disappointing news.

Apparently I had been asking too much. It was obvious the federal courts had adopted and were adhering to a strict "Hands off!" policy.

From June to November—five more months of careful planning, endless research, writing and rewriting.

The petition was filed.

And then . . . the Supreme Court slammed the door in my face for the *fourth* time.

I filed the necessary application for what is called a further stay of mandate.

Next, I prepared and mailed to the Supreme Court an application for extension of time from December 29, 1953, to January 15, 1954, to file the petition for rehearing.

That petition was granted.

The petition for rehearing was denied. My stay was terminated. Another date for execution will soon be fixed.

I refuse to throw in the sponge. I still hope to survive. I intend to keep fighting until I win or until the gas chamber door slams shut in my face. Accordingly, I have never for an instant stopped digging for evidence, for ammunition. I am prepared to start all over again back in a lower state court with a new proceeding, a new legal attack.

Failing altogether in the courts, I would like to ask the governor for executive clemency. I think that I am now worth more to society alive than dead. The long years lived in this crucible called Death Row have carried me beyond bitterness, beyond hate, beyond savage animal violence. Death Row has compelled me to study as I have never studied before, to accept disciplines I never would have accepted otherwise and to gain a penetrating insight into all phases of this problem of crime that I am determined to translate into worthwhile contributions toward ultimate solution of that problem. This book is a beginning contribution; I would like to believe that it also signals the beginning for me of a journey back from outer darkness. Yet I realize that I may well be out beyond the point of no return.

I should add most emphatically that I thank myself alone for my plight; I certainly don't blame the courts or the governor for it. Obviously the courts didn't invent Caryl Chessman, the "psychopath" with the violent criminal past. They only dealt with him—a man, they were repeatedly warned, who was cunning, sinister, dangerous, and who, it seemed, gave not a damn for courts or society or anyone or anything, his articulate protestations to the contrary notwithstanding. Talk is cheap, and claims of innocence are no novelty. A Chessman waiting to die, a Chessman confronted with the imminence of death, a Chessman bent upon cheating the executioner and who can do so only with the aid of some court—isn't such a Chessman apt to make any claim he believes will serve his ends? Can't such claims be conveniently ignored, brushed aside, in the interests of justice?

And Chessman—this Chessman with which the courts have been dealing for these many years—he is but one of a constantly growing criminal horde. Isn't it possible that his execution will serve as a grim deterrent to the others? That it will serve a useful purpose?

No, it isn't possible; it isn't remotely possible. His execution will deter no one, it will gain society nothing, it will prove nothing. It will simply mean that he will be dead and that, in his case, the problem he typifies has been evaded. That will leave us right back where we started, with a corpse, a liquidated half-million-dollar investment, and at least two more recruits to the criminal ranks ready and eager to take the dead Chessman's place.

You can hardly call that progress, can you?

All right, then let's meet head-on the problem of our Chessmans. Let's see if there isn't something constructive we can do about them.

Let's recognize that the personal fate of Chessman may not be of importance to anyone but Chessman himself. But let's recognize that the thousands of youngsters following in the footsteps of Chessman are of prime importance to all of us.

So there is a little more, a little more than just the life of a man about to die; more than a tale of blazing guns, screaming tires, reform-school educations, and the *plop!* in the pan beneath my final chair.

The winter day outside is gray. A driving rain lashes the barred windows. Gusts of wind vent their strange fury against the building.

It's late afternoon and outside it is beginning to turn dark. The face of Death Row is a scowling, brooding face.

Night soon will be here. For me, it may be a night that will never end.

Does that matter?

Do your Chessmans matter?

The decision is yours.

THE END